Practice rese partnerships in social work

Making a difference

Christa Fouché

BASW
BRITISH ASSOCIATION
OF SOCIAL WORKERS

First published in Great Britain in 2015 by

Policy Press   North America office:
University of Bristol   Policy Press
1-9 Old Park Hill   c/o The University of Chicago Press
Bristol BS2 8BB   1427 East 60th Street
UK   Chicago, IL 60637, USA
t: +44 (0)117 954 5940   t: +1 773 702 7700
pp-info@bristol.ac.uk   f: +1 773-702-9756
www.policypress.co.uk   sales@press.uchicago.edu
                                       www.press.uchicago.edu

© Policy Press 2015

British Library Cataloguing in Publication Data
A catalogue record for this book is available from the British Library.

Library of Congress Cataloging-in-Publication Data
A catalog record for this book has been requested.

ISBN 978 1 44731 401 1 paperback
ISBN 978 1 44731 400 4 hardcover

The right of Christa Fouché to be identified as the author of this work has been asserted
by her in accordance with the Copyright, Designs and Patents Act 1988.

Cover design by Policy Press
Front cover: image kindly supplied by istock
Printed and bound in Great Britain by Hobbs, Southampton
Policy Press uses environmentally responsible print partners

FSC
www.fsc.org
MIX
Paper from
responsible sources
FSC® C020438

SOCIAL WORK IN PRACTICE series

Series editors: **Viviene Cree**, University of Edinburgh and
Steve Myers, University of Salford

This important series sets new standards in introducing social workers to the ideas, values and knowledge base necessary for professional practice. These core texts are designed for students undertaking professional training at all levels as well as fulfilling the needs of qualified staff seeking to update their skills or move into new areas of practice.

Editorial advisory board:

Suzy Braye, University of Sussex

Jim Campbell, Goldsmith's University of London

Gina Hardesty, Independent Consultant

Ravi Kohli, University of Bedfordshire

Jill Manthorpe, King's College London

Kate Morris, University of Nottingham

Joan Orme, University of Glasgow

Alison Shaw, Policy Press

Charlotte Williams, RMIT University, Australia

Published titles in the series
Social work - Viv Cree
Social work and multi-agency working - Kate Morris
Youth justice in practice - Bill Whyte
Radical social work in practice - Iain Ferguson and Rona Woodward
Religion, belief and social work - Sheila Furness and Philip Gilligan
Communicating with children and young people - Michelle Lefevre
Social work and lesbian, gay, bisexual and trans people - Julie Fish
Supporting people with alcohol and drug problems - Sarah Galvani
Social work in the community - Barbra Teater and Mark Baldwin
Residential child care in practice - Mark Smith, Leon Fulcher and Peter Doran
Effective writing for social work - Lucy Rai

Coming soon
Social work and people with learning difficulties - Susan Hunter and Denis Rowley

Dedication

To the memory of Dr Annemie de Vos, who inspired research-mindedness and provided me with the foundations for everything I know about research. Thanks, Hanneke and Annesu, for sharing your mother with me and with many other emerging researchers.

To Professor Irwin Epstein and Dr Helen Rehr (in memoriam), whose practice-research endeavours continue to sustain an academic minority.

To Marcel and Maryke, who shared this journey in so many ways, and to family and friends who endured it, I am forever grateful.

To Susan, who gets to share all the challenging journeys: thank you!

Contents

List of figures and tables

Figures

Tables

List of examples

List of reflection exercises

Glossary

Action research
A study with the focus on the involvement and participation of various stakeholders in a particular research project; a single activity which is simultaneously a form of inquiry and a form of practical action.

Applied research
Research aimed at solving practice problems.

Collaborative research
An orientation to research that enables and encourages individuals with diverse and complementary knowledge and skills to plan, design, implement and disseminate a scientific process to generate new knowledge.

Community of knowing
A group of individuals with a shared practice interest and/or passion for research in which they share expertise and the creation of new knowledge through both social gatherings and formal structures. There are a number of determinants that impact on the effectiveness of communities of knowing.

Community-based participatory research (CBPR)
Research that is based on a commitment to sharing power and resources and working towards beneficial outcomes for all participants, especially 'communities' (see also *Action research*).

Evaluation research
The systematic use of research methods to make judgements about the effectiveness and the overall merit, worth or values of some form of practice.

Evidence-based practice (EBP)
The use of the best available scientific knowledge derived from randomised controlled outcome studies and meta-analysis of existing outcome studies as one basis for guiding professional interventions and effective therapies, combined with professional ethical standards, clinical judgement and practice wisdom.

Interpretivism
A view in the social sciences that social research may not be subject to the same methods of investigation as the natural world, and that the influence of social actions on people should be considered (see also *Positivism*, as interpretivism is also known as anti-positivism).

Learning organisation
An organisation that actively engages in promoting the development of knowledge by extracting, storing and nurturing the knowledge that exists in individuals and systems.

Mixed–methods research
Both a philosophical assumption (methodology) that guides the many phases of the research process and a method that focuses on mixing both qualitative and quantitative techniques of data collection and analysis.

Participatory action research (PAR)
See *Action research*. Used by some authors as a synonym for action research.

Partnership
A relational activity that enables sustained change and long-term benefits for all involved.

Positivism
A view in the sciences that logical and scientific knowledge (objective and measurable) is the exclusive source of all authoritative knowledge (see also *Interpretivism*).

Practice–based research (PBR)
Research that is inspired by social work practice and is derived from practice wisdom. PBR sets out to answer questions that have been raised in practice.

Practice research
A collaborative partnership by a range of stakeholders to advance understanding of practice issues and to make a difference to practice.

Qualitative research
Pertains to quality (information-richness) or data as (mostly) words.

Quantitative research
Pertains to quantity (counting) or data as numbers.

Reflective practice
Practice accompanied by 'thinking in action' or 'thinking on action', with knowledge developed from the personal experience and the expertise of practitioners and service users.

Reflexive practice
A form of practice that looks back on itself, that is premised on self-analysis.

Research design
A step in the research process where operational decisions are being made; also the act of designing the study in its broadest sense – that is, all the decisions made in planning the study.

Research
A systematic process to generate new knowledge.

Research-based practice (RBP)
Practice that starts from social science or social work theory and aims to research practice.

Systematic review
A critical assessment of all primary research studies that address a particular issue by pooling the findings of all identified studies in order to clarify what is known about it.

Introduction

The purpose of this book is to elucidate the joint responsibility of various stakeholders to enable research in practice. It aims to highlight the development and nature of practitioner research and the relationships inherent in the creation and dissemination of knowledge. It will demonstrate the nature of relational research to 'make a difference' to service delivery. To this end, this book is divided into three parts.

Part One: The relationship between practice and research

This first part highlights the delicate yet dynamic relationship between practice and research. It is argued that all practice research takes place in a particular context and that an understanding of the context is essential to committing to ways of making a difference in this regard. The focus in this part will be not on the pragmatics of conducting collaborative practice research, but on its inherent, often non-negotiable, context. This part may not be of great interest to emerging practice researchers; Parts Two and Three will have more relevance for this group. Chapter One considers how the relationship between social work and research has developed and the significance of this relationship. It contextualises practitioner research and highlights why it continues to be important for social work practitioners to acknowledge their contribution to the practice–research–theory cycle. Research knowledge is positioned as one type of knowledge that can potentially make a difference to practice. Chapter Two focuses on the various political, ethical and cultural drivers that shape the social work research landscape and the internal and external reasons impacting on practitioners' decisions to conduct practice research. Chapter Three turns to the practicalities of forming and maintaining relationships to successfully engage in practice research, from both managerial and practitioner perspectives.

Part Two: Designing practice research

As an extension of Part One, on the relationship between practice and research, this part is more practice oriented, aiming to focus on the pragmatics of designing and implementing a practice research project in collaboration with others. It uses three chapters to discuss how the research process and research methodology can be managed within networks and through collaborative relationships to make a difference in practice. It is argued that developing networks in practice research parallels social work practice and builds on existing practice knowledge and skills. In Part One, Chapter Two makes reference to the context of research as a determining factor in the critical appraisal of existing information. In Part Two, Chapter Four expands on this notion by outlining techniques for conducting a review of relevant literature and appraising existing material, with a focus on the effective use of collaborative relationships. Chapter Five introduces a discussion of applied, practice-focused designs that most effectively allow for collaboration, and includes action research and evaluation research as two popular examples. The scope of this chapter does not allow for a detailed understanding of each of these designs, nor of the many other applied research designs, but, rather, encourages readers to creatively explore research designs appropriate to developing collaboration in the context of practice research. Chapter Six concludes this part with a focus on the selection of the most appropriate methods for obtaining data for practice research projects. Both traditional and more contemporary methods are discussed, while acknowledging the strengths and weaknesses of each and, in particular, their relevance to collaborative research.

Part Three: Nurturing networks

Flowing from the previous part, where the focus was on the pragmatics of designing and implementing collaborative practice research projects aimed at making a difference in practice, Part Three highlights the benefits and responsibilities associated with relationship-based research. In the conduct of small-scale research, more questions than answers tend to develop, necessitating other, sometimes more advanced, research activity. Similarly, in the course of collaborative work, the players of various roles and a range of potential contributions to research are identified and this creates a platform for, and indeed expectations of, on-going activity. It is argued that a focus on the momentum generated by research is essential so as to enable the real transformative potential of networks. The chapters in this part focus on activities to maximise the findings from collaborative research and propose strategies to sustain the momentum generated. To this end, Chapter Seven encourages a consideration of the dynamics involved in the utilisation and dissemination of findings. Different avenues for dissemination are highlighted and the strengths and weaknesses of each of are outlined. A focus on the particular issues and elements of providing and receiving research mentoring in practice and the value of mentoring relationships to enable on-going research activity in practice follows in Chapter Eight. The notion of nested mentoring is proposed to support collaborative practitioner research activity so as to impact on practice. The concluding

Chapter Nine summarises the main themes of the book across the three parts and speaks to various stakeholders, including educators, practice managers, funders, practitioners and postgraduate students about their responsibility to develop and maintain a commitment to effective social work practice, to collaboration in social work practice research as a strategy to realise this and to developing capacity for practice research partnerships to make a difference to social work practice.

Part One

The relationship between practice and research

The nature of practice research in social work

Introduction

Have you ever considered why you do what you do? It is widely accepted that social work, by its very nature, has to deal with people's experiences of abuse, violence, neglect, hardship, and suffering. Social workers find ways to help people manage this by working within and across systems, agencies and policies 'at the points where people interact with their environments' (International Association of Schools of Social Work (IASSW), 2005, p 2). Very often this is done with limited resources, under huge public scrutiny and at relatively low rates of remuneration. It is quite sensible, then, to raise a question about why: why would you? Yet, research indicates that social workers generally have high levels of job satisfaction and often have long careers in their chosen field of practice (Collins, 2008; Fouché et al, 2013).

You will have your own reasons for being in social work. But generally, answers to this question lead to the potential for making a difference; people engaged in social work are passionate about social justice, human rights and equality and will go to great lengths to promote 'social change, problem solving in human relationships and the empowerment and liberation of people to enhance well-being' (IASSW, 2005, p 2). It flows naturally, then, that social workers wanting to make a difference will want to do no harm and, in fact, be able to convincingly state that they have effected competent change. Isn't the very core of professional practice a commitment to competence? So the next question is: how do we know that? How do we know that what we do is, at the very least, doing no harm, but indeed making a difference? And what gives social workers the authority or right to act as if they will enable a positive difference? Is it good intentions, core values, statutory power, professional registration, accredited qualifications, certain competencies or knowledge bases? These are on-going questions and debates which will not be solved here, but it is important to at least acknowledge that the effectiveness of social work practice is a principal concern to the profession and cannot be ignored. This leads us to the need for evidence.

Commonly, social workers are positive that (most) clients express their satisfaction with services received. Or that they leave the agency with a need met. Client satisfaction is indeed a very good measure of the extent to which social workers have made a difference. However, in considering the range, scope and extent of resources utilised to enable such satisfaction, we can't help contemplating factors such as levels of satisfaction and levels of need. Consider the following example:

Example 1.1: Making a difference

John has recently become unemployed and is experiencing hardship. He is thankful for (satisfied with) the support received from social services agencies, including food parcels, emergency housing and low-cost healthcare. Social workers have made a difference, measured by John's improved circumstances and expressed satisfaction. But could/should more have been done to increase satisfaction and/or reach others like John? Would another type of intervention have reached John and others like him with fewer resources? Potentially, a measure of outcomes may be more, or at least equally, important in considering the effective use of resources and a measure of the difference made.

All of this places an obligation on practitioners to conduct a 'search' of their practice; a search for evidence of the extent to which aims are achieved (or not), needs are met (or not) and resources effectively utilised (or not). As Groundwater–Smith et al (2013) urge, practitioners should be encouraged to express not only their opinions, but how they arrived at those opinions. And if you are of the opinion that change has occurred, the question is: 'Is this change really an improvement and for whom is it an improvement?' (Groundwater–Smith et al, 2013, p 22). This search and re-search of practice highlights the interface and relationship between social work practice and research. This chapter will look at how this relationship has developed and its significance, and will contextualise practitioner research with reference to the current climate, including the call for reflective practice and research–mindedness. You will be encouraged to ponder the implications of that in your own context through a series of reflection exercises throughout the book.

Reflection exercise 1.1: The place of evidence

1   How do you know that what you do is at the very least doing no harm, but at best making a difference?
2   What gives you the authority or right to make decisions about the best intervention?
3   Is the effectiveness of social work practice a principal concern to you?

The development of practitioner research

A number of factors have driven the recent interest in research: economic and managerial realities (effectiveness, cost-effectiveness and efficiency); wider accountability agendas; public confidence; user demand; context of registration and professionalism; global push around evidence-based, evidence-informed activity; influences of other professions; and a growing need for understanding increasingly diverse client groups. In response to these pressures, research can add to existing knowledge; address particular issues of concern; find out what our clients think of services; explore particular needs in an area; influence policy makers; convince funders; provide voice for users; change the ways in which things are done; or develop and test new interventions. There is a robust tradition in social work on research informing practice. Yet, the domain of responsibility for producing and utilising such research seems unclear. As Orme and Shemmings (2010) remind us, social work has been identified as having a deficit in research capacity both in research produced and in its utilisation by practitioners. Few professionals actively engage in or draw on practice-related research findings, with a few studies over a period of time successively reporting on this: a survey of social work journals by Rosen et al (1999) revealed relatively little research on interventions, and that much of that research had basic methodological flaws; Sheldon and Chilvers (2000) reported that of the social workers surveyed (2,285), 18 per cent have read absolutely no practice-related material in the previous six months. It is most important to note, though, that these reports also make reference to the respondents reportedly being dissatisfied with the situation. Even though research probably occupies the minds of educators and students more, Mills et al (2006), in a demographic review of the social sciences, identify that only a small number of social work academics in the UK were effectively undertaking research.

The expectations for evidence, accountability and demonstrable outcomes are nothing new. Way back in 1915, at an early international conference on social work, Abraham Flexner described social work as 'hardly eligible for the status of a profession' and faulted social work for 'not having a specific, separate, scientific body of knowledge' (Kirk and Reid, 2002, pp 1–6). In 1964, the US professional body the National Association of Social Workers (NASW) conducted its own investigation into developments with regard to the professional standing of social work and concluded that: 'Social Work has not produced a systematic body of knowledge, although it exhibits many of the characteristics of a profession' (NASW, 1964, p iii). By 1973, a seminal development in these debates was published, namely the article by Joel Fischer (1973) entitled: 'Is social work effective?' Subsequently to this publication, a number of studies were reported and debates published during the 1970s and 1980s on 'what works', convincing the profession that indeed social work is effective. These included articles on developments of 'scientifically based' practice. One of these was an article by Wood claiming that the principles of quality practice include clients' experience of the intervention (Wood, 1978). This introduced an important direction in the development of the debates on effectiveness of social work by valuing the client experience. The focus then turned to articles offering alternative research designs or 'improvements' in existing designs, aimed at increasing social workers' capacity to demonstrate effectiveness (Reid and Hanrahan, 1982). This eventually led to the introduction of the 'scientist–practitioner vs. practitioner–scientist' paradigm in the 1990s. This paradigm has resurfaced in many guises over the years, but basically remains the same at its core, namely that practitioners have a responsibility and obligation to generate and use research in practice.

It is interesting to note that the nature of these discussions varied across the globe, influenced by the local standing of social work in different contexts. Consistently and increasingly, the nature of that responsibility has also been debated, as will be highlighted in the section below. Most recently, the practice–research paradigms included those on evidence-based practice (EBP), evidence-informed or evidence-influenced practice and its many critiques. The EBP movement originated to some degree in the US and the field of evidence-based medicine (EBM), which is defined as treatment based on the best available science. In the 1990s EBM became 'the fashionable coinage to describe a process of self-consciously incorporating research evidence into medical practice' (Pope, 2003, p 269). As Corby (2006) summarises, the main tenets of the evidence-based movement were that professional interventions should be based on research findings about what was effective and that therefore research should reflect these concerns and form the basis of professional training and practice. This clearly builds on the considerable activity over many decades to develop a research–informed knowledge base for social work.

This paradigm has rapidly expanded to other social and human service professions and was eventually defined in the *Social Work Dictionary* (Barker, 2003, p 189) as 'the use of the best available scientific knowledge derived from randomised controlled outcome studies and meta-analysis of existing outcome studies as one basis for guiding professional interventions and effective therapies, combined with professional ethical standards, clinical judgement and practice wisdom'. Gilgun (2005) later aligned this to the four cornerstones of social work: research and theory; practice wisdom; the person of the practitioner; and what clients bring to practice situations. Not surprisingly, there has been a good deal of spirited debate both for and against EBP. Some authors are highly critical of this movement, emphasising the methodological weaknesses and poor fit with social work activities because of the complexities inherent in practice (Webb, 2001; Hammersley, 2005), while its proponents see it as a rational, science-based activity and a moral obligation (Gambrill, 2003; Thyer, 2004). Gray et al (2009) provide a comprehensive and analytical discussion of the nature of evidence on social work and the many debates and interpretations of EBP, concluding that it is a subject fraught with controversy. Of note is their observation that EBP is very different from empirical clinical practice and is not simply about how social workers use evidence to inform everyday decisions. By positioning EBP as a much more complex process of formalisation, they question it as a paradigm in the 'scientist-practitioner' debates. This is very different from the stance of another strong proponent of EBP, Thyer (2004), who regards this movement as expanding on prior initiatives, including the model of scientist-practitioner training. These on-going discussions are important and relevant to our consideration of the tenuous relationship between social work practice and research over many decades. However, there is no need in the context of this book for further exploration of these debates and opposing points of view, other than to encourage you to consider these EBP debates as one of many over the years to contextualise the nature of practice research. As such, the discussion can now turn to a discussion on practice research.

According to Epstein (2001), there are two main approaches to social work research: research-based practice (RBP) and practice-based research (PBR). The distinction between these two approaches lies in the underlying view of how to conduct research. RBP starts from social science or social work theory and its aim is research on practice. In RBP there is high regard and priority for randomised control groups, requiring some service users to not receive treatment. It seeks to collect data in the future and depends on using standardised quantitative research instruments. This approach is collaborative but may put the needs of research over what is best in practice. This form of research can be costly and disruptive to both social work practitioners and service users (Epstein, 2001) and is associated with the empirical EBP movement in the US and, as will become clear below, is also associated with the 'narrow stream' approach outlined by Shaw (2005). PBR, conversely, is inspired by social work practice and is derived from practice wisdom. PBR sets out to answer questions that have been raised in practice. This approach does not require experimental control groups. It can either use available clinical information or seek to go about collecting data in the future. This approach can be quantitative or qualitative but requires employing instruments that are tailored to practice needs. It is also collaborative, but the needs of practice overrule research requirements. Epstein (2001) argues that PBR therefore is more manageable for practitioners and service users, as research is derived within the natural processes of the organisation and does not impose ideas or techniques from outside of practice. In more recent publications, this notion of PBR has been narrowed to 'research conducted by practitioners for practice purposes' (Dodd and Epstein, 2012, p 5). A range of publications by the National Research and Development Centre for Adult Literacy and Numeracy (NRDC) focus on practitioner-led research initiatives (see Hamilton and Wilson, 2006; Hamilton et al, 2007; and Hamilton and James, 2007). However, for all sorts of reasons social work practitioners rarely conduct research on their own – other than for advanced qualifications – and the challenge remains for how to generate and use research in practice. Shaw and Holland (2014, p 16) warn, though, that 'knowing' and 'doing' research and practice are not two wholly distinct areas that need mechanisms to connect them, but are to a significant degree part and parcel of one another.

Shaw (2005) introduces the notion of 'narrow stream' and 'broad stream' approaches to practice research in the UK, which is very similar to the debates regarding RBP and PBR introduced by Irwin Epstein in the US. According to Shaw (2005), narrow-stream EBP is primarily driven by academia; is powerfully associated with the empirical practice movement in the US; engages in a more confined use of the term 'evidence-based practice'; and its supporters are in favour of particular interventions, normally demonstrated to be effective via experimental designs. Broad-stream EBP, on the other hand, is practice driven with a focus on accountability; emphasises partnerships between practitioners and researchers; supports easier access to data; promotes the dissemination of research findings in easy-to-understand formats; focuses on outcome issues in practice; and has introduced debates on terminology in this regard, including notions of evidence-informed or evidence-led practice rather than EBP (Shaw, 2005). Practice research in this book will be presented as a collaborative effort by a range of stakeholders to advance understanding of practice issues and to make a difference to practice.

Reflection exercise 1.2: Your relationship with research

1   What is usually your initial reaction when you hear someone reporting on the findings of research?
2   Do you personally think research has a place in practice? Why?

Parallel to these debates in the UK and US, dialogues about reflective practice, reflexive practice and research-mindedness were continuing. From the beginning, the inherent goal of the scientist-practitioner paradigm was to stimulate research-mindedness and critical thinking among professional practitioners. In the current climate, practitioner research is very prominently linked to the call for reflective, critical reflective and reflexive practice as well as research-mindedness (Orme and Shemmings, 2010; Thompson and Pascal, 2012). Reflective practice is regarded as practice accompanied by 'thinking in action' or 'thinking on action' (Schön, 1983), with knowledge developed from the personal experience and the expertise of practitioners and service users (Gilgun, 2005). Reflexive practice is a form of practice that looks back on itself, that is premised on self-analysis. Reflexivity is a key part of making sure that reflective practice is *critically* reflective practice, according to Thompson and Pascal (2012). This construct has its origins in the Latin word *reflexus*, meaning 'to bend back' or to 'stand apart from'. Reflection can, as such, be described as the ability to step back and pose questions about why things are done in a certain way. Reflexivity will help us ponder questions on how we could have done it differently.

It is not difficult, then, to see its relationship with practitioner research – where we aim to answer questions that have been raised in practice. By engaging in reflective practice, we 'take a step back' to reconsider what we have done and to examine ways to do it better. This exploration assumes a 'mindedness', an individual's capacity for reflection. Research-mindedness therefore requires practitioners to display an understanding of the use of research to inform practice. A considerable number of authors have in recent years made mention of research-mindedness in their writing with a 'research mindedness in social work and social care' test funded by the Social Care Institute for Excellence (SCIE) to enable practitioners to assess their own research-mindedness (see http://www.resmind.swap.ac.uk/index.htm). Based on these and other insights, Table 1.1 offers a series of questions to enable a self-assessment of research-mindedness. Check your response to these questions and your own level of research-mindedness.

In some contexts, practice guidelines (once again following the lead of medicine) are offered as a solution to a practitioner-scientist approach by proposing that research findings be incorporated into and interpreted by guidance for practitioners (Rosen and Proctor, 2003). All of these approaches to the place of science in social work have their champions and critics; the arguments for and against cases are compelling. As Payne (2005) summarises, research-mindedness has been criticised for lack of rigour; EBP has been criticised for its failure to recognise the limitations of the positivist position in a human activity; practitioner research has been criticised for producing large numbers of poorly constructed studies; and practice guidelines have been criticised for incorporating material to comply with the policy demands of governments rather than evidence of effectiveness. Suffice it to say that, for the purpose of this book, the core debate remains that practitioners have a responsibility and an obligation to generate and use research in practice, and even though the nature of that responsibility is debated, there is some level of agreement that careful collaboration is required to ensure the best possible outcome in and for practice. This will be core to the discussions in this book as we explore the nature of and strategies for practice–research collaborations.

Table 1.1: Self-assessment of research-mindedness

Research-mindedness questions	Not at all	To some extent	Very well
I understand the place of research in social work practice			
I know how to access research studies which are relevant to my own practice context			
I understand the political, cultural and ethical issues involved in practice research			
I know how research informs my practice			
I have an understanding of the benefits and challenges of different research designs			
I know how to interpret research findings and research limitations			
I know how I can play a role to advance research in practice			

The significance of the practice–research relationship

From the perspectives outlined above, it is easier for the split than the interconnectedness between research and practice to be evident. The continual tension between 'practice' and 'research' seems to be a long-standing one in social work, but not exclusively so, as is clear from similar discourses in nursing (see Giuliano, 2003) and education (see Groundwater-Smith et al, 2013). Indeed, the 'Teacher Research Movement' (Marilyn, 1999) has been as widely debated as social work, with very similar outcomes. Cochran-Smith (2005) presents sharply diverging viewpoints on the teacher-educator functioning simultaneously as researcher and educator, and concludes that there has been, and still is, reluctance among many educators (as we find with social work practitioners) to embrace research. This is echoed by many social work authors, leading to what Trevithick (2000, p 9) calls the 'stereotypical view' where research is considered to be irrelevant, obscure, abstract and untranslatable in terms of direct practice. Smith (2009), on the other hand, states that academic researchers can legitimately be criticised for failing to seek proactive engagement with the world of practice and for not producing findings which are relevant or accessible to practitioners, policy makers or service users. Furthermore, many social work and governmental agencies do not appear to have a substantial commitment to the research process, either in the sense of commissioning and utilising studies or in terms of the support and resources they could provide to encourage practitioner research (Smith, 2009). A number of strategies to make social work practice more scientific have been offered over the years, including programme evaluation (Suchman, 1967), research utilisation and dissemination (Grasso and Epstein, 1992), intervention research (Rothman and Thomas, 1994), single-subject designs (Bloom et al, 1999) and so on. According to Shaw et al (2010) these efforts are the 21st-century descendants of Abraham Flexner's work, which considered social work hardly eligible for the status of a profession.

As recent as 2008 though, Orme and Powell made the claim that social work lacks the necessary breadth and depth to respond to the demands of being a research-based discipline at the present time. The message seems consistent, albeit from various corners of the earth via divergent academic and practitioner views: practitioners have not experienced the benefits and clarity that research can bring to practice situations and researchers often enforce this paradigm by producing findings that reflect their lack of understanding of practice. While some authors regard research as mirroring practice, or at least regard it as another social work method alongside case-work, group and community work (D'Cruz and Jones, 2004), most caution on expectations for conflating the skills of practitioner and researcher (Shaw and Faulkner, 2006). Some academics (see Gray and Schubert, 2012, p 204) place the blame squarely on the shoulders of practitioners, stating that despite on-going attempts to ground practice more firmly on sound research, social workers continue to resist scientific models of knowledge development as antithetical to their humanistic theoretical frameworks and practice-based approaches.

Trevithick (2000) has written at length about the anti-intellectual stance within social work, highlighting that practitioners, for various reasons, do not work in a learning culture where curiosity, enquiry and exploration are encouraged or where opportunity, encouragement, time and resources to update knowledge are seen as priorities. This stance is also sustained by academics, who, at times, have gone about the task of linking theory to practice quite insensitively, sometimes dictating to practitioners how they should work and producing research findings critical of practice, tending to ignore more positive accounts of social work. These views can easily distract from the many positive developments that some practitioner-researchers embrace, and provide ammunition to those opposing research in practice. This book sides with Neiman: 'The gap between what is and what should be is too deep to ever be reached completely, but what we can hope to do, is to fill it in' (Neiman, 2008, p 141). So how can this gap be filled? It requires attention to the relational qualities of research. As much as competent practice is the result of collaborative efforts of people with diverse competences, so will a collaborative effort of people with diverse competences strengthen the development of new knowledge.

Reflection exercise 1.3: The significance of the research–practice gap

1   What is your view on the tension between practitioners and researchers; who is to be blamed for this tension?
2   What is the best strategy, in your view, to bridge this gap? Should it even be bridged?

A number of increasingly complex models to capture this notion of knowledge creation, transfer and use have been offered over the years. Davies et al (2000) present a simplified model of the changing nature of EBP that captures well this tension between research and practice/experts and users of research, while Gray and Schubert (2012) propose a more complex model. There are seemingly core components to these and other views on EBP, illustrated in Figure 1.1.

From this illustration it is clear that the researcher–practitioner relationship traditionally involved one of experts disseminating the knowledge they created to users – with an expectation for it to be adopted in practice. This also reflects the unidirectional relationship between practitioners and researchers, where practitioners learn from researchers, but researchers do not consider the practice expertise of clinicians in their research. Orme and Shemmings (2010) warn that making research results available is not always enough and they encourage researchers to undertake research that is meaningful to practitioners both in its focus and in the way it is undertaken. The contemporary view of practitioner-research advances this notion by encouraging interconnectedness and a shared responsibility for appraising existing knowledge and creating, validating, disseminating and adopting knowledge.

The contemporary model is a very significant development in the advancement of practice research, as it introduces the notion of 'relationship'. Collaborative efforts seem to be increasingly regarded as the way to 'fill the gap'. However, the focus then shifts to how best to ensure real collaboration in the practice–research interface. Some researchers still implement this collaborative model rather uni-directionally, at times. Galinsky et al (1993), for instance, stated in the early 1990s that even in collaborative efforts, researchers often fail to view practitioners as full partners in research. In fact, this is true today and it is common practice in many healthcare settings for social work practitioners to serve as data collectors rather than true research collaborators. When I attended a presentation by a prolific author

Figure 1.1: The changing nature of practice research

Traditional model of practice research

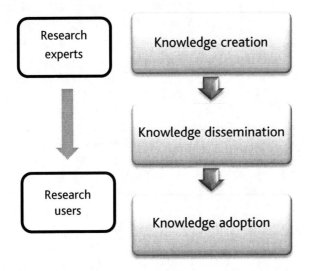

Contemporary model of practice research

on practice research at an international conference recently, I was absolutely amazed by the focus of 'collaboration' on 'how we can get practitioners to buy into our design'! Groundwater-Smith et al (2013) argue for a truly reciprocal relationship that recognises that the boundaries between actors are of a more permeable nature. They also encourage practice–research partnerships that go beyond a combined exercise comprising a sharing of resources, to embrace a relational activity that enables sustained change and long-term benefits for all involved. According to Groundwater-Smith et al (2013, p 1), true practice–research collaboration is when practitioners and researchers 'together systematically investigate issues and challenges that matter to them'. This is the type of collaboration we will explore in this book. Before we continue discussions on making a difference through practice research, we need to briefly consider the bigger picture: how this relational activity is about more than practice research, but contributes to the interface with other knowledge to advance social work as a profession.

The theory–practice–research interface

It is timely to remind ourselves that this discussion on the relationship between practice and research started with the need for evidence. Social work is located within some of the most complex problems and perplexing areas of human experience and for this reason social work is, and has to be, a highly skilled activity (Trevithick, 2000). We have seen that effecting competent change in practice requires a search for evidence on what constitutes competent change. But a skilled practitioner relies on more than research to inform practice decisions, assessments and interventions. Trevithick (2008) categorises knowledge under three overlapping headings, namely theoretical knowledge, factual knowledge and practice/personal knowledge. This framework proposes that all forms of knowledge are considered relevant and should be used in ways that can guide understanding and action. This is not a notion supported by everybody, with some positivists advocating passionately against practice wisdom. But for the purpose of this discussion about how practice research can make a difference, it is important to understand that research knowledge does not, by default, take precedence over other types of knowledge. Even though Orme and Shemmings (2010) suggest that research underpins all knowledge, factual (including research) knowledge is only a part of the knowledge base informing competent practice. As such, in considering the need for research, one has to also consider the place of other knowledge. This calls attention to the importance also of theoretical knowledge.

Debates on the relationship between theory and practice in social work can be seen to parallel those debates on the relationship between research and practice. Being guided by theory is, as with research, strongly associated with the effectiveness of practice. As Fargion (2007) reminds us, by citing a range of publications on this topic, some regard the gap between theory and practice as inherently problematic and fault practitioners for being neither interested in their theoretical training, nor prepared to allow theory to guide their conduct. Others are critical of the potential impact of theory over social workers' practices and regard the output of researchers and academics as less relevant than other forms of knowledge, including practice knowledge developed through concrete experience (Sheppard, 1995, 1998). The synergy with the present debates about the practice–research gap is clear. However, in reality the opposing approaches to the place of theory in practice are not so divergent but, according to Trevithick (2008), merely an indication of the way different authors place an emphasis on certain features over others. Those authors who emphasise the importance of a more scientific approach to knowledge take the view that systematically produced knowledge is linked to more competent practice. This type of knowledge is referred to as theoretical knowledge (Trevithick, 2008), formal or product knowledge (Sheppard and Ryan, 2003), expert or specialist knowledge (Fook, 2002) or propositional knowledge (Fox et al, 2007). According to Fargion (2007), in this approach, boundaries between scientific knowledge and common sense (practice knowledge or practice wisdom) are mainly vertical and they mark out a hierarchy. The second approach places an emphasis on knowledge gained through action and experience and regards scientific or formal knowledge as useful only once it has been used in practice. Trevithick (2008) refers to this as practice or practical knowledge, also regarded as process knowledge (Fox et al, 2007) or action knowledge (Osmond, 2005). This approach tends to underline the struggle for social work to be accepted as different but equal among the social sciences, and boundaries are mainly horizontal (Fargion, 2007).

Reflection exercise 1.4: The value of knowledge in practice

1   Do you consider practice knowledge/practice wisdom more important than theoretical knowledge in delivering services to vulnerable populations? Why?
2   In your view, what is the real value of theoretical knowledge to practitioners?

As briefly outlined above, there are multiple types of knowledge of which empirical or research knowledge is but one. As such, not only do we have to consider how relational activity can fill the gap between practice and research, but also how such collaboration can address the gap between practice and theory. This does not imply multiple foci in our relational activity, but in essence an interconnected 'wheel of science' (Babbie, 2001), or what Smith refers to as the 'theory–research–practice triad' (2009, p 2). This connection between theory, practice and research has been eloquently presented in the seminal 1996 publication edited by Fook, *The Reflective Researcher*, and expanded in the 2011 contribution by the same author (Fook, 2011) highlighting that generating theory from practice positions the practitioner within the research process. 'A process of reflection on practice might thus involve the potential for theory development, research enquiry and practice improvement', according to Fook (1996, p xiii). Trevithick (2000) reiterates this by stating that, between theory and practice, lies the activity of formulating and testing working hypotheses (research). You may start to wonder what all of this has to do with practice research. Let's consider Figure 1.2 to illustrate the research–practice–theory interface.

You can consider the wheel presented in Figure 1.2 by starting at any of the three points. As a practitioner, you will be most likely to consider practice observations, so let's discuss the wheel by starting there. Practitioners are likely to see the same type of problem or behaviours on a frequent basis – from, for instance, teen mothers, adult drug users or older people with dementia. Experienced practitioners analyse a problem to the point where they recognise familiar patterns. These may present either as similarities across cases/populations/interventions or as anomalies – where a situation was not quite what you expected or didn't fit the pattern. Fox et al (2007) suggest that once a practitioner has used pattern recognition to define the problem, the focus shifts to resolving the difficulty; you may begin to develop a way of working to address some of these patterns or anomalies.

Figure 1.2: Practice–research–theory wheel

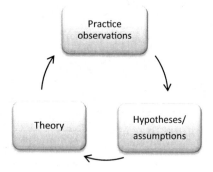

Example 1.2: Developing a hypothesis

As a community mental health worker you are involved with a group of women, aged 45–55, referred to mental health services for the first time for presenting with depression. In reflecting on this situation, you realise that there has been an increase of middle-aged women presenting with depression and a high percentage of these women have blamed their condition on menopause and hormonal imbalances. You are wondering about the possible link between depression and menopause.

In terms of the practice–research–theory wheel, you have just started developing a hypothesis. A hypothesis is a statement of relationship between two variables – in this case, the relationship between middle-aged women's depression and menopausal symptoms. There are a number of ways to do this, or to investigate this relationship, or to test the hypothesis. More about this later, as this is the interface with practice research. But let's first discuss the implications for the wheel: once you have explored this relationship in any significant way, you will have developed insights – either supporting your hypothesis or not. Either way, the outcome will have changed your understanding pertaining to depression and the importance (or not) of menopause in depression experienced by middle-aged women. By making these results known, you will contribute to theory! So the third part of the wheel will be informed by and will impact on not only your own but also other practitioners' understanding of depression in a particular population. This new insight will impact on assessments and interventions; it may assist you in including targeted questions about menopause in working with older women experiencing depression, and this in return may alter your intervention – you may incorporate strategies to deal with grief associated with loss of child-bearing in your work with these women. In doing so, you or one of your colleagues may observe a different pattern with women from a certain ethnic group. You express your observation to each other and question the link between depression and menopause for African women. You have just developed a new hypothesis: findings on one question raise more questions, and you find yourself in a perpetual cycle – a practice–research–theory wheel.

There are two crucial parts to this wheel – the axis, if you will – that will determine whether the wheel turns or not. One is that the hypothesis needs to be expressed and investigated; the other is that the findings from investigation of the hypothesis must be made known. Hopefully, you will see that this is the collaboration required for effective research-theory building and practice-research developments. To investigate hypotheses is not something that practitioners regularly do; it is not considered a key performance indicator! However, there are multiple ways to enact that and these will be discussed in the chapters to follow. Similarly, disseminating findings from tested hypotheses seems so very academic and unlike something practitioners will do as 'standard practice'. Yet, the development of social work as a profession and the possibilities to effect competent change depend on it. Note how the enactment of this 'wheel' depends on multiple relationships to 'make a difference' to service delivery.

Conclusion

This chapter has examined the development of practitioner research globally, highlighting calls for collaborative efforts in practice research. Research knowledge was positioned as one type of knowledge that can potentially make a difference to practice and was presented in the context of a practice–research–theory cycle. Critical questions about views on the need for evidence and the drive to make a difference have been offered. There are many excellent examples of ways in which key stakeholders, including practitioners and academics, have successfully connected in practice-research networks and these will be highlighted in the chapters that follow. Chapter Two will focus on the various political, ethical and cultural drivers that shape the social work research landscape and the internal and external factors impacting on practitioners' decisions to conduct practice research.

Further reading and resources

Fischer, J. (1973) 'Is casework effective? A review', *Social Work*, vol 18, pp 5–20.

Kirk, S.A. and Reid, W.J. (2002) *Science and social work – a critical appraisal*. New York: Columbia University Press.

Further reading on the relationship between social work and research may not be of high interest to emerging practitioner-researchers, but you may well be intrigued by the significance of this relationship. If so, these two publications are very useful in providing additional information and position practice research in a more academic way.

The context of practice research

Introduction

Have you ever felt frustrated by knowing what to do to solve a problem or deliver an effective service, but not being able to act on those insights for lack of authority or resources, or because of the challenges of professional boundaries or job security? No social activity takes place in a vacuum and there are always a number of dynamics to consider and relationships to negotiate in order to make a difference. We may even want to consider who decides that a difference is needed, and what the best alternative would be. Research is no exception; even with an understanding of and commitment to practice research, there are many dynamics to consider in the design and implementation of research. Like practice, social work research is subject to a range of influences, including: access to information and resources; highly politicised practice contexts with issues of trust and power to be managed; the funding context as a controlling factor in research agendas; and the influence of the consumer movement or multi-cultural priorities impacting on the nature of research topics and designs. The context of research itself is also a determining factor in the critical appraisal of information and in the dissemination of findings. Indeed, Shaw and Holland (2014) emphasise that research is largely bare of meaning when stripped from its context, as it occurs in time and place.

As we have pondered in the previous chapter, there is limited evidence of sustainable success in reaching the aspirational goal of combining the professional practitioner's role (to intervene in clients' life situations) with the researcher's role (to produce new knowledge) in any one person at a given time. A range of successful collaborative initiatives relating to practice research have been implemented, though, in different countries across various disciplines: some report excellent examples of ways in which key stakeholders, including practitioners and academics, have successfully connected in practice research, and most report success in achieving their goals of increased practitioner research activity. A systematic identification and analysis of such practice research studies undertaken within a social services context has been reported by Mitchell et al (2009). Yet, in considering these reports more closely, it is evident that almost all have benefited from funding support and it seems unlikely that these successes would be maintained beyond the life of the initiatives – unless another round of funding were forthcoming. A number of more formal government-funded initiatives have also been developed, mostly in the UK, with the aim to address the so-called deficit in research capacity. According to Orme and Shemmings (2010), these initiatives had a positive impact, but the development of research infrastructure to support practice research remains a priority.

Different authors identify various reasons for this situation, highlighting both the opportunities for and barriers to this state of social work's engagement with research. Many of these can be considered as contextual: the context in which practitioner research is either enabled or hindered. Mitchell et al (2009) highlighted three barriers for social workers conducting practitioner research, based on a systematic search of articles on barriers to and facilitators for the conduct of practitioner research, namely resources, professional identity and organisational systems and culture. Resources involved a lack of time; research confidence and expertise; difficulties in arranging cover; practical support; and reliance on external collaboration and support. Professional identity included social workers viewing themselves as helpers rather than as intellectuals by questioning how research knowledge fits with other sorts of knowledge, including intuition, experience, authority and policy. Organisational systems and culture were related to difficulties faced in terms of workload, role expectation and lack of support. This chapter will highlight the various factors that affect the social work research landscape and practitioners' capacity to conduct practice research. All of these both encourage and discourage collaborative practice research in various ways. The strategies and techniques to manage any one or a combination of these will receive attention, supported by questions for you to reflect on.

Reflection exercise 2.1: The context of research

You are committed to consider evidence in your practice or to engage in practice research of your own. Or you are a practice manager or social/ health services manager and you are approached by research-minded staff who ask to be allowed to incorporate more research-related tasks into their daily practice activities.

1   What do you anticipate will be the main enablers and barriers to such research-minded practice?
2   Are you clear on the procedures for obtaining approval and access to data and/or participants to enable practice research in your agency?

Contextual factors impacting on practice research

The contextual opportunities for and barriers to social work practitioners' engagement with research are varied. For the purpose of this discussion, these will be roughly categorised under three headings: political, ethical and cultural, as proposed by Campbell and Fouché (2008). However, these categories are not mutually exclusive, nor exhaustive of the description of contextual influences. Practitioner research is enabled or hindered by a multitude of individual factors and those highlighted below do not fully reflect situations where a spark between like-minded colleagues or the actions of a laterally thinking leader or the long-term insistence of a passionate colleague magically bring practice research initiatives to life. The relational aspects of these factors will receive focused attention in the next chapter.

Political factors

The context of social service delivery changes constantly, being impacted on by changes to global development agendas, ruling political parties, policy directions and budget decisions. You will have experienced the impact these changes have on funding and funding priorities; to demonstrate that funded initiatives deliver outcomes linked to the latest policy or budget priorities. A number of factors including managerialism and neoliberal politics have ensured that agency-based research agendas are now firmly focused on effectiveness, evaluation and monitoring (Gibbs, 2001). However, the pressure is mounting for research aimed at demonstrating impact and outcomes, and comes both from politicians having to manage on-going economic challenges and from administrative leaders' need for knowledge about the efficacy of social work (Uggerhoj, 2011). But these are often competing demands. McLaughlin (2007) provides a detailed account of the state of social work in the UK and very convincingly explains how the modernisation agenda changes not only the social work landscape but also that of the research. Warren (2007) highlights the legislative and policy framework impacting on the increasing significance of service users' involvement. He convincingly explains how these changes impact on the monitoring and evaluation of service-delivery processes, with the expectation of involving service users as partners. In varying forms, and probably at different times, this is the context of social work practice and research.

Politicians, managers, practitioners and academics are likely to have different expectations of research and it is not uncommon for real challenges to emerge at the stage of dissemination. What to report, what not to report, how to report and when to report can become really contentious issues. We will explore this more in following chapters on the planning and dissemination of research. But it is important to note that different players, agendas and dynamics contribute to the complexity of research in practice. Even researching one's own organisation will be influenced by a range of political factors. McLaughlin (2007) refers to claims that researchers (seemingly educators) are sometimes seen as politically naïve and failing to fully understand how an organisation operates, whereas managers (seemingly senior practitioners) are 'tuned to the importance of information and the uses and abuses to which it might be put' (McLaughlin, 2007, p 163). This is potentially true in the model of researchers as experts working with practitioners as research novices or in a context where researcher-educators have never been managers, practitioners or board members themselves. McLaughlin (2007) concedes that such a view neglects that both social work and research are essentially mediated activities; research impacts upon practice and practice influences research. The essence of practice research is partly to mitigate some of these claims and partly to ensure that, even where there is limited understanding by the one or the other partner, that the sum of the whole will be more than its individual parts. If we consider for example the findings of a recently completed cross-country audit of the role of hospital-based social workers, the difference between collaborative practice research and an expert-driven investigation will become clear.

Example 2.1: Problem solving through collaboration

A collaborative study involved academics and social work practice managers in the design of a tool to conduct an audit on social work competencies in a hospital setting. At the planning stage the political drivers, including pending changes in IT systems and in the way activities would be recorded, were considered. The 'politically naïve' researchers were included in a discussion of the dynamics of the organisation and appropriate practice responses. Discipline-specific sensitivity/turf protection related to the naming of competencies such as 'counselling', 'pastoral care' or 'physical exercise', historically seen as the domain of a particular discipline, was sensitively managed. The timing of the audit was also adapted in terms of other managerial priorities. Similarly the 'research novice' practitioners were guided through aspects of methodological rigour and the scientific process so as to enable robust findings. This included discussions about the importance of recording reliable data, even though this might cause inconvenience to daily operations and potentially exclude 'important people' who might happen to be unavailable on a particular day. To this end, the collaboration mitigated problems that could have arisen if the audit had been implemented by 'outsiders' and the findings been reported to practitioners.

However, research-related initiatives are often situated in research offices separate from practitioners and the coalface of practice and are conducted by research 'experts' – very much in the old model of EBP as discussed in the previous chapter. Funding is allocated to these research 'machines', which only rarely involve practitioners or front-line workers and if they are involved, this will be to manage randomised control trials or to act as resources for data collection. Influencing agendas, funding allocation and research practices as a practitioner will be relatively difficult in the absence of strong political connections. The same is also true for academics. Globally, tertiary institutions get funded for their research activities and even though funding arrangements and their respective criteria are diverse, there is an explicit link between research output and funding and status. Broad (1999) made mention of these dynamics in 1999 and they hold true today: whereas in the past it may have been possible for academics to go into an agency to research an aspect of practice as part of their paid employment, the reality of the current funding situation in universities means many research centres are run as small businesses. It is unlikely, at a time when agencies are facing cuts in funding for core services, that expenditure for research can be justified.

Whereas the practice of tenure drives research agendas in US universities, repeated funding-related assessments of research performance in universities in other countries, including the UK, Australia and New Zealand, impact on the nature and focus of research and the status of professions. The notion that certain research outcomes are considered for funding that are not always compatible with outcomes in applied disciplines such as social work is common. Funding for research-related activities is allocated in a political context, with governments, philanthropists and foundations setting funding priorities by considering a range of influences – not all of which are beneficial to social work research. While the purpose of any research (and in this context, practice research in particular) is to ultimately make a difference to the lives and well-being of service users, the issue of practice relevance needs to be balanced with scientific or methodological rigour. Powell and Ramos (2010) remind us that real tensions can arise for a researcher in generating knowledge that is both rigorous and relevant. As Lyons (2000) comments, it seems likely that social work, along with some other forms of professional education, is between a rock and a hard place in terms of maintaining both academic credibility and professional relevance.

Social work scholars in universities often face low recognition and support for community-based research. Despite often encouraging and promoting research that can be seen to have practice value or is useful to service users, universities tend to reward projects that attract prestigious funding and result in highly visible, peer-reviewed publications. If the research also happens to be useful to practice, it is a bonus. Successful collaborative research requires an investment by the researcher in the invisible work of trust building, negotiation and consultation, thereby potentially sacrificing more observable outcomes such as scholarly publications. Scholars who focus on issues emerging from practice needs will often experience reluctance from funders to support the endeavour. Given the lack of support and few successful models of university–community research, some social work academics choose more traditional approaches, which directly impact on the nature of practice research. The political context discourages practitioners from partnering with universities, due to lack of trust that the research will deliver a useful outcome for practice. It isn't difficult, however, to find a core group of practitioners who willing to work within the constraints and without incentives, so as to learn more and do whatever they can to provide a better service to clients. There is a core group of researchers passionately committed to making a difference to practice and putting their efforts into advancing practice research. And in some contexts, notably in the UK, change is evident.

This growing recognition of practice research partnerships is partly driven by the interest in knowledge exchange and partly by the focus on social impact and social outcomes. It has changed the understanding of research and contributes to the focus on translational research (or the so-called 'bench-to-bedside' programmes), as will be considered later, in the discussion of research dissemination. Funders increasingly require an indication of how the research will benefit communities and, as such, these partnerships are becoming more meaningful for practice stakeholders. The concerns of universities about the 'employability' of graduates and the link with industry have also seen movement towards recognition of and support for community-based research. The 'Capstone project', while it differs from university to university, is a good example of this. Students are encouraged to connect projects to community issues and to integrate outside-of-school learning experiences. But that does not imply that practice-generated research is becoming free from political dynamics.

Orme and Shemmings (2010) remind us that funding impacts on power relationships and often determines ownership of the research. Funded research, in particular, can put constraints on what is researched, the process and the dissemination of outcomes. However, all practitioners might be expected to engage with research topics that are meaningful to the organisation if they expect to receive support to progress the research. This will have implications not only for what is researched, but also for what happens to the results of the research (Orme and Shemmings, 2010). This dynamic also impacts on the appraisal of research. The process for appraising research will be discussed in Chapter Four, but it is important to take note that the context of research strongly impacts on the nature of research dissemination. There is a saying in the media: 'no show, no story' – implying that, if a celebrity does not physically appear, there is very little to report. However, in research a 'no show' is as important as a 'show'. The very competitive publishing environment does not easily allow for a failed project or findings of little significance to be published. Yet, it is from failed attempts and results that do not quite turn out as expected that we find the most learning. Even the publishing context, therefore, will impact on the nature and quality of practice research.

This all clearly indicates how the political context may impact upon collaborative practice research. Although some of its aspects may be discouraging, positive opportunities are also generated within this context through the political interest in partnerships and knowledge transfer. Social workers, more so than a range of other social scientists, are well placed to apply for grants that require well-developed relationships between academics and industry partners. Philanthropic organisations in particular tend to prefer funding those social programmes that have an in-built evaluation component, which creates research opportunities and raises the profile of the practice–evidence link in community agencies. Within this context, there is opportunity for practitioners and academics to tackle this complexity and to partner not only in order to conduct the research, but to influence funding priorities and knowledge transfer that will impact on the effectiveness of professional social work.

Reflection exercise 2.2: Political factors in practice research

How can you communicate lessons learned from a failed project to interested stakeholders, without doing more harm than good?

Ethical factors

Ethics is a topic that covers questions relating to what kinds of lives we should lead, what counts as a good society, what actions are right and wrong, what qualities of character we should develop and what responsibilities humans have for each other and the ecosystem. Social workers have an ethical responsibility to service users, the wider community and employing agencies to provide the best possible service. This responsibility gets communicated in various documents on social work practice standards and codes of conduct. In the context of research, ethics as a subject area traditionally covers topics such as the overall harms and benefits of research; the rights of participants to information, privacy and anonymity; and the responsibilities of researchers to act with integrity. All research raises questions about ethics: about rigour, responsibility and respect for the practices of researchers. As a result, there are strict systems in place to encourage and enforce ethical research conduct. There are increasing constraints on what research can be undertaken, by whom and with whom. Nobody will dispute the importance of this, but the way they are exercised has become a major factor impacting on how practice research is shaped and conducted.

Fox et al (2007) state that the number of hoops that practitioner-researchers need to jump through varies considerably and depends on the research site and the nature of the research. These act as both challenge and catalyst. They may range, at one extreme, from obtaining approval from an organisation, to receiving formal approval from a list of individuals and institutions, at the other extreme. Not only does this uncertainty about acceptable ethical processes in practice impact on research planning, but so too do the risk-averse practices that accompany these processes. According to Dodd and Epstein (2012), the benefit of participating in research is sometimes overlooked by ethics approval committees in their quest to ensure that research subjects are not burdened or harmed by research participation. It is not uncommon for research projects to be rejected or put under extreme scrutiny if the topic is too sensitive or participants are regarded as vulnerable. As a case in point, a researcher has experienced endless difficulties in convincing an ethics committee of the merits for survivors of a natural disaster of partaking in an exploratory study on their lived experiences. Once the research was under way, though, participants embraced the opportunity for their voices to be heard and not one reported harm or burden, nor accessed any of the support services offered in anticipation by those considering ethical dilemmas.

According to Coghlan and Brannick (2005) and Williamson (2007), there are a number of specific ethical considerations related to undertaking insider research (which practice research can be viewed as being, especially when you are researching your own organisation), including negotiating access with authorities and participants; ensuring participants' right not to participate and/or to withdraw from the research without fear of negative consequences; and keeping good faith in the reporting of the data in order to protect on-going relationships. Gray (2004) adds balancing the day-to-day practitioner role with that of the researcher role as a major issue. This may raise particular challenges regarding confidentiality, with the danger of 'role blurring' (Williamson, 2007, p 17). Role blurring is particularly relevant when using a number of applied research designs (to be discussed in Chapter Five) such as participatory research, where the boundaries between researchers and 'research subjects' begin to blur. According to Wysocki (2008), it is important for practitioners to be guided by the ethical codes of their regulatory bodies and those that they are contractually bound to by their employers. But not everybody agrees with this rather pragmatic point of view. Guillemin and Gillam (2004), for instance, question the relevance of professional codes for research practice when stating: 'professional ethical codes are largely not practical or applicable and can serve only as general guidelines' (Guillemin and Gillam, 2004, p 263). This view poses a huge challenge for practitioner researchers, who sometimes have to convince an ethics approval body that they are, indeed, competent to conduct ethical research within the very same context in which they are considered particularly capable to practise ethically as social workers. Ironically, a practitioner with a day job in the field of victim support for child sexual abuse has been scrutinised by an ethics committee on the potential danger of interviewing child prostitutes. Moral and political issues are central to the conduct of research and the role of the researcher, and not just a matter for consideration in the research approval process.

One solution and a growing expectation is that this ethical responsibility will be exercised through partnerships, consultation and collaboration (Fox et al, 2007), including with vulnerable and marginalised groups such as mental health users, people with learning disabilities, disabled people, refugees and older people. Whereas traditional research may mostly make use of consultation with these groups, practice research encourages collaboration and consideration of reciprocity in user involvement. According to Blaikie (2010), over and above service users or clients, these partnerships may also include the range of possible audiences that the researcher has to, or wishes to, take into consideration, when implementing the findings. These audiences include authorities such as governments and universities; agency managers or boards on whose behalf the research is being conducted; sponsors who are (or may be) funding the research; colleagues; scientific communities (particularly the editors of journals); and employers. However, in exercising this option with the involvement of diverse partners, a wide range of different expectations of and demands on knowledge, research findings and research designs must be managed. Again, applied practice research creates specific challenges in this regard, which may not be adequately addressed by institutional frameworks for ethical conduct in research.

As with the political factors, it is clear that these ethical challenges may at times seem to discourage practice research. But, the opportunities and benefits that arise from these challenges should not be underestimated. The challenge of managing boundaries as a practitioner-researcher also implies the existence of relationships with potential respondents. This will ensure access to contexts where research would potentially otherwise be limited, and enhance data collection through existing relationships of trust. There are many examples of research undertaken with drug users, prostitutes and gang members based on existing trust relationships. The advancement of our understanding of end-of-life discussions and of the experiences of parents with terminally ill children will hardly be possible unless there is some role blurring between those doing the research and those being researched.

The ethical challenges of role blurring should also be balanced against the benefit for service users of participation in research. A project with welfare recipients on their experiences of 'being poor' highlighted the benefits of participation: being supported to explore their experience; being heard; having an in-depth interview (data collection) that they had consented to; and being part of action for change. This all seemed to be more important than the blurring of boundaries between researchers and research subjects. Coy (2006) highlights examples of where professional judgement is required despite the conditions of the ethics approval, namely that research participants be given professional support when this is assessed as being more important than data collection. Participants' stories may remain untold when professional judgement calls for anonymity and confidentiality beyond that anticipated by an ethics committee. In fact, a recent research study with HIV-positive migrants and refugees posed a range of ethical dilemmas that were successfully managed by the experienced social work interviewers but were never anticipated at the stage of ethics approval. Naturally this doesn't mean that boundaries should not be noted and managed, but in practice research relationships between researchers and research participants can be a strength rather than a weakness. A practitioner-researcher's commitments to ensure that ethical issues are resolved on an on-going basis, rather than (only or mainly) as an approval process, will ensure that we make a difference. The desire to ensure quality research and to protect clients, but also not to discourage practice research, requires a fine balance. A good start is to consider the use of a 'letter of agreement between participating parties', as opposed to a 'consent form for participants', when preparing an ethics application. Such an agreement will always be particular to a project and to the negotiations – much like a contract for service.

Reflection exercise 2.3: Ethical factors in practice research

What would a letter of agreement look like if you were to partner with an agency/university/researcher for a practice research project?

Cultural factors

Indigenous and bicultural perspectives have criticised some paradigms (mostly positivist) as Westernised, racist and demeaning of other cultures (Tuhiwai Smith, 2012). According to Gibbs (2001), this implies that new definitions of research problems, alternative research designs and data-collection methods, as well as indigenous people's control over research findings and publication are expected. Naturally this raises a range of challenges for practice research. Past and present immigration policies mean that client groups increasingly include greater numbers of migrants and refugees from non-traditional source countries and there are competing demands on resources to better manage these multicultural priorities. Guidelines for research and evaluation with specific cultural groups have been developed internationally to assist researchers with applying the principles of partnership and participation when undertaking projects that require cultural input (for example, *Guidelines on Pacific Health Research*, published by the Health Research Council of New Zealand, 2005; *Guidelines for Ethical Conduct in Aboriginal and Torres Strait Islander Health Research*, published by the National Health and Medical Research Council of Australia, 2003; *Statement on Cultural Competence in Evaluation*, published by the American Evaluation Association in the US, 2011; and *Celebrating our Cultures: Guidelines for Mental Health Promotion with Black and Minority Ethnic Communities*, published by the National Institute for Mental Health in England, 2004). Most of these documents emphasise the development, cultivation and maintenance of relationships as integral to all ethical cultural practice and highlight values of reciprocity, respect and equality. Alongside the ethical factors referred to above, we also need to consider the issues regarding effective collaboration with service users from particular cultural, marginalised and vulnerable communities.

Cultural factors impacting on practice research also include educational and organisational contexts. According to Orme and Shemmings (2010), one of the complex reasons why the use of research by practitioners is still patchy relates to the lack of attention to research in the education and training of social workers and to the culture of organisations. The level and content of qualifying professional training and the recruitment of staff to universities primarily as social work educators have contributed to the limited development of methodological expertise and rigour in building the research capacity of social work (Orme and Powell, 2008). Although this claim is made for universities in the UK, this holds true internationally. The fact that schools of social work are hardly respected for their research expertise and comparatively assessed as not performing well on research performance measures has major implications for advancing practice-research agendas.

Regarding the organisational context, McLaughlin (2007) highlights a number of 'social worker issues' (p 152), including work pressure, the value of research as 'real' work and research literacy, as a set of barriers within organisations to research-informed practice. Practitioners need to work in a learning culture where curiosity, enquiry and exploration are encouraged and where opportunity, encouragement, time and resources to update our knowledge are seen as priorities. This would, hopefully, encourage many more practitioners to engage in research and this, in time, may provide the link that is needed in the theory–practice divide (Trevithick, 2000). Orme et al (2010) warn that so long as workload demands remain high and research findings are obscure, meaningless or hard to access there will be limited response to them among practitioners. Organisational culture will also determine the role of gatekeepers and access to information, resources and participants, which can impact on the planning and conduct of practice research. In one health practice context, the mere dynamics involved in accessing the data routinely entered into a database were enough to discourage any enthusiasm. A request had to be submitted through layers of managerial permissions and the approval eventually came with so many provisos that hardly any critical analysis was possible, while access to information entered by other health professionals was denied. For knowledge production in practice research, organisational flexibility is needed (Kristiansson, 2006, in Uggerhoj, 2011) and boundaries between disciplines, both social and economic, need to be crossed (Gibbons et al 1994, in Uggerhoj, 2011). Furthermore, practitioners have to have the time, the means and the motivation to access, understand and utilise the findings of research (Orme and Shemmings, 2010). Similar to the other contextual factors, these challenges may at some times discourage practice research and at others enable opportunities to advance practice research.

> ### Reflection exercise 2.4: Responding to contextual factors
>
> 1   When you consider the practice context where you will potentially engage in research, what do you think is needed, ideally, to effectively respond to the call for more and better practice research?
> 2   What do you think should be done, realistically, to enable this to happen?

Responding to contextual factors in practice research

If we accept that various contextual factors pose challenges, but also allow opportunities for practitioners and academics to partner for ethical and culturally sensitive research and to influence funding priorities, then we need to find effective ways to enable that. As with all social work practice, contextual factors are non-negotiable; some are more challenging than others, but all require attention in a quest to make a difference. There are no easy answers; managing contextual factors requires particular skill in mediation, negotiation and even radical practice. Many books have been written on empowerment, advocacy and radical social work for this very reason. This is less so in the research context. Maybe we do need more publications on radical ways to demand resources and organisational support and to enhance professional identity as practitioner-researchers! McLaughlin (2007) very eloquently states: 'Research like social work is a messy social and political activity ... it is highly contested, fraught with ideological, ethical and moral debates' (p 184). But, as has become clear in the discussion so far, a great many of these contextual factors also provide the impetus and opportunity to advance practice agendas and, indeed, practice research opportunities. To manage the contextual factors, layered macro- and micro-level interventions interwoven with a commitment to collaboration, and a resolve to improve the knowledge and effectiveness of professional social work, are required. Some of these interventions will be located outside of the domain of individual researchers and practitioners, while others are more pragmatic and manageable at an individual level. But jointly we can make the difference – as we always have regarding social work practice complexities.

Mitchell et al (2009) raise a number of important questions (strategic, organisational and programmatic) to be addressed if practice research is to continue to flourish. These questions span the contextual factors highlighted above and prompt us to consider how to respond to them in the planning, conduct and dissemination of practice research. There are on-going debates in response to each of these questions, so the answers will be diverse. However, you are encouraged to consider your responses to these questions as appropriate to your context and, more importantly, to use these questions as a base for considering your own contextual factors for practice research. Note in particular how all of these responses are dependent on relationships, networks and partnerships, to make a difference in practice. The development of practice networks will be discussed in more detail in Chapter Three.

Strategic responses

Reflection exercise 2.5: Strategic responses to contextual factors

Practice research can be driven and controlled by an organisation, practitioners, service users or by external researchers and develop as a bottom-up initiative, or it can be directed by management. What would work best in your agency, and why?

As with the historic development of the interface between research and practice, we can track the development of strategies to advance research-mindedness or research-related activity in practice over many decades. A full history is not relevant, but there is a lot that we can learn from this history, especially regarding strategic responses. Early initiatives involved the development and implementation of research projects in collaboration with academic schools of social work and social service agencies (Rehr and Berkman, 1978; Rehr and Caroff, 1986). The partnership involved collaboration between schools of social work and agencies beyond traditional internship arrangements by successfully integrating training curricula and collaboration between schools and agencies. Academic–practitioner partnerships tend to be piecemeal rather than strategic. These partnerships typically involve academics posing research questions that are then investigated in practice. They may allow opportunities for researchers and practitioners to take each other's perspectives and to participate in interpreting the results of the research. Alternatively, they may involve practitioners discussing research questions and designs with a consulting academic, based on the perception that academics are the more knowledgeable group and the transfer of knowledge is one-directional. Very few partnerships will involve both practitioners and academics in the design phase or in the reporting and dissemination of the findings (Rynes et al, 2001), and even fewer will involve sustained and on-going relationships. All the examples of successful practice research initiatives include some element of academic–practice partnerships (Mitchell et al, 2009), and if you are in a position to influence or initiate real partnerships, formal secondments or joint appointments, it will really make a (world of) difference.

Academic–practitioner partnership models have been successfully implemented in the US (between, for example, Mt Sinai Hospital and the City University of New York) and have recently gained momentum in Australia, where a number of health settings now offer joint staff appointments with university staff or contracted arrangements to facilitate the integration of research and practice. The relationship between allied health staff at the Peter MacCallum Cancer Centre and the University of Melbourne and between the Hunter New England Health Service and the University of Sydney are good examples. We need more of these initiatives and the model should be implemented more widely in sectors other than health. The nature of these partnerships will naturally be shaped by political factors and changes within tertiary and political systems, including the announcement of strategic directions for funding, the availability of resources for specified outputs, or modified expectations for performance evaluations and promotions, as highlighted earlier. It should be regarded as acceptable and expected for academics and practitioners to alter partnerships consistent with changing opportunities and dependencies.

A natural follow-on from these early initiatives involves research training in the workplace. Adequate educational preparation and on-going training are core professional concerns. Building a research culture in many organisations and sectors will be from a low base and will require concerted professional attention if it is to harness the energy and enthusiasm of practitioners. This may require a new set of relations to be negotiated between the profession and the tertiary education sector.

Organisational responses

Reflection exercise 2.6: Organisational responses to contextual factors

Networks, collaborations and learning circles to advance practice research can be fostered at all levels of an organisation, and practice research can be nurtured in different ways. What would work best in your agency, and why?

The role of the employing organisation is important if particular practice projects and practitioner research more broadly are to be nurtured. Instead of situating problems and solutions at the level of individual practitioners and their teams, it is important to recognise the responsibility of organisations and how, at this level, resources can be managed. This would be more effective in organisations already known as learning organisations and those committed to organisational excellence (Corby, 2006). The successful completion of a research project can be assisted by appropriate workplace support, including managerial and Board support. In one example, with the support of management, a practice team was able to set aside occasional days and use this reserved time for data collection and analysis. These shared times of research activity also proved valuable for purposes of morale building. Within this organisation there was also positive affirmation from the Board for the research activities that were being undertaken and a belief that such developments were worthwhile and should be supported. Given that research is frequently a marginalised process within many organisations (Shaw, 2005), such practical and emotional support was extremely welcome for the team involved. Conversely, there are examples of practice research teams that felt such support was not forthcoming, or was actually being withheld. The implication for these teams was that research had to be undertaken in personal time and was not a core part of professional social work. This compromised both the momentum and availability for implementation and the nature and extent of dissemination. McLaughlin (2007) regards the notion of a learning organisation as one of the most important ways to align differing interests between social work researchers, social work practitioners and organisations. However, many agencies seem reluctant to embrace a learning culture and to support collaboration across boundaries.

In many organisations, core activities, defined as allocating caseload, seeing clients and getting work 'done', trumped all else. McLaughlin (2007) highlights one of the barriers to research as the perception that reading a book or journal implies that 'real' work is being neglected. There is a need for practice research to be seen as a constituent of real work and for job descriptions and professional development to include space for research. It is important that opportunities are created at an organisational level to access research, read research, discuss research and participate in a range of research-related activities, from planning through to dissemination. This collaboration throughout the entire research process, which entails not only discussing findings but also trying them out, facilitates knowledge-based learning processes (Uggerhoj, 2011). Examples of successful practice research initiatives often include some element of mentoring and team learning (Mitchell et al, 2009), and more such initiatives are needed. Supporting staff members to become team builders, to embrace innovation and to encourage continuous service improvement are key elements in a learning culture. To obtain the expert input and continuing support, universities need to partner with practice to offer continuing educational opportunities.

Literature and research on organisational learning and continuing professional development provide models for improving the use of research in practice. Drawing on theories of organisational learning, Orme and Powell (2008) have encouraged strategies to address staff development issues for academics and practitioners and the creation of vibrant learning communities across academic and practice settings. These authors' ideas include a focus on the relationship of individuals (practitioners and/or academics) with their employing organisation and the relationship between academia and practice. They suggest that parallel and complementary arrangements have to be developed for social work academics (primarily educators) and practitioners to engage in research. Walter et al (2004) presented three models that embody different ways of thinking about and developing the use of research in social care. One of these, the organisational excellence model, places the responsibility for research development on the organisation and recognises that individual practitioners are both constrained and empowered by the context in which they work. This fits well with the organisational response to contextual factors. However, Walter et al (2004) promoted a whole-systems approach, stating that initiatives to improve the use of research are more likely to be successful if they complement one another. This notion of a whole-systems approach fits well with the collaborative, practice research promoted in this book. The organisational responsibility includes attention to people, procedures and systems. The focus on people includes giving support, helping to build teams and encouraging networking of appropriate resources within agencies. Procedures pertain to building into employees' performance appraisals or development plans the expectation (or even the requirement) to critically reflect on practice or identify researchable questions, if not the explicit expectation of engaging in research. Attention to systems includes providing mentoring replicated on successful supervision models by either appointing internal mentors or contracting external mentors. But it isn't only about organisational responsibility, it is also about strategic responses and individual- and grassroots-level initiatives.

Programme and individual responses

Reflection exercise 2.7: Programme responses to contextual factors

There are various grassroots-level activities to support practice research: what is the most appropriate model of mentoring; the most appropriate content and delivery mode for training; the best way to disseminate research findings among practitioners; and what guidance is needed for ethical review? What would work best in your agency, and why?

At a grassroots level, responses to the practice–research context relate to the development of individual competence, the expansion of researcher roles and the maximisation of opportunities. Engel and Schutt (2013) remind us that, whether we plan to conduct our own research projects, read others' project reports or just think about and act in the social world, knowing about research methods has many benefits. This knowledge gives greater confidence in opinions, improves the ability to evaluate others' opinions, encourages improvements to the social programmes in which we work and provides better interventions with clients. But the development of competence includes more than research skills – it requires a certain level of information literacy. Individual practitioners need to take responsibility for developing skills in accessing online resources, joining topic-specific blogs or online forums and registering for e-mail alerts on new material relevant to their practice context. Most importantly, research competence is also a determining factor in the critical appraisal of information and in the dissemination of findings, as will become clearer later. We have alluded to the fact that all the contextual factors will have an impact on what can be said, how it can be said and how it can be disseminated. But if you are unable to source relevant material and appraise the material for its scientific merit, no number of strategic or organisational responses will advance your involvement in practice research. However, this does not mean that the responsibility for the whole of the research endeavour falls on any one individual. Once again, the notion of partnerships becomes important.

This points to group capability and opportunities that can be maximised in practice teams with varied strengths, opinions, perspectives and experiences.

Practitioners have vast insider knowledge and experience, which makes them excellent advocates of new research topics. They can potentially persuade both the administrators of their organisation and researchers with an interest in their field to start a new study. Due to increasing ethical and bureaucratic limitations, academic researchers encounter increasing difficulties in accessing potential samples. Collaboration with practitioners would offer such access, enabling practice-related research projects. Practitioners can also enhance their own skills by participating in research education. The purpose and context of research will, and should, influence methodological choices (Smith, 2009). This will be considered in more detail when aspects of designing applied research are discussed.

Example 2.2: Success factors for practitioner research

As an example of one initiative aimed at supporting practice research, the use of a structured approach or a 'framework of opportunity' contributed to the management of obstacles and opportunities and eventually to the success of the initiative (Fouché and Lunt, 2011). Reference to this initiative will be made at various places in this book to illustrate a particular discussion. Based on learning from this initiative, a structured approach displaying the following characteristics has proven effectiveness: a time-limited focus, a shared vision, work breakdown structures and cohort membership. The review conducted by Mitchell et al (2009) identified similar success factors for undertaking practitioner research, including working in a close team environment (that is, small teams of practitioner researchers or forms of peer support) with group ownership and passion for the practice focus of their projects, and project milestones to address time management and forward planning. Another factor highlighted by Mitchell et al (2009) is the support of the employing organisation, reminding us again of the interconnected nature of contextual responses.

Conclusion

All the stakeholders in practice research are interdependent and influenced by the context in which they operate. Politicians, managers, practitioners, educators, service users and funders have an interest in the efficacy of social work and in the advancement of knowledge-based practice, but we are all bound by political, cultural and ethical factors. Social workers are restricted to their organisational and professional context and therefore need to take into account not only their own needs and those of their clients, but also the organisational obligations and available resources. Educators and university researchers are interested in the research process itself and in the contribution the topic makes to existing knowledge, but are restricted by their own research field and by the university's requirements for academic justification (Uggerhoj, 2011). Yet, the possibilities to effect competent change depend on effective management of the context, as much as on the research agenda. The effective management of the practice and research contexts depends on multiple relationships to 'make a difference' to service delivery. In this chapter, a commitment to collaboration was posed as one of the strengths for working with and within the multitude of contextual influences. The next chapter will put the nature of these relationships and networks under the spotlight.

Further reading and resources

Social Care Institute for Excellence (SCIE) Resources: http://www.scie.org.uk/about/Index.asp.

There are many topics in this chapter and the following chapters that can benefit from additional reading. Material relevant to each chapter will be recommended as appropriate. However, we will recommend and refer to various resources developed by the SCIE throughout the book and, as such, this is posed here as a useful resource to explore and consider for your practice research journey.

SCIE is an independent charity working with adults, families and children's social care and social work services across the UK. It gathers and analyses knowledge about what works and translates that knowledge into practical resources, learning materials and services. SCIE is committed to co-production and has developed a set of principles and a strategy to achieve this.

3

Practice research relationships

Introduction

To what extent do you believe in the value of relationships? It is generally accepted that relationships are core to the practice of social work and most readers will probably regard relationships as hugely important in their personal and professional lives. Payne (2005, p 20) reminds us just how significant these are by emphasising the importance of interactions in 'making' social work: 'theory is constructed in an interaction between ideas and realities, mediated through the human beings involved. How clients experience their reality affects how workers think about their practice theories; agencies constrain and react to both and together they make some social work.' Cree and Davis (2007, p 158) report on a study about perceptions of social workers in the UK, stating that, among other things, social work is about 'being alongside people in their lives' and about 'building relationships'. This is true for research as well. Research as a process of knowledge generation is inescapably a value-laden activity within which the researcher plays a significant role (Powell and Ramos, 2010). But social research, by its nature, involves more than just the researcher; human participants such as vulnerable or marginalised individuals or groups and organisational resources are core to social research. In other words, social research is about people!

Social research is a dynamic and interactive process. It can take place only with the trust and cooperation of those who take part in the research. Therefore the relationship between the researcher or research team and those who are 'researched' is fundamental; the more collaborative the research, the more fundamental the relationships. Current approaches in social research reveal tensions between research that gets close to practice and is empowering in nature and that which is regarded as objective, scientific and displaying methodological rigour. Naturally, the robustness of research is, and should always be, of concern. It will be clear to the reader by now that this book unashamedly falls in the category of collaborative, committed and empowering research for the benefit of practice. However, it does not approve of research that is non-scientific and lacking in rigour. The extent of collaboration does not make research more or less robust and certainly is not an indicator of its potential authenticity or significance. But collaborative, practice research is multi-faceted and unpredictable by nature and brings with it a complexity that makes it different from research that is not collaborative and that is more tightly controlled. Therefore, the nature of relationships in research and the use of networks should be explicitly acknowledged in this context.

Smith (2009, p 21) very strongly makes the point that social work research is not, cannot and should not be treated as a pure or discrete exercise of discovery: 'the field and subjects of inquiry will always include people who are likely to be affected by its outcomes, and may well be directly involved in its processes'. This implies that multiple, interrelated research relationships exist in conducting and advancing practice research. The previous two chapters comprehensively highlighted the influences on practice research and the importance of collaboration to make a difference in practice. This chapter will turn to the practicalities of forming networks to successfully engage in practice research and the complexity of maintaining these relationships.

Reflection exercise 3.1: Forming and maintaining relationships

1   Consider the different types of relationships you manage in your professional role and the value of these relationships in enabling you to get tasks done or goals achieved.
2   How/why did these relationships form?
3   List the factors that you regard as crucial in initiating, developing and maintaining positive relationships in practice.

The scope of practice research relationships

All responsible and accountable research requires attention to relationships. As practice researchers are encouraged to develop as many collaborative networks as possible to enable robust research that will benefit multiple stakeholders, consideration of relationships becomes exponentially complex, but important. According to D'Cruz and Jones (2004), consultation and collaboration with others extend the sources of knowledge and range of perspectives that may contribute to the question-setting process. Discussion with others from both within and outside the social work research community can develop alternative ways of thinking about the research question and design, and can enable insights into the multiple factors impacting on the research. Moreover, according to Powell (2007), undertaking research as part of an interdisciplinary team can also offer creative opportunities for extending ways of 'thinking and doing' research, despite the challenges and potential pitfalls. The nature of these relationships and the related obligations can be considered in the following broad categories: funders; employers (including community or agency representatives); colleagues (fellow researchers or practitioners, including other social workers; other teams and other professions); participants and/or service users or the intended beneficiaries of the research; the researcher; and ethics reviewers.

Funders

Many funders of social research, internationally, including philanthropists, government agencies and targeted funds or awards, are increasingly focused on supporting partnerships and multi-agency or collaborative initiatives in addition to ensuring the demonstrated benefits of research. To this end it is not uncommon for requests, proposals or applications to require information about outcome benefits, post-contract outcomes, implementation pathways and evidence of service users' or key stakeholders' involvement – all highlighting the expectation of collaboration and networking. Any strong and credible user linkages that have clear potential to lead to uptake of research results and to establish and grow effective relationships with user communities – including indigenous communities – are increasingly encouraged. This does strengthen the funding possibilities for social work, as mentioned earlier, although there is little evidence to suggest that we capitalise on the collaborative nature of our profession. Funders report frustration in having to deal with power issues, turf protection and the appearance of collaboration without real substance.

Unlike many other professions, social work is, at its core, about relationships, and I am often amused by colleagues in other disciplines asking how we initiate and manage our multiple relationships to ensure that we meet the funding expectations. My simple response is always that it is what we do best. But it also creates real tension in the development of a proposal for funding. Due to the collaborative and thus unpredictable nature of practice research, it is not always possible to meet the 'scientific' (that is, positivistic) assessment criteria for proposals. Many attempts at obtaining funding for innovative practice research projects have been challenged with feedback such as 'lacking details on design, including number of participants and method of data collection'; or 'no clear outcomes articulated'. In the initial phases a practice research design such as action research or data mining will naturally lack this level of detail. Real collaboration will assume that alternative ways of thinking about the research question and design and about the factors impacting on the research will be the focus of the initial phases of the project. However, the tension lies in the fact that a (especially funded) project cannot get under way until these details have been decided and presented as a set of milestones to be contracted – very much along the lines of traditional, non-collaborative research. An important way to manage this is to present collaborative research as a robust methodology in its own right – as will become clear later. But more importantly, building relationships with potential funders is a crucial component of advancing practice research. Not only will it assist social workers in developing insights into the mechanisms for funding allocation, but it will increasingly allow opportunities to make this tension known. This is true for both practice managers and academic researchers.

There is a wealth of material on strategic sense making within funding relationships (see for example Grimes, 2010). Even though this pertains mostly to developing operational funds for the not-for-profit social services sector, it is suggested that performance measurement (a focus and result of practice research), can be an effective mechanism for entering into funding relationships. Grimes (2010) made the point that organisations are often involved in several different partnerships and funding relationships, but that increasingly this may happen across organisations, in which successes and failures are shared. The relevance of this for advancing practice research is evident. Similarly, the relationship between funders and academic researchers is widely debated – albeit from opposing viewpoints. It is important, though, to note that findings from a study conducted in Norway (Gulbrandsen and Smeby, 2005) indicated a significant relationship between industry funding and research performance: professors with industrial funding describe their research as applied to a greater extent, they collaborate more with other researchers both in academia and in industry, and they report more scientific publications as well as more frequent entrepreneurial results. In terms of the status of social work research internationally, the evidence of significant industry funding for social work academics seems to be sporadic.

Employers

Limited numbers of social work practitioners are actively involved in exploring and accessing research opportunities, including access to funding. There are many opportunities available to various sectors, be it allied health funding, NGO development support or workforce and professional development resources. These are universally underutilised by social workers – the focus is mostly on the 'usual' well of dedicated and easily accessible support. But the same hurdles highlighted in previous chapters that prevent social workers from doing research (including time and resources) are probably also the barriers to accessing funding for research – which, ironically, will provide resources to enable more time for research. However, good relationships between funders and employers and between employers and practitioners will enhance understanding of practice research needs and benefits. Moreover, resources to support and enable practice research, including time, access, approval and information, will be possible only if there is a good relationship and shared understanding between employers and employees. At a very basic level, it is the responsibility of the practitioner to be clear about the needs to enable practice research and that of the manager to explore opportunities to meet those needs. However, as highlighted earlier, the extent to which these discussions will deliver any tangible results will depend largely on the advances the employing agency has made as a learning organisation. The notion of a learning organisation remains one of the most important ways to align interests between researchers, practitioners and organisations (McLaughlin, 2007).

Colleagues

For many practitioners it will be a logical first step to consider close colleagues for collaboration in practice research. Mostly, these will be colleagues from the same team. It may include social work colleagues in the same organisation, practice team and site, or in the same field of practice. For others this may involve other disciplines, other sites, other agencies or other geographic locations. This will be specific to each organisation and its particular way of service delivery. Most important, though, is that there are many permutations of collegial networks. Even though we will naturally approach those most accessible or those we have reason to be in contact with on a regular basis, practice research requires us to explore those networks aimed at best serving the practice project. One of the secondary benefits of practice research is regularly reported to be enhanced relationships and networks (Lunt et al, 2008; Epstein, 2009). This holds equally true for practitioners, researchers and educators. Practitioners are often better placed than academic researchers to develop collaborative relationships with professionals and service users. But academics have strong relationships with colleagues in various disciplines and with postgraduate students (often practitioners themselves), and access to dedicated support, such as from statisticians. The real challenge is in finding the will and passion to engage with 'fit-for-purpose' teams to best serve the needs of the project. This will not happen without encountering difficulties. As Orme and Shemmings (2010) warn: the moment we undertake research that requires generating knowledge *from* practice and potentially undertaken *by* those involved in the situation, it is bound to raise all sorts of issues. These include issues of power, authority and gatekeeping. Our skills in managing clients and organisational dynamics will serve us well in managing these challenges!

Participants

Respondents in traditional research and in most types of quantitative research are sources of information or subjects of the study. Sometimes, these respondents are also referred to as participants; this is technically correct, as they do participate in the process of data collection. But true participation by those whose experiences are under investigation or whose information is collected for the purposes of creating new knowledge involves more than data collection. The involvement of participants and intended beneficiaries of the research in shaping its focus has become a key principle of 'research that creates change' (Munford and Sanders, 2003). The participation of service users has become an important consideration when undertaking collaborative research. Service users have naturally always had perspectives about their experience of policy, practice and services, as they are, after all, on the receiving end. But increasingly, governments across the globe have undertaken to provide a legal and policy framework that requires more active user participation; service users need to be involved as partners rather than simply being consulted about service delivery and developmental processes (Warren, 2007). This is increasingly true for all research activities, but undeniably relevant for practice research. The level and nature of engagement will vary, but thinking about service users as participants and about different levels of potential participation will highlight the importance of the research–participant relationship. This will encourage consideration of how research participants are valued in the shaping, designing, implementation and dissemination of research. According to Warren (2007), different levels of participation can be enacted at different stages of the process with different groups of service users, including at the level of information giving and receiving; consultation, where service users' views are taken into account; full participation, where service users are regarded as equal partners in decision making; and empowerment, where they have power and control over the decision making.

There are naturally many pitfalls in enabling these levels of participation, particularly where service users include indigenous communities or tribal peoples. The complexities and potential pitfalls in involving indigenous people in research start with the purpose of participation and the real reason why participation from participants is sought. It is common to find examples of the 'tokenistic' inclusion of people to advance the research agendas of others. Linda Tuhiwai Smith (2012) promotes the decolonisation of research methodologies, arguing for a more critical understanding of the underlying assumptions, motivations and values that inform research practices. There is also increasing involvement of service users in health and social care education with the benefits reported as being increasing levels of skills, confidence and capacity (Anghel and Ramon, 2009; Fox, 2011). Yet, there is little research that reflects on the personal costs of involvement for service users, and this question needs to be raised when involving service users in research. The participation of service users and indigenous communities is a very interesting and contentious topic that cannot be done justice to in this chapter. Readers are encouraged to read more on this (consult the list of further reading at the end of this chapter). McLaughlin (2012) reminds us that service–user research should be regarded as an alternative research approach with its own strengths and limitations, and that the involvement of service users in research should always be carefully considered.

The researcher

It is important to acknowledge the various roles of the researcher that are created by the multiplicity of their relationships. In traditional research, the role of the researcher is relatively clear: as the expert, implementing an agreed research design by engaging with subjects, albeit in the same complex context. In collaborative practice research, the roles and activities become varied and more complex as a result of the possibilities of contexts and the relationships highlighted above. The researcher as academic or the researcher as practitioner in partnership with funders, service users, other beneficiaries of the research, employers and colleagues can be active in various research–related roles (Campbell and Fouché, 2008): as generator of research questions, hypotheses and opportunities; as collaborator in the design or implementation phases; as gatekeeper, informant or participant; as facilitator in steering or reference groups; as purchaser or manager of projects involving external researchers; as active practitioner–researcher conducting relatively small-scale projects in the workplace; and as 'consumer' of research as they seek to apply findings in their practice. The researcher as academic partner in practice research projects can perform multiple roles over the course of the project, including: as expert, by providing knowledge around either subject matter or methods of inquiry; as mentor and critical friend, by having a profound understanding of practice and possessing the capacity to bring this understanding to bear on the professional learning; and, as enabler, by utilising strategies to motivate and facilitate learning and the provision of resources (Groundwater-Smith et al, 2013).

Ethics reviewers

There is growing interest in the place of ethical review (typically encapsulated within requirements to submit research proposals to a formal ethics committee) and broader processes of governance in research. Practice research is not excluded from this; in fact, the nature of such research raises ethical dilemmas related to conflict of interest, confidentiality and informed consent. Engaging in research where the boundaries between researchers and research 'subjects' begin to blur will always pose challenges. Grinnell and Unrau (2005, p 41) warn that, for practitioners, relating to clients both as clinician and in a research context has the potential to constitute a problematic dual relationship and pose a challenge to the duty of care. This dual relationship also holds true for colleagues in the reporting of results, disclosing results to participants and acknowledging colleagues' contributions. Ethical implications regarding 'insider research', including ensuring participants' right not to participate or to withdraw from the research without fear of negative consequences, are also important for the practitioner in own-account research (Coghlan and Brannick, 2005). Practice researchers should respond to calls for ethical review and greater formal consideration of research projects, as discussed earlier. But within this process, a number of challenges and frustrations are often reported. Ethics reviewers become crucial partners in managing these.

Lunt and Fouché (2010) recommend that, while all practitioner-researchers should sign up to 'ethical' research, their review of ethical issues should be supported by streamlined procedures and practices that leave scope for multiple expertise. They advise against a singular approvals body and for increased discretion in line with professional codes of ethical conduct. A focus on the outcome, rather than the process, of ethical reviews and a realistic assessment of the potential for harm will embrace the unique character of social work practice research activities. This implies a collective responsibility and attention to the relationship between the research team (in its broadest sense) and those governing the ethical conduct of the research. Moreover, the nature of all the relationships and permutations created by such collaboration also carries ethical obligations. This complexity, along with those alluded to in the range of relationships highlighted above, will be considered next, before we explore strategies to manage it.

Reflection exercise 3.2: Managing relationships in practice and research

1   What do you regard as core factors that will enable practice-research relationships?

2   What can you (realistically) do as a practitioner to engage in networks and partnerships while systemic change may still be in the making?

The complexity of relationships in collaborative research

There is no doubt that collaboration brings with it a range of opportunities, including the opportunity to share ideas and creative solutions. Practising in isolation has been found to be a main predictor of underperformance, according to Norman et al (in Brehaut and Eva, 2012). The limitations of partnerships are also widely acknowledged, however, most notably their time-consuming nature (it is so much easier to get decisions made if you don't have to consider others!). The complexity that is inherent in partnerships is discussed by several authors. Trust is regarded as the fundamental component of collaboration, with Frank and Smith (2006) emphasising that a lack of trust undermines any partnership. Where partners come together in the true spirit of genuine collaboration and joint enterprise, highly successful working relationships can be developed that continue for many years and produce cumulative benefits. However, where the presence of any member of the team is viewed with suspicion, these collaborations produce tensions. Suspicions can be grounded in various factors, but lead to power struggles and impacts on the research process.

In addition to trust, Miller and Ahmad (2000), Himmelman (2001), Glendinning (2002), Frank and Smith (2006), Radermacher et al (2011) and others highlight a range of interrelated factors impacting on collaboration: the need for collaboration/forming partnerships with others; personal relationships between the key stakeholders driving the collaboration; compatibility of values and interests; previous experience of working collaboratively; differences in power; issues of accountability; and, most interestingly, the availability of resources (limited resources reportedly restrict opportunities for collaboration or partnering). Groundwater-Smith and colleagues (2013, p 67) reported on findings from research on university–secondary school partnerships and highlight that much about these partnerships rested upon the prior experiences and general attitude of team members in relation to 'the academy'. It is not uncommon for practitioners to voice that academics live in 'ivory towers' – implying they are ill informed about the realities of practice – even though many social work academics have spent many years in practice and often continue to hold practice positions. Similarly, academics can easily hold the moral high ground, lacking the capacity or willingness to become truly connected to the practice context and an understanding of how agencies operate – implying that practitioners are not adequately theoretically informed or research minded.

Naturally there will be issues of power and authority with academics, managers, service users and practitioners in the same room trying to negotiate design and implementation details – even when these are supported by adequate levels of trust and good personal relationships. Gatekeeping is a strong and powerful strategy exercised by all these stakeholders to push their own agendas. As extensively outlined in previous chapters, all research – and practice research even more so – takes place in a political, ethical and cultural context. Micro-politics in a particular agency and in practice teams parallel these dynamics and it would be ignorant to think they can be avoided. Clarity about the level of participation required from various stakeholders in different aspects of the project and the scope of ownership entailed by this will overcome some of these challenges. The nature and scope of involvement in research is viewed differently by different stakeholders and is mostly driven by what the participation in a research project is meant to achieve and the degree of influence participants are allowed (Roy, 2012).

Ownership is, to a large extent, a rather straightforward matter as far as agency research and traditional academic research is concerned; the researcher (or researching agency) owns the data and, most often, authorship of the results that are disseminated in various forms. In collaborative research, especially externally funded projects, this issue becomes more complex. Ownership, according to Orme and Shemmings (2010), involves issues of funding and power; funding is commonly linked to accountability and therefore drives the outcomes and often the design, but also asserts the power of decision making. Findings from practice projects often highlight strengths, demonstrate effectiveness or impact and put practitioners and organisations in a good light. They may additionally offer a range of secondary benefits in terms of service improvement and capability building. However, projects also produce unfavourable outcomes. Sometimes a programme evaluation, undertaken to demonstrate the benefits of the programme for continued funding, may highlight that the programme is not effective. Or controversial findings are disseminated in a way that impacts on the reputation of the agency. This is naturally possible with all types of research, but is particularly pertinent for practice research, where unfavourable outcomes may potentially have negative consequences for how the funders, participants, the public and other stakeholders view the respective social service, programme, client group or intervention under study. This is a real fear for some agencies and managers and often (understandably) results in resistance or behaviour aimed at controlling the process of data collection and the dissemination of findings.

In a top-down approach, the funding body will own the data and have the power to decide on subsequent actions, including on the dissemination of findings. In a bottom-up approach the power is shared between the community and the researchers; the academics/researchers are consulted for their research knowledge, but the community decides design, methods, goals and implementation. The community then owns the data. With top-down methods, the data and power to make decisions are in the hands of the policy makers, whereas the community holds this power and data when a bottom–up approach has been used (Roy, 2012). Orme and Shemmings (2010) remind us that underpinning all of this are the ethical implications of ownership not only of data, but of all of the research process. Those who participate in the research own the knowledge that the researcher(s) wishes to access, and it is crucial that the process is managed in a way that has integrity for all those involved, and also for the findings and the knowledge claims. However, the point of this discussion is to highlight that considerations of ownership are far reaching and must be negotiated at an appropriate time so as to ensure equitable involvement for all stakeholders and best use of the research findings. The earlier these issues are agreed upon, the better, as any delay in the discussion adds exponentially to the difficulty of discussions concerning ownership.

Rather than positioning this complexity as a challenge to undertaking practice research, this book calls for complexity to be managed as part and parcel of practice research. This is no different from how social workers will consider social work practice. Social workers do not distance themselves from complex interactions or disengage from networks with multiple agendas; they find ways through them and work within them. Those practice skills will serve practice researchers well. Uggerhoj (2011) argued that contradictions in research collaboration are unavoidable and even necessary in supporting a process for developing new knowledge created by multiple partners. Dilemmas resulting from collaboration do not need to be 'resolved' before we continue the process, as this may prevent individual partners from feeling that their needs are being met – potentially resulting in one or more stakeholders withdrawing from, or even opposing, the research project or aspects of the project. Differences need to be included in the practice–research process to ensure equal participation and influence from each partner (Uggerhoj, 2011). These differences are varied and situation specific, but a few common issues can be expected, and strategies to manage these will be considered below.

Example 3.1: Ownership of research data and findings

A not-for-profit agency obtained funding to advance an innovative idea to collect information on service users over a 12-month period in order to gain a deeper understanding of the experience of families living in poverty. A research team under the guidance of a research manager (employed by the agency for this purpose on the research grant), researchers from different universities (paid from the grant received) and employees of the agency (as part of their daily activities) refined the design, implemented the project and contributed to the dissemination of findings. The scope of involvement and degree of influence over the design varied, based on individual availability and capability. Participants were interviewed fortnightly and a rich dataset was developed. The project focused on a range of issues affecting clients, such as housing, debt, food insecurity, health, education and employment. The success of the project was partly attributed to the collective skillset of the team: access to service users; capability to collect data; logistical support to schedule interviews over the long term and to offer participants tangible recognition of their contributions; data management; data analysis; and eventually dissemination to various audiences in multiple formats. A question arose about the ownership of data and the nature of on-going dissemination from the data as opposed to about the data. Ownership was eventually resolved with a 'letter of understanding' based on considerations of accountability to the agency, service users and the funder; agency reputation; and to a lesser extent, level of participation; but also academic freedom for advancing conceptual debates on issues related to the data. The issues of ownership were not addressed at the beginning of the project and therefore this made for some tense discussions later on; but they were addressed early enough in the process (at the time of developing a dissemination plan) to allow for agreement to be reached.

'Communities of knowing' in practice research

Once complexity and challenge in collaborative research have been accepted as a non-negotiable part of the endeavour, we may now want to shift our focus to proven strategies for developing and maintaining these collaborative initiatives. Informal groupings have always existed in organisations and their value has been embraced. Efforts to add value to organisations have seen 'communities of practice' increasingly acknowledged as valuable resources – mostly in the field of management practice. The term was coined by Etienne Wenger and Jean Lave in the early 1990s and, in later years, expanded in partnership with Richard McDermott and William Snyder. There is currently a plethora of information on communities of practice and their value to organisations and, increasingly, on the nature of online communities of practice; and there are some seminal publications by the above authors and a growing pool of literature by others specialising in the field of knowledge management (Lave and Wenger, 1991; Wenger, 1998; Wenger and Snyder, 2000; Wenger et al, 2002; Coakes and Clarke, 2006).

Typically, a community of practice exists as a social gathering or technological network aimed at the sharing of expertise and the creation of new knowledge, often tacit in nature (Lave and Wenger, 1991). Wenger et al (2002) define communities of practice as groups of people who share a concern, a set of problems or a passion about a topic and who deepen their knowledge and expertise in this area by interacting on an on-going basis.

> Over time they develop a unique perspective on their topic as well as a body of common knowledge, practices and approaches. They also develop personal relationships and established ways of interacting ... even develop a common sense of identity. They become a community of practice. (Wenger et al, 2002, p 5)

It is clear, therefore, that communities of practice are vehicles for the creation and dissemination of knowledge. These communities find value in their interactions and become informally bound by the value that they find in learning together. Communities of practice are thus often considered in the context of organisational learning. The concept of community of practice is well embedded in social work too – mostly in the context of community development, but seldom in relation to research. Cordoba and Robson (2006) are among the few authors writing about the role of communities of practice in research. But the link to knowledge generation and the possibilities of utilising the notion of communities of practice to advance collaborative research seems sensible. There is also a link with material related to participatory research – an approach to research that is based on a commitment to sharing power and resources and working towards beneficial outcomes for all participants, especially 'communities'. This will be explored more in the discussion of applied research designs in Chapter Five.

Wenger et al (2002) are of the opinion that few would dispute the potential benefits that communities of practice can bestow on the individuals making up these communities and the organisations that these communities of practice reside in. But Davidson and Voss (2002) warned against the temptation to therefore formalise communities of practice. They warned that formal networks go stale almost as soon as they are established, but informal networks, precisely because they are dynamic, never do (Davidson and Voss, 2002). By its very nature, then, the success of communities of practice depends on their informal nature. Muller-Prothmann (2006) makes the case that the majority of individual knowledge transfer does not follow formal hierarchies or processes, but is instead driven by personal and informal communications. This is the point of difference – and potentially the added value for practitioner research – between communities of practice and communities of knowing.

One of the earlier authors on knowledge communities defines them as 'groups of people with a common passion to create, share, and use new knowledge for tangible business purposes' (Botkin, 1999, p 30). Knowledge communities, also referred to as 'communities of knowing' by Boland and

Tenkasi (1995), are therefore primarily focused on the sharing of knowledge. Based on an informative study about the differences between knowledge communities, communities of practice and knowledge networks, Muller-Prothmann (2006) made the case that it is difficult to precisely distinguish knowledge communities from communities of practice. He acknowledged the growing literature on these related concepts, but also the confusion over their conceptual and applied distinctiveness. He concludes that, whereas communities of practice are organised for the purpose of practical implementation of knowledge derived from experience, knowledge communities can be defined as 'relationships of trust between people within a wider domain of knowledge' (Muller-Prothmann, 2006, p 268) and these are organised for the generation of new knowledge. Most importantly for our purpose and the consideration of a strategy to advance relationships in practice research, he reported that members of communities of practice tend to work together, whereas knowledge community members do not necessarily work together.

If we then combine our understanding of the (mostly informal) practice nature of communities of practice with the (mostly formal) knowledge focus of communities of knowledge, we may have an effective vehicle in 'communities of knowing' for understanding, developing and nurturing relationships to advance practice research. Communities of knowing develop where a group of individuals with a shared practice interest and/ or passion for research enter into dialogue (driven by personal and informal communications) and take ownership for the sharing of expertise and the creation of new knowledge through both social gatherings and formal structures (including scheduled meetings, learning and dissemination opportunities). There are a number of determinants that impact on the effectiveness of these communities of knowing, namely the context, the processes to develop and support these communities, as well as the attitude and capability of members (Figure 3.1). These will be discussed in more detail below. It is interesting to compare these determinants with the elements of effective community action identified in a meta-analysis of community action projects conducted by Greenaway and Witten (2006), namely: building skilled leadership; accessing adequate resourcing; enabling infrastructural development; creating committed strategic support and advocacy; enabling effective coordination; vision building; skilled facilitation of people and processes; networking to build relationships, communication and knowledge; accessing mentors; effective planning; and making opportunities for critical reflection.

Figure 3.1: Determinants of successful communities of knowing

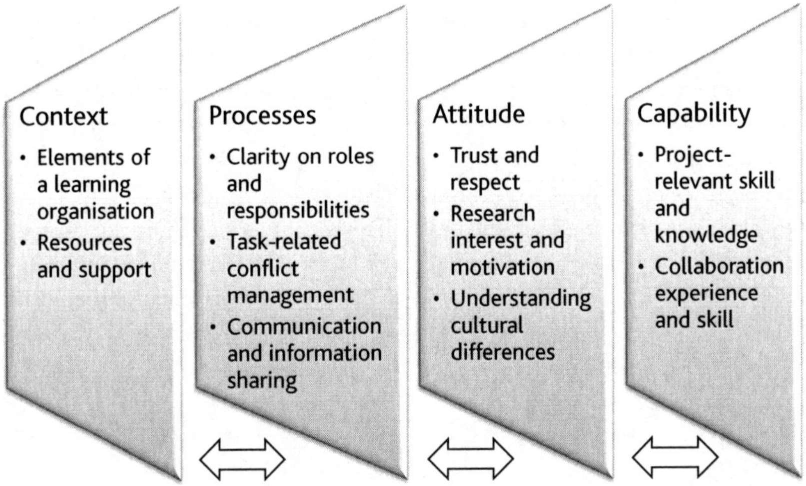

Context	Processes	Attitude	Capability
• Elements of a learning organisation • Resources and support	• Clarity on roles and responsibilities • Task-related conflict management • Communication and information sharing	• Trust and respect • Research interest and motivation • Understanding cultural differences	• Project-relevant skill and knowledge • Collaboration experience and skill

Context

As we have discussed in the preceding chapters, successful practice research is embedded within the organisational structure and related resources and support. Sabah and Cook–Craig (2010) and Cook–Craig and Sabah (2009) make a case for virtual communities of practice and suggest that adopting an organisational learning model and launching virtual communities of practice may encourage learning, making use of evidence and developing practice innovations. Orme and Powell (2008, p 998) propose that, to facilitate the creation of vibrant learning communities across academic and practice settings, it is necessary to include a focus on the relationship of individuals (practitioners and/or academics) with their employing organisation and on the relationship between academia and practice. This means that a specific context is required for social work academics and practitioners to engage in research. Academic–practitioner research partnerships in themselves are not new and, though constructed in varied ways, have shown a steady increase over the years. The nature of these partnerships is shaped by developments occurring within tertiary education and political systems, and it is common for academics and practitioners to alter partnerships, consistent with changing opportunities and dependencies. However, these partnerships tend to be piecemeal rather than strategic. Universities and practice agencies can facilitate practice research by offering strategic opportunities and incentives to those willing to undertake collaborative research.

Processes

To ensure success in research collaboration, there is a need for clarity on commitments, roles, responsibilities, expectations and resource needs to ensure effective use of members' capabilities. It is best to acknowledge the team dynamics and the value of different voices/types of expertise and respective contributions earlier rather than later in the process. To enable this, clear communication processes are required, including facilitated meetings and sensible information exchange. Powell and Ramos (2010) highlighted the importance of skills in negotiation and facilitation in the team, as relationship challenges are integral to practice research and some level of conflict resolution will be required in the process.

Attitude

Trust and respect for each other play a critical role and cannot be taken for granted in research collaborations. It is about like-minded people being willing to share expertise and create knowledge, without prejudice or fear of being shamed. Naturally, an interest in and motivation for engaging in research would be assumed. Groundwater-Smith et al (2013) encourage understanding of each other's institutional, cultural and political contexts and practices as a key aspect of these partnerships, and warn that it is important to approach collaborations without preconceived ideas as to how the relationship will unfold.

Capability

In the context of management research, Amabile et al (2001) identified team characteristics as a potential determinant of the success of cross-professional research collaborations. These characteristics include project-relevant skill and a common core of knowledge, as well as knowledge comprising diverse and complementary backgrounds and skills. Complementary knowledge, experience and skills pertain to the use of technologies for supporting data collection and dissemination (such as Twitter, Facebook and SurveyMonkey), specific software packages (for example databases such as NVivo and SPSS) and knowledge of and experience in writing funding proposals. According to Patton (2002), the credibility of the researcher in such a team is dependent on their training, experience, track record, status and presentation of self. He states that 'credibility involves intellectual rigor, professional integrity, and methodological competence' (Patton, 2002, p 570).

Reflection exercise 3.3: Strategies to advance communities of knowing

1   Do you have a couple hours to spare this year? How can you support those who are willing and able to develop communities of knowing or are already engaging in practice research relationships?
2   Do you have more than a couple hours? What can you do to identify people with practice research passion and to support communities of knowing?

Example 3.2: Growing Research in Practice (GRIP)

A structured group approach to advancing practice research, as highlighted in Example 2.2, is reported by Fouché and Lunt (2009). The authors reflect on the range of inputs and synergistic group processes that allowed for a series of outcomes that would not have been possible within an individualised initiative. This project was called Growing Research In Practice (GRIP) and comprised five core components: (1) the GRIP team: comprising four academics from two universities and two skilled research-practitioners; (2) selected groups of social service practitioners engaged in their respective practice projects; (3) support from funders; (4) strategies to collectively implement and share resources; and (5) the intention of gaining knowledge on the effectiveness of these components in the development of practice research activity. The partnership enabled eight practice teams with self-selected membership to conceptualise, implement and disseminate small-scale research projects driven by their own practice questions and agendas. The strategies and resources included workshops, mentoring and a symposium organised by the GRIP team. The initiative was developed from knowledge on the value of groups (McCafferty, 2004), the benefits of group supervision (Proctor, 2000), as well as a firm belief in the concept of mutual aid (Steinberg, 2004). The model was based on social group-work principles, including, among others, support, collective decision making and cohesiveness, and with the understanding that each member of the group was an important influence on the group's behaviour. Group members were regarded as providers and recipients of resources in achieving the common group and individual goals of, in this case, research-mindedness and research activity (Northen and Kurland, 2001; Steinberg, 2004). The emphasis on the group meant that the research activities and decisions for most groups would be fitted into the daily flow of work and the workplace. Dynamic forces for change included opportunities for: group control; reality testing; a universal perspective; a sense of hope; acquisition of knowledge and skills; mutual support and mutual demand; and cohesiveness.

As summarised by Davies et al (2007), just producing evidence does not necessarily result in change. It is crucial who disseminates this evidence, who regards it as important and how it is understood to be relevant to practice. Engaging practitioners in research will ensure that the work done is relevant and geared to their needs. It will increase the sense of ownership of, and commitment to, the research itself, and to any development and other policy and practice proposals which are based on the research. It also enables full-time researchers to become more familiar with the type of information that practitioners require and the range of ways in which research findings might be packaged and communicated. In addition to focusing on individual practitioners, an important aspect of many practitioner-research programmes is to also engage the senior management of organisations in the programme, thereby increasing their involvement in and awareness of research activities, agendas and outcomes. The purpose of this is to encourage them to provide the essential infrastructures for practitioner research. Moreover, it is equally important that senior managers become more active in disseminating such research and act on its outcomes. This will impact on decisions about policy directions and funding priorities.

Conclusion

This chapter has encouraged us to progress from debates about the importance of research in practice and who should take responsibility for advancing research, to dialogue about strategies and models whereby networks are utilised and the nature of learning organisations is questioned and developed. There is a vast amount of valuable material on this – albeit in the fields of organisational and knowledge management (see Allee, 2000; Davidson and Voss, 2002; Benson-Rea and Wilson, 2003; Coakes and Clarke, 2006). The use of organisations and inter-organisational networks for learning and knowledge development holds valuable information relevant to advancing the social work research agenda. The focus of knowledge management has progressed from an early emphasis on technologies and databases to an appreciation of how deeply knowledge is embedded in people's experience. Additionally, there is a growing body of knowledge on the value of networks (see Bessant and Tsekouras, 2001; LaMendola et al, 2009; Knights and Scarbrough, 2010). The scope of this book does not allow for an exploration of the strategies, stages and tasks to initiate, develop and maintain networks, communities of practice, knowledge communities or indeed, as proposed here, communities of knowing. But an appreciation of the importance and value of these communities will set us on the track to discovering these knowledge pools, expertise and resources.

In this chapter a collaborative effort for practitioner research has been promoted, while individual initiative is acknowledged: it takes a special person to move people from anxiety about research to joint exploration and knowledge building. As such, this first part of the book, on the dynamic relationship between practice and research, calls each one of us to consider our place (and those of others) in the advancement of knowledge for practice. A common management saying, 'none of us is as smart as all of us', seems a pertinent reminder in this context. Part Two will focus on the pragmatics of designing and implementing a practice research project from this base of collaboration and communities of knowledge.

Further reading and resources

Warren, J. (2007) *Service user and carer participation in social work*, Exeter: Learning Matters.

This book provides a useful perspective on the principal elements of service user involvement and participation and supplements the content on participant involvement in this chapter. The book is part of a series written specifically to support students on social work degree courses in the UK and, as such, may be difficult at times for an international audience. However, the book effectively introduces concepts on service user involvement and highlights the knowledge, attitudes and skills needed to enable this.

Smith, L.T. (2012) *Decolonising methodologies: Research and indigenous peoples*, London: Zed Books.

This book sets the scene for an extensive critique of Western paradigms of research and knowledge from the position of an indigenous and 'colonised' Maori woman. Smith's book challenges traditional Western ways of knowing and researching and calls for the 'decolonisation' of methodologies, and for a new agenda of indigenous research. Linda Tuhiwai Smith's book can inform non-indigenous researchers who may be involved in research initiatives with indigenous communities; in particular, it covers what a non-indigenous researcher needs to be aware of when researching with indigenous peoples; how non-indigenous researchers can improve their practices with indigenous peoples; and, most fundamentally, whether it is appropriate for non-indigenous researchers to be involved in research with indigenous peoples.

Coakes, E. and Clarke, S. (eds) (2006) *Encyclopedia of communities of practice in information and knowledge management*, Hershey, PA: IGI Global.

This publication is an amazing resource (all 100 chapters!) on communities of practice and knowledge communities by a selection of international experts across many disciplines. It provides robust discussions on generic aspects of communities of practice, and also highlights their organisational aspects.

Huxham, C. and Vangen, S. (2013) *Managing to collaborate: The theory and practice of collaborative advantage*, New York: Routledge.

The authors of this book suggest that managing to collaborate involves managing in order to collaborate. One has to think about this somewhat, but it is a powerful message that they then explain in the context of collaborative advantage and collaborative inertia. For those interested in the dynamics of collaboration and the reasons why collaboration sometimes does not achieve anything, this will be a useful book to consult.

Part Two
Designing practice research

Framing the project

4

Introduction

What do we want to achieve when we 'research'? The most difficult aspect of research is not the fieldwork or even the analysis of data, but the first step of figuring out what you want to know. People new to research often find the time–consuming process of determining the focus of a research project surprising. Mostly, people think that this can be decided quickly and easily and that the bulk of the work centres on the empirical phase or fieldwork. Consequently, the important first step of framing a research focus is overlooked in favour of designing the fieldwork and getting people involved in the project. It is not uncommon for a practitioner, when asked what they want to research, to shape a practice question with ease – sometimes linked to their frustrations in practice: we want to show that the resources are inadequate; we want to get data to convince management that we need to expand this service; or we need evidence on the value we add to the service. Other times, practitioners may use language originating from funding proposals or performance indicators: we want to demonstrate that this intervention is effective; we need to evaluate the impact of the programme on clients' lives; we want to capture the stories of clients; we want to show the effect of the current policy on the delivery of services. But eventually, the whole project will stand or fall on the way it was framed, and unless this is done well in the first instance, one will eventually have to return to a robust framing of the project; it happens without fail! It is therefore a good strategy to assign adequate importance to the framing of the project, which is the focus of this chapter.

Let's begin at the beginning and consider the nature of research. Orme and Shemmings (2010, p 11) suggest that research can be divided into three categories: the very general and loose application we all use, such as in 'doing the research' before committing to an expense such as buying a car or a house; the formal type that conjures images of people in white coats going about their business in laboratories; and a third, 'mid-point', the category that includes reading documents and gathering data to inform an opinion. It is within this last category that we place social research, even though the first is the one most often reported in the media, contributing to the 'bad' reputation of research and researchers. According to Leedy and Ormrod (2005), all research starts with a problem, and they continue to define social research as a process with a specific outcome, namely new knowledge, obtained through an orderly investigative process. D'Cruz and Jones (2004, p 5) refer to this as 'seeking knowledge for a purpose'. Davidson and Tolich (2003) highlight social research as a collection of methods and processes for producing knowledge about the social world; about people and interactions. There are probably as many definitions of research as there are books on the subject, but at its core, and for this discussion about framing a project for practice research, it is important to focus on the corresponding criteria: research is essentially an *orderly process* of investigation resulting in the development of *new knowledge*. Recently there have been attempts to define the unique nature of *social work* research, as opposed to general social science research. *The Sage Handbook of Social Work Research*, edited by Shaw et al (2010), captures the essence of these debates and is worth reading if this distinct focus is of interest. Orme and Shemmings (2010), very pragmatically, are of the opinion that as long as research is contributing to the improvement of social work practice, then particular approaches to research are not important. Interestingly, these arguments parallel debates about the unique nature of social work theory and the notion that social work ideas connect to (and originally came from) wider bodies of knowledge and theory and may contribute to those wider bodies (Payne, 2005, p 28). This, in my view, is also true for social work research and will not be debated in any more depth here. Robust research does not make a distinction whether it is *nursing* research or *social work* research, or any other research for that matter; it may well be conducted by a nurse or social worker, but it remains research – an orderly process aimed at developing new knowledge.

Some authors expand this discussion about the nature of research to refer to the difference between applied and basic research. For the purpose of this discussion, the core distinction between these types of research will suffice: basic research can be regarded as research for the sake of research (pure, basic or strategic knowledge development), whereas applied research is regarded as research with the aim of solving a practice problem. Hall (2008) considers basic research to be designed to advance knowledge and understanding regardless of its application and to lay the foundations on which other research is built. He highlights the focus of applied research as being on problem solving (Hall, 2008). Applied research, according to Sarantakos (2005), is directly related to social and policy issues and is aimed at solving specific problems and establishing policy programmes that will help to improve social life in general and specific conditions in particular. Practice research will therefore clearly be applied in nature, as it will be undertaken for practice purposes. But practice research has the added focus of being conducted by practitioners or, at the very least, as is encouraged in this book, in real partnership with practitioners. As such, particularly relevant here is Epstein's definition of practice-based research as the use of 'research-inspired principles, designs and information gathering techniques within existing forms of practice to answer questions that emerge from practice in ways that inform practice' (Epstein, 2001, p 17).

A further distinction in the understanding of research (sometimes referred to as the approach to research or the research strategy) is the difference between quantitative and qualitative research. Again, for the purpose of this discussion, a core distinction between these types of research will suffice: quantitative research pertains to quantity (counting), or data as numbers, whereas qualitative research pertains to quality (information-richness), or data as (mostly) words. The distinction between quantitative and qualitative research involves more than just the type of data, however, and a number of research publications go into some depth about ways of knowing about the social world. We won't go into these discourses here, but it is important to understand that quantitative research is structured, definitive and linear in nature and uses objective measures to enable forced responses to be analysed through statistical procedures (Dudley, 2010; Bryman, 2012). Qualitative research, on the other hand, is aimed at discovery, is more unstructured and circular in nature and collects data in word form on topics that are not necessarily predetermined. This allows for word analysis by considering patterns and themes (Dudley, 2010; Bryman, 2012). In the so-called 'paradigm wars' there has been on-going debate about the preferred approach to be used, and quantitative research has often surfaced as the more pure science. However, the robustness of the study is more important than the approach taken. Some excellent qualitative studies have produced more insights than have badly executed quantitative studies. And naturally, some topics lend themselves better to one approach over another, and that is – and should be – the determining factor in which approach to use.

Whittaker (2012) contended that quantitative research is generally more valued by governmental bodies, as it focuses on the 'what works' agenda and is more easily generalisable. This is indeed the case – not only for government agencies, but also for a range of managerial agendas – and is often crucial in multi-disciplinary teams. Social work has tended to favour qualitative approaches; practice research in particular has a more natural fit with methods of interviewing and narrative data. It is important that we don't opt for this approach by default, but that we consider the best fit for the topic under investigation and the contextual influences that may necessitate more data of the one type than of the other. This is particularly true in the current climate of social work research, where 'hard data' as well as 'clients' voices' are required to evidence the effectiveness of services or demonstrate a contribution to complex social outcomes. According to Whittaker (2012), this decision to proceed with qualitative research is at least partly influenced by the lack of capacity within social work to undertake quantitative research. Collaborative efforts and a team member with capability in a particular approach will not only contribute to solving this problem, but will also build capacity in the team for future endeavours. Hans Rosling is known for his inspirational talks on the value of statistics, and his TED talk on 'Let my dataset change your mindset' (http://www.ted.com/talks/hans_rosling_at_state.html) sends a powerful message on the use of quantitative data – also relevant for social work agendas.

Applied, practice research can utilise either one or a combination of these approaches, and does in fact most often rely on a combination of the two – the premise being that a combination of approaches provides a better understanding than either one alone. The core differences between these two approaches having just been outlined, it seems illogical that you could use both in one study, and for some there is strong objection to mixed-methods approaches. However, in recent times there has been a trend towards combining these methodologies, and increasingly the focus has been on the most effective ways to do this, rather than on the underpinning philosophy about whether it should be done (Onwuegbuzie and Leech, 2005; Creswell and Plano Clark, 2011). Mixed-methods research is both a philosophical assumption (methodology) that guides the many phases of the research process and a method that focuses on mixing both qualitative and quantitative techniques of data collection and analysis. We will revisit this discussion when addressing design issues.

Reflection exercise 4.1: The nature of applied research

1   Do you feel more drawn to qualitative or quantitative research? Why?
2   Which type of data will best serve the needs of your organisation?

It is within this context that we consider the framing of a practice research project. This chapter will outline the basic process for designing, implementing and reporting a small-scale research project as an introduction to more detailed discussions about designs and methods for data collection in the following chapters. As a first step in the research journey, this chapter will outline techniques for conducting a review of relevant literature and appraising existing material. An understanding of the scope and nature of existing knowledge is a prerequisite for any practice research. As has become clear throughout the book so far, the focus will again be on the effective use of collaborative relationships and communities of knowing to enable this. The inherent challenges in shaping collaborative research, such as ownership and reporting of the data, as well as equitable participation in co-production, will be explored.

The research process

Where do you start when you are assigned a new client in social work practice? Most often, you will aim to get to the heart of the problem by doing a thorough assessment and building on existing knowledge before you jointly consider the best way forward. Practice research parallels social work practice, and therefore the processes are the same in many ways: in starting a research project, you will build on existing knowledge and find ways to properly define the problem or frame the issue before any actions are taken. The process is impacted on by contextual factors as highlighted in Part One and, as such, the initial phases of shaping small-scale practice research projects involve negotiating a number of conditions to ensure that we eventually make a difference in practice. To be most effective, this calls for partnerships from the start.

At its core, research parallels the steps of problem solving: commencing with an idea that develops into a design to be implemented, resulting in reporting of the process and the outcome. Babbie and Mouton (2001, p 72) state that all empirical research conforms to a standard logic that they call the 'ProDEC' framework, the four elements that are standard in all forms of empirical research: a research problem (Pro), research design (D), empirical evidence (E) and conclusions (C). However, this process is not a linear one and the framing of a project is often more involved than one may initially anticipate. Leedy and Ormrod (2005, p 6) elaborate on this cyclical nature of research by stating that a neatly closed circle is deceptive.

> Research is rarely conclusive. In a truer sense the research cycle might be more accurately conceived of as a helix, or spiral, of research. In exploring an area, one comes across additional problems that need resolving, and so the process must begin anew. Research begets more research. To view research in this way is to invest it with a dynamic quality that is its true nature – a far cry from the conventional view, which sees research as a one-time act that is static, self-contained, an end in itself.

This process is always a trade-off; in deciding to take a certain course of action, you have decided not to take another. It is similar to having the option of taking different roads to your destination. If turning right or left at a crossing won't make any difference to getting to where you are going, you have options. However, by deciding to turn left, you have, in effect, decided not to turn right. And by deciding to turn left, you have excluded a range of possibilities associated with the right-turning option. At the same time, though, you are forced into implementing the actions that come with the left-turning decision. In a research context, the choice of an overall research question will focus your literature search and your choice of design. As Smith (2009, p 150) states: 'From this point in, the research project is shaped by an unfolding process of compromise and adjustment between what the investigator sets out to achieve and the slippery but sometimes intractable nature of the real world with which s/he is engaging.'

As with practice, the problem-solving process is made up of a series of interwoven decisions, each one impacting on and being impacted upon by the next. There are multiple phases and steps in the research process outlined in the literature – not unlike the phases and steps of social work practice. Some authors discuss the process nature of research without distinctly referring to steps (see, for example, Corby, 2006; Fox et al, 2007; Orme and Shemmings, 2010), whereas others simplify it to a few basic steps (Dudley, 2010) or break it down into a more complex series of phases and steps (see, for example, De Vos et al, 2011; Whittaker, 2012). For a practice researcher trying to find their way through research literature applicable to a variety of disciplines, the descriptions of a research process as perceived by different authors may be very confusing. The reason for this confusion lies in the fact that different authors use different terms for basically the same aspects of the research process, and sometimes different terms for the same aspects from a quantitative or qualitative perspective. When these various views of the research process are compared, it is clear, however, that they do not, in essence, differ very much from one another (Table 4.1). All of these phases of the research process can be simplified to five main elements: (1) framing; (2) designing; (3) collecting; (4) analysing; and (5) reporting. The focus of this chapter is on the first phase – the framing of the project.

The literature is confusing in the terms used to shape the first phase of the research journey. Some authors refer to this phase simply as 'getting started' (Babbie, 2007, p 109), moving into a phase of conceptualisation, while others propose very distinct activities in identifying a general topic area and refining this into a research question or problem (Hall, 2008) or, in the case of quantitative research, hypotheses (Bryman, 2012). Yet others prefer a very distinct description of the selection of an appropriate topic and the development of a research question or research problem (Carey, 2012). But, in essence, all these authors are in agreement: this first phase is about the need for the study, that is, what do you want to know? And to produce a definitive statement in this regard, the decision making will flow from a general topic of interest through a refining of a question or problem statement to a discussion of core concepts. This will be underpinned by an exploration of existing knowledge – for some authors a distinctly separate step in the research process (Hall, 2008; Whittaker, 2012), and for others, implicit in the whole process. Before the techniques for conducting a review of relevant literature and appraising existing material are addressed, the process of developing a definitive focus for the project will be discussed.

Table 4.1: The research process as represented by different authors

Orme and Shemmings (2010)	Dodd and Epstein (2012)	Hall (2008)	Bryman (2012)	Babbie (2007)
Ethics and ethical approval	Establishing the practice-research problem	Planning applied social research	Literature review	Interest, idea, theory
Reviewing the literature	Practice-based research study purposes		Concepts and theories	Conceptualisation and operationalisation
Methodologies and method	Practice-based research designs	Designing applied social research	Research questions	
Statistics and quantification				
Selecting research strategy/design	Data-collection methods			Choice of research method
	Qualitative or quantitative data gathering	Conducting applied social research		
Samples and surveys	Sampling		Sampling cases	Population and sampling
	Ethics and protection of human subjects		Data collection	Observations (data collection)
				Data processing
Talk and discourse	Analysing and interpreting results	Analysing applied social research	Data analysis	Data analysis (and drawing conclusions)
	Disseminating results	Communicating applied social research	Writing up	Application

Focusing the topic

Uncertainty is a basic principle of scientific inquiry. For some researchers the topic of study is a constrained choice, as it is undertaken on behalf of funders or as a commissioned piece of work. The origins of a good practice project lie mostly in reflections on practice or conversations with a colleague. These may pique interest in a particular population, behaviour or condition; a particular service or programme; a problem you have faced or been made aware of; previous research findings or something reported in the media; or a hypothesis developed from practice observations.

Example 4.1: Focusing on a practice topic

As a practitioner, you may be involved with older people and concerned about the support they receive when moving into residential care. You will need evidence if you are to influence service delivery in this regard, so you decide to undertake a small study.

Your interest may predominantly be in the older person, so your focus may immediately turn to their experiences. But there are a number of people involved in the transition to residential care, so a number of *potential populations* may be the target and may change the focus of the study. Are you interested in the experiences of the older person, their primary caregiver, extended family, community support worker, hospital social worker or other health professionals? What would be the best contribution that each of these populations could make? Any one or a combination of these may influence your research.

If you are to consider different *behaviours or conditions*, your topic may yet again be influenced in various ways. Are you interested in the older person's levels of anxiety, depression, happiness, general well-being, or is the focus on physical, financial, social and emotional support needs?

Similarly, in focusing the topic a *particular intervention* may be considered: is your interest related to the effectiveness or outcomes of services offered, or are you interested in the gaps in service provision?

Your focus may be on a *problem you experience* – for example, accommodation options for migrant older people without in-country family support – and this may provide a particular impetus.

Previous research findings or a recent media report on the experiences of an older person in residential care may indicate a range of psychosocial challenges experienced by this population, and you may find that the migrant population you are working with does not display the same characteristics. This may lead you to focus the research accordingly.

You may recall that in the discussion of the practice–research–theory wheel we have suggested that *hypotheses* are developed by asking questions about practice and recognising patterns across cases. You may well have developed a hypothesis that certain personality types respond differently to a major life event, such as moving to residential care, and focus your topic on this.

Smith (2009) warns against research in an area where the researcher has a high personal investment – not so as to discourage practitioners from undertaking research on subjects which matter to them for intensely personal reasons, but to consider ways of constructing safeguards and managing the potential influence of personal investment on process and findings. Research topics may also originate (although less so for practice research projects) from theory (as indicated in the discussion of the practice–theory–research wheel) or from intellectual curiosity. Dodd and Epstein (2012, p 28) capture this well in stating that many students, when faced with the task of identifying a research topic, are known to draw a complete blank; whereas for experienced practitioners 'the struggle is not coming up with a topic to study, but coming up with one – and only one – topic to study'. If you value reflective practice, practice research is the perfect vehicle.

This said, however, it is important to recognise that our choice of research topic – and all our decisions thereafter – is affected by who we are and what we are bringing to the research. Howard Becker (1967), in his seminal work, 'Whose side are we on?' encourages us to consider why we choose a particular topic and how that will colour the framing of the research and the reporting of findings. He proposed that it is impossible to conduct research that is uncontaminated by personal and political sympathies, and that these sympathies may cause us to take sides. The question, he argued, is not whether we should take sides but, rather, whose side we are on (Becker, 1967, p 239). It might be that we acquire sympathy with the participants under study, or refrain from studying a certain group of participants, or inadvertently distort our questioning to investigate only the kind of thing we are already in sympathy with, or distort our findings because of our sympathy with one of the parties in the relationship under study. This becomes particularly significant in practice research, and more so when we are researching our own organisations. Gray (2004) explains that when undertaking insider research one is required to balance the day-to-day role with that of the researcher role and this raises challenges in managing the change of role from practitioner/insider to researcher/outsider. This role blurring can impact on the framing of the question. The benefits of insider research in directing a question are significant too. Brannick and Coghlan (2007), in exploring the dynamics of insider research, came to the conclusion that there is no inherent reason why 'being native' should be an issue, despite issues of role duality and organisational politics. They affirm the value of insider research in providing ease of access and a pre-understanding of the context, and this allows framing of questions that may be impossible without insider knowledge. The solution to managing the impact of insider research – or 'one-sided' studies, in the words of Becker (1967, p 247) – on the framing of practice research is to know the limits of what we study and the boundaries beyond which our findings cannot be safely applied.

Once you have a list of potential areas of study, the best way forward is to brainstorm and debate your way through it. Practice wisdom and the collective insights of colleagues and managers about what is needed and what has been done before will be priceless. You may find that you have more than one research question – which is not uncommon. If so, you need to ensure that they sensibly link to each other under an overarching question, so as to prevent the implementation of a number of research projects at once; unless, of course, that is what you are aiming to do. Building a 'big picture' has been a very helpful strategy in many practice agencies – in order to attempt not only to narrow the brainstorming to 'the one' project to be done, but to actually develop a complex wish-list of projects that will benefit the agency. This will not only provide a strategic direction for scientific inquiry, but also enable the focused involvement of students, colleagues and even contracted staff (if resources allow) to serve the needs of the agency rather than the needs of the individual conducting research for higher qualifications or other purposes. Dodd and Epstein (2012) encourage consideration of relevance and impact so as to further narrow the research. It is useful to assess whether the findings will have the potential to impact on practice or policy decision making, and the differential impact that alternative or serendipitous findings may have.

The most practical way to focus the many options is to think about a question. As the research question typically deals with information needed to solve practice problems, the terms 'research question' and 'research problem' are often used interchangeably. The question will largely control the way that the rest of the research process is conducted; it will guide decisions about methodology, data analysis and conclusions. To continue the example [4.1] above, the question might be: 'What are the views of stakeholders involved in the transition of an older person to residential care about the factors impacting on a positive transition?' In the course of a qualitative study, research questions may become more concrete, more focused and narrowed, and may be revised as the study progresses, but a research question must be formulated as clearly and unambiguously as possible, as early as possible in the life of a project. In a quantitative study, the research question will be more explicit and will take into consideration concepts and variables used. Again in relation to Example 4.1 above, the question might be: 'To what extent do psychosocial factors impacting on a transition to residential care differ for migrant older people?'

The importance of research questions is discussed by O'Leary (2010, p 33) as assisting in defining an investigation, setting boundaries, providing direction, enabling researchers to keep focus, as a guide for writing, and to act as a frame of reference for assessing the project. The discussion in

Chapter Two on the context of practice research made it clear that numerous constraints may impact on the topic; we won't revisit that, but it is crucial to remain very aware of those potential constraints in the consideration of a project. Similarly, as has been highlighted previously with regard to the value of communities of knowing, this is an excellent time to join forces with academics or outside facilitators who are able to help shape the planning from a neutral point of view, taking the position of a naïve inquirer and challenging practitioners who are passionately committed to the topic and deeply immersed in the dynamics of the organisation, so as to focus on a topic that will allow for robust investigation. O'Leary challenges researchers to use a 'real-world research question checklist' (O'Leary, 2010, p 35) comprising the following:

- Is the question right for you?
- Does the question have significance?
- Can it lead to tangible situation improvement?
- Is the question well-articulated?
- Is the question researchable?
- Does the question have a level of (political) support?

With a question in place, the next useful step is to consider the purpose of the research or the type of study that will best serve to answer the question. This does not refer to design, but merely to the selection of the most appropriate action/verb. Research can help to gain insight into a situation (exploratory research); to describe an experience or phenomenon (descriptive research); to test the relationship between variables or explain the cause–effect relationship between variables (explanatory or correlational research); to measure the implementation of social interventions (evaluation research); or to develop a new technology, programme or intervention (intervention research). As might be expected, the purpose of the study will help to direct the choice of design. Smith (2009) warns that small differences in the formulation of questions have substantial implications for the conduct of the study. Exploratory studies will require more flexible designs as opposed to comparative studies, which are dependent on highly refined standardised designs. Where a purpose is defined as evaluative in nature, or maybe is aimed at designing a new intervention, the nature of the design that follows may take the study in a particular direction that excludes alternative designs. In some instances the topic chosen will be the main determinant of the approach selected.

Example 4.2: Purpose determines approach

Are you interested in a study on: the job satisfaction of social workers; termination of pregnancy (TOP); or dementia?

By applying different verbs, you can shape potentially very different projects.

I aim to: *explore* social workers' job satisfaction; *describe* factors that influence social workers' job satisfaction; *explain* the relationship between job satisfaction and productivity; *evaluate* the policies aimed at increasing job satisfaction; or *design* a programme to advance job satisfaction.

I aim to: *explore* pregnant women's experiences of receiving counselling for TOP; *describe* health professionals' role in the provision of TOP counselling services; *explain* the relationship between TOP counselling and women's loss and grief experiences; *evaluate* the effectiveness of TOP counselling services; or *design* a counselling service that will meet the needs of women requesting TOP.

I aim to: *explore* the range of activities for people attending dementia day programmes; *describe* the use of internet and social media in supporting the families of people living with dementia; *explain* the relationship between quality of care for people living with dementia and support available for caregivers; *evaluate* the effectiveness of dementia day programmes; or *design* a programme to advance quality of life for people living with dementia.

The place of literature in research

Focusing on literature to support practice research may not be the initial response of a practitioner. Even though there are a number of reasons not to engage with literature, accessing existing publications has many advantages. It is generally accepted – with the notable exception of a small number of qualitative researchers who are inclined towards postmodernism – that literature serves certain general functions, irrespective of the design selected. Monette et al (2008) regard the purpose of using the literature at this framing stage as being to become familiar with the current state of knowledge regarding the research problem; to learn how others have delineated similar problems; to narrow the focus of the project and to ensure that no unnecessary duplication takes place. Davidson and Tolich (2003) regard the latter as the most important focus at this stage, and suggest that, once the research question begins to take shape, the library should be the first stop to answer the question of what others have written on the topic. In the process of uncovering related literature on the topic, the literature may also divulge procedures, techniques and designs worth copying or, as Monette et al (2008) have mentioned, pitfalls to avoid. In a project on service users' experiences of family meetings in a health setting, a practice team shaped a great study and a mixed-method design to collect data. However, their literature search (in partnership with academics) revealed relevant and powerful material which they never knew existed. As Hall (2008) has warned, the assumption that a new project must be undertaken for every problem encountered is under question. Not only do we need to know what has gone before, but to test hypotheses/assumptions/practice premises may require a revisiting of existing data rather than a new investigation or a research project soliciting primary data. We will discuss this in more detail when we consider designs.

There is a rather confusing array of terminology to explain what the engagement with literature for a research project entails. The terms 'literature search' and 'literature review' are often seen as synonymous, but, strictly speaking, the former refers to the process of identifying material that is relevant and the latter refers to a critical evaluation of that material. Whittaker (2012), for instance, defines a literature review as a comprehensive summary and critical appraisal or written synthesis of the literature. Dodd and Epstein (2012, p 64) distinguish between *conducting* a review and *writing* a review, where the former includes the search and critical appraisal, but not the summarising and synthesising, which is regarded as part of the writing task. In this section we will consider the literature search, and in the next will focus on the critical appraisal of information, with the assumption that the reading and summarising of literature is often interwoven with the search activities; these activities are seen as fluid, rather than linear. Dodd and Epstein (2012, p 63) are less supportive of a literature review (as opposed to a search of the literature) in the initial stages of a practice research study and encourage a strategic approach to the timing of the literature review so as to avoid practitioners feeling overwhelmed by this academic task. They imply that a well-informed practitioner who reads professional journals and books should already have a sense of the relevant literature and the state of knowledge in their field of practice. For these practitioners a review of the literature will be of lesser importance initially – even more so if a qualitative study is undertaken. This may not be true for many practitioners who find it difficult to remain knowledgeable about the latest material on a particular topic. Either way, practitioners must implement the best strategy in their context for finding the most important literature in the most expeditious way.

Reflection exercise 4.2: The place of literature in practice research

1   What are the strategies you use or can use to access current publications in your field of practice?
2   Do you receive any e-mails or electronic notifications of new material published on topics of interest to your practice? If not, how can you enable that?

It is surprising in how many instances the activity of literature review, in and of itself, contributes to the research-mindedness of practitioners. As highlighted previously, this is one of the secondary benefits of practice research. If this activity is conducted in partnership or within existing networks, the burden of the literature reviews is shared, an opportunity is created to discuss the material and learning is exponential. In some instances, a discovery is made that an answer to the research question does, in fact, exist. This is great news and allows practitioners to build on that knowledge to advance their understanding of the topic. When the skills are mastered to focus research topics and undertake a literature review, the potential for finding answers to other practice problems is tremendous. This reiterates the benefits of one of the strategies for advancing research-mindedness: journal clubs, discussions of literature and access to readings are hugely beneficial for developing research-minded practice.

Example 4.3: The influence of literature review on research focus

In a project on 'What is effective social work practice in a family meeting in an acute hospital setting?' the practice team's literature review revealed a broad body of literature that examined family conferences and end-of-life meetings. This material placed a strong emphasis on communication skills and structures to support families. These insights assisted the team to refocus their study on the nature of family meetings in terms of communication skills and structures provided.

A project aimed at exploring how social workers acquire knowledge and skills in the area of case-noting was driven by a supervisor's frustration with bad practice in this regard. The practice team leaders wanted to explore ways to enhance good practice. However, in the literature review it became clear that there was limited information on record-keeping and documentation practices, but a growing body of material on computer- and paper-based systems and tools available to social workers to record their client-related interactions. This information assisted the team to refocus their study on the relationship between the availability of different tools and case-noting practices.

A literature review is an important step not only in the formulation phase but also in the entire process of designing the study and is not, in fact, completed at any point in the research process. Literature is invaluable, even after data collection, to explain the relationship between the findings and existing knowledge. In this regard Dodd and Epstein (2012) do indeed have a point: by initiating the literature review too early, a practitioner may become so overwhelmed by the mere volume of information that the research process may come to a premature halt. It is important not only to develop a focus for the topic under study, but also to develop a focus for the literature search and review so as to prevent this from happening. To this end it is crucial to have a search strategy. I always find the conversation between Alice and the Cat in Lewis Carroll's *Alice's Adventures in Wonderland* (1920) a timely reminder of the need for direction. In this classic children's fiction, the perpetually lost character, Alice, stops at a crossroads and the following conversation ensues between her and the cat:

> 'Would you tell me, please, which way ought I walk from here?'
>
> 'That depends a good deal on where you want to get to.'
>
> 'I don't much care where….'
>
> 'Then it doesn't much matter which way you go.'
>
> '… so long as I get somewhere.'
>
> 'Oh, you're sure to do that, if only you walk long enough.' (Carroll, 1920)

This popular quote highlights the need for a purposeful direction to manage new territory – or face spending many hours 'getting somewhere' in the alternative.

Literature search

If the research question and the researcher's preference – based on experience, interest or circumstances – are tentatively geared towards a quantitative study, the literature search will be focused on the definition of central concepts and selection or construction of measuring instrument(s). Trevithick (2000) states that reference to present and past research findings attempts to test out hypotheses by looking for evidence for and against the hypothesis and to develop new hypotheses or theories based on that evidence

(Trevithick, 2000). As such, practitioners may not only uncover higher-level information on the topic, but also ways to measure practice activities that have the potential to change practice. If the study leans towards qualitative research, the review of the literature may be less rigorous in terms of core constructs, but the use of literature to refine the question and situate the proposed project with existing knowledge will not be different.

The refined research question will comprise certain concepts (such as those used as Examples 4.2 and 4.3): job satisfaction; dementia day programmes; family meetings; termination of pregnancy; or case-noting. An important starting point for the literature search is to define these core concepts. For the purpose of the study, it is crucial to ensure that there is a shared understanding of the concepts. When using concepts, one can't assume that respondents or consumers of the research will know or use those concepts in the same way as the researcher. The understanding of concepts can be tested through a review of the literature and through discussions with other people. If your topic is aimed at exploring the experiences of children after the death of a sibling, you may be very clear about what you want to achieve. But in considering the core concepts in this statement, namely children, death and siblings, there may be some confusion. Are young adults included in the definition of children? Are you interested in the opinions of biological siblings, half-siblings and adopted siblings; geographically close or distant; any age group? Does death include both sudden death and death following a terminal illness? Decisions about the definitions of these concepts will enable a more focused review of the literature. Furthermore, a brief overview of the relevant material is an important point of departure. Orme and Shemmings (2010, p 63) encourage a 'helicopter' view at first, so as to establish what is going on before, an in-depth, detailed 'microscope' view is considered.

Different sources have different strengths and weaknesses, and the best source to access for information pertaining to a particular topic will be dependent on the nature of the research question. It is important to decide what you need and how best to access it. Most reflective practice researchers will be aware of, and have access to, journals, websites and other electronic resources in their area of practice interest. However, yet again, if this activity is conducted in partnership or within existing networks an amazing pool of knowledge on available resources can be generated in a very brief period of time. Based on discussions by Dudley (2010, p 79), Whittaker (2012, p 27), Orme and Shemmings (2010, p 63) and Hall (2008, p 37), the most relevant sources can be reduced to the following.

Internet

In the past, scientific communication occurred largely by means of journals and books. The internet, with its easy accessibility and the breadth of information it contains, can greatly expedite a literature search. Unlike the information in standard printed reference materials, this can be updated as frequently as is necessary. For most people, the logical place to start will be with a Google search and this may well produce very useful material. However, a disadvantage of the internet is that there is a lot of unreliable information available; this makes the quality of judgement crucial, as will be discussed below. The internet is a powerful means of making new and recent information (such as official documents, policy documents, speeches or press releases) available expeditiously. Reliable, reputable material in the form of research reports on topic- or service-specific portals, or through the Social Care Institute for Excellence (SCIE) website (http://www.scie. org.uk/), can also be accessed in this way. Orme and Shemmings (2010) remind us that some of these sites offer automatic e-mail information alert services, which are extremely valuable for alerting busy practitioners when new material relevant to their context becomes available.

Computer-accessible journal articles

Professional journals are viewed as one of the most important sources of information for researchers, as they provide information on the most recent research and developments in a specific discipline. Recent debates on a certain topic, as well as reflection on current research on that topic, are normally reported in article format. They seldom appear in the form of a book. Journal articles comprise current opinions and information on the topic and will easily help to identify leaders in the field. Progress in technology for the storage, retrieval and transfer of information is increasing the amount of knowledge accessible to researchers, and conducting electronic searches is becoming increasingly user friendly. There are numerous search databases or systems, each with a unique search 'protocol'. It is most effective to have a knowledge worker, librarian or colleague with expertise in identifying search terms and search parameters and in accessing databases on the practice research team. It is important to use broad-enough terms for your search results to be comprehensive, but not so broad as to overwhelm. This reiterates the importance of a clear focus not only to the topic but also to the literature search.

Scholarly books

Authored books not only serve as 'evergreen' or primary sources on a particular theme but should also contain a selected bibliography of basic textbooks and reports on research projects dealing with the subject. Dudley (2010, p 79) refers to this as 'footnote chasing', the process of locating useful material by searching the reference sections of literature that focuses quite specifically on a topic of interest. Edited books normally bring together experts writing on a particular theme and are useful for identifying different angles on a topic that may produce new insights for the shaping of the project.

Research reports, dissertations and monographs

This category of sources contains descriptions of the methods and findings of original research. The fact that these sources describe not only the results of research but also the methodology utilised, and make this information available for public scrutiny (and thus for criticism and replication), contributes to the particular credibility of such sources. Specialised computer indexes accessible in accredited libraries list these sources of information comprehensively, and it is worth finding partners with access to and experience in searching such databases.

Practice material

For practice researchers the value of material generated in practice should not be underestimated. These sources, also included under 'grey' material (see below), are difficult to access from outside the organisation but are often easily accessible through colleagues with institutional knowledge and a memory of projects completed, contracted or funded during the lifetime of an agency's development. Dudley (2010) reminds us of the utility of consultation as a search technique. By simply communicating with others through e-mail, discussion groups or professional listservs, both published and unpublished material can be uncovered. This includes conference materials, often available in unpublished form.

Presentation material

A large amount of information and knowledge is generated and made available during conferences, symposia and workshops, and is included in the category of 'grey' material, unless published in conference proceedings. Most papers presented orally at national and international conferences and symposia are made available to conference audiences and other interested parties. Although most papers are evaluated beforehand with a view to selection, a researcher should utilise such information with caution and critically evaluate the credibility of its source.

Two problems commonly present in conducting a search of the literature: there is either too much or too little information. When the result is that 'nothing has been written on this topic', it is surely not a bad thing, as this highlights the importance of your study. At the same time, though, it may be really difficult to progress a study without any significant existing information. However, it is rarely the case that no information pertaining to or relevant to the topic will be available. In the unlikely event of such an instance, it is important to widen the search parameters. Ensure that you have accessed 'grey material' (not necessarily in electronic databases, but tucked away in the agency archive) and talked to key individuals in the field. When the response is that 'there is too much written; it has all been done before', this too can be either positive or negative. An overwhelming amount of data may imply that to do yet another study on the topic may not be sensible, but it may also be a rich source of information that will enable a particularly effective focus of the topic. If this is the case, it is important to focus the search more clearly and map the types of literature of real value to the study. It is also useful to consider publication dates, and possibly to limit the search to the most recent sources. The notion of 'saturation' is useful to assist with the decision on when to stop. Introduced as a research concept by Glaser and Strauss (1967), saturation allows a researcher to make the decision to stop searching the literature (theoretical saturation) or collecting data (data saturation) if new material is regarded as no longer contributing to any additional insights.

An often-forgotten piece of advice is offered by Dodd and Epstein (2012): the importance of creating and maintaining a system for organising the information. This is particularly important when a practice research project is conducted by a team. It is immensely frustrating to have discovered a very useful bit of information on a website or in an article, only to be unable to relocate that information. A useful strategy is to create a shared document where full information about resources, including web addresses and the dates when they were accessed, is recorded, along with a brief summary of the relevant content of the site or other source. A sensible networking strategy is to appoint a 'custodian' with meticulous record-keeping skills to maintain such a document; this will not only enable effective sharing of information but also save time. Similarly, there are all sorts of strategies for reading, summarising and synthesising the sourced material. Using a template to create a summary of a document, article, book chapter or website is a very effective strategy. Basic headings such as the reference, summary of key points and brief reaction to the material might suffice. More detailed headings may be required to capture the information, especially when the task is shared and others may need more than a basic summary to understand the gist of the reading. At this point, the focus of the engagement with the literature is more on the reviewing and writing than on the search and surveying. According to Dudley (2010), it should become clear at this point that some articles or reports are more useful to the project than others, and this may lead to a decision to narrow the number of documents for review, or to find more documents on a particular aspect of the review. Combining the summaries into an overall integrated discussion should produce an understanding of the current state of knowledge on the topic.

Critical appraisal of information

An important element in engaging with the literature is to judge the quality of the information before utilising it in decision making. Critical appraisal refers to the process of systematically examining research evidence for its validity, results and relevance before using it to inform a decision, but is also about appraising the face value of the publication. As another parallel to social work practice, it is one thing to accumulate information, but quite another to weigh the worth of some opinions against those of others. In a family group conference, for instance, does the conference facilitator give more value to the opinions of the lawyer or to those of the nurse practitioner? Or is the opinion of the father valued more than that of the mother? All practitioners will be able to clarify this: sometimes it is about the one with most authority, but mostly it is not about *who* is saying it, but about *what* is being said. Similarly, summaries of literature will guide us sometimes to those 'experts' with sound wisdom and sometimes to those that make most sense to us.

The discussion on the context of practice research in Chapter Two set the scene for an understanding that published material comes from a particular perspective, is published at a particular point in time and does not necessarily reflect an impartial perspective. Whittaker (2012) warns that authors may have an allegiance to a particular point of view and may therefore even ignore literature that does not support their stance. As such, we cannot take at face value even highly regarded opinion pieces. Furthermore, we may want to consider that certain topics, views or results may be 'out there', but not in print. Not all articles submitted for publication appear in print! Some articles are rejected when they do not adhere to the 'popular' voice and sometimes the findings of projects never appear in a manuscript that is submitted for consideration. How often do we see articles in social work journals on experiments that did not work or on services that did not meet the need? It can be assumed that the evidence for those instances will exist – even though it may not appear in scientific journals or books.

An increasingly popular method for judging the rigour and quality of research studies is a systematic review. Although the methodology involved in a systematic review is not something that aligns easily with practice and it will therefore hardly be an activity undertaken by practitioners, having access to a systematic review is invaluable. A systematic review is a critical assessment of all primary research studies that address a particular issue by pooling the findings of all identified studies in order to clarify what is known about it. Access to a systematic review will not only deliver a critical appraisal of all the studies conducted on the topic, but will also provide an exhaustive list of those studies. The Cochrane collaboration (www.cochrane. org) and the Campbell Collaboration (www.campbellcollaboration.org) can be accessed for systematic reviews on a range of topics. However, not all documents pertaining to a topic will be research studies and not all of these will have had a current and robust systematic review completed. Bear in mind that anyone is at liberty to make information available on the internet or through other avenues, such as self-publishing. All available information is not necessarily controlled, reliable, verified or correct.

There are numerous resources, guidelines and checklists to support a critical appraisal as, you will quickly find out if you do an internet search on this phrase. Naturally, different studies, methods or resources are judged differently for quality, and the range of templates and guidelines accounts for that. The main elements involved in critical appraisal are relatively common, though, across most studies. Shaw and Norton (2008, p viii), in a critical study on the quality of research in UK universities, discovered that the quality of research can be divided into intrinsic (judgement of the rigour of the study or the methodology) and extrinsic quality (judgement of the value of the study or 'value-for-use' or 'value-for-people'). The latter is probably of higher importance to practitioners, although there will potentially be agreement that valuable research should also be done to the best possible standards. Extrinsic quality has been discussed throughout this book, in that applied research, by its very nature, will be higher in extrinsic value than basic research. In fact, one of the drivers for applied research, as discussed earlier, is for research that will benefit society. As will be very clear by now, this whole book is underpinned by the intrinsic value of practice research to have value for people and value for use. Shaw and Norton (2008) conclude that the following are the five core elements for judging intrinsic quality: a well-considered and argued epistemological and theoretical position; well-informed research that draws on the existing knowledge base; choice of methods related to the question and justifiable in the context of the aims and objectives; appropriate analytical techniques used and justified; and conclusions that are valid, in the sense of being carefully founded and plausible. If we consider these in a practice context, judging quality can be summarised by answering three critical questions.

Who says it?

In responding to this question, you move into an evaluation of the author, agency or publishing body. If you are able to ascertain who conducted the research, what their goals were and who sponsored or funded the research, you will be able to determine the context and potential agendas for publication, thus getting a sense of bias or political influence. It is critical to determine if the author has even disclosed this information. It is also important at this stage also to consider any disclaimers. A report published under the auspices of a research council or funding body can easily be regarded as more scientific or of higher value than other reports or documents. However, it is not uncommon to find a disclaimer in the front of a report where the agency technically distances itself from the views expressed by the author and you will be better advised to consider the standing of the author than that of the council, association or funding body. Publication of a document under the auspices of an external body should encourage you to question the political context of that document.

How do they know?

This question is all about assessing the quality of the evidence presented to support the research question. Understanding how research works is one way to become a more sophisticated consumer of other people's research. As mentioned above, a systematic review is a popular method of judging the rigour and quality of research studies, but this isn't always necessary or feasible. Asking questions about the nature and quality of the methodology can provide a good indication of the project's value. Orme and Shemmings (2010) encourage consideration of trustworthiness, generalisability and ethical conduct. Basic consideration of the design, the sample and the methods will also provide material for appraisal: does the evidence originate from credible sources, and how was the information obtained and analysed?

Does it make sense?

Consider carefully the arguments made by the author and whether these are logical and flow from the data. If you discover a document, article or opinion that is vastly different from what you know about the field, you need to ask yourself why that is. You need to ascertain whether this is a 'front-runner', that is, a person with new and fresh views on dated debates, or whether this is a controversial and contentious piece of writing aimed at generating debate. This will enable you to decide on its value for your study. If the author(s) present(s) material that is different regarding any existing debates, Carey (2012, p 50) encourages consideration as to whether this unique or distinct stance is adequately supported by evidence and how it compares to other publications, arguments and research findings. In pondering this question, you will also depend on your practice wisdom and tacit knowledge of the field.

Formulating a research statement

Now that we have discussed the selection of a topic and the processes for refining the topic, including surveying the literature and appraising existing knowledge, it is useful to formulate a definitive statement about the focus of the project. This is also the time to reconsider whether it indicates relationships to be explored. A research statement clearly and concisely presents the premise and focus of the project. A global competition called the '3 Minute Thesis' is an excellent example of the clarity needed to present the focus of a project to a lay audience. These annual three-minute speech competitions challenge postgraduate students to effectively communicate the most important ideas and findings of their research to a non-technical audience – with only a single presentation slide. The winning presentations all have an exceptionally clear message with what is referred to as a 'top and tail' element: what is informing the project and what the student hopes to achieve with the outcome. You are encouraged to consider framing your project so as to incorporate these elements.

The process of framing the project can be visualised as a funnel (Figure 4.1) so as to concentrate or focus a substance (research ideas) in a particular direction, from a wide mouth (broad options) tapering to a small hole (focused research statement). This will enable consideration of how information addressing this focus can be obtained, and will lead logically into decisions on the methods of data collection – to be explored in Chapter Five.

Figure 4.1: Focusing a research project

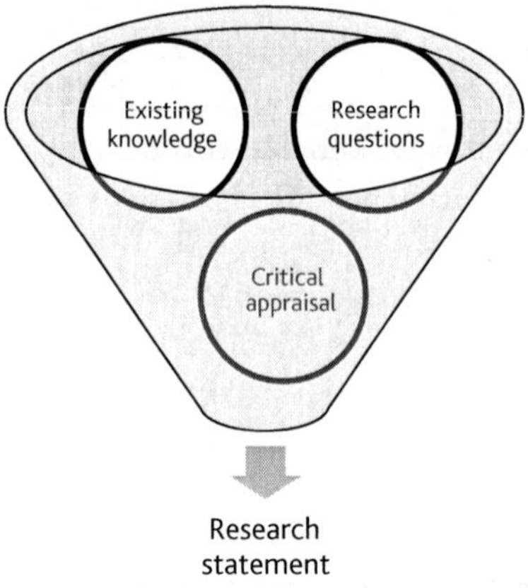

Research
statement

Conclusion

This chapter focused on 'framing' as the first pragmatic step in a practice research project conducted in collaboration with others. We have considered the importance of existing knowledge for robust research, techniques for conducting a review of relevant literature and appraising existing material. The focus has been yet again on the effective use of collaborative relationships and communities of knowing to enable this. It has been argued that developing partnerships in practice research parallels social work practice and builds on existing practice knowledge and skills. The next chapter will expand on this notion by introducing a discussion of applied, practice-focused designs that most effectively allow for collaboration.

Further reading and resources

Social Care Institute for Excellence – Managing knowledge and research resources, http://www.scie.org.uk/topic/developingskillsservices/managingknowledgeresearch

As mentioned in Chapter Two, the resources on this website are extensive and useful for various practice contexts. One of the categories of resources is related to knowledge management and includes resources aimed at assisting practitioners to use knowledge more effectively. Many e-learning resources are also available that are aimed at exploring the principles of knowledge management for individuals and organisations.

5

Designing applied research

Introduction

How best to do it? This is the question that follows any good idea. Yet, so many people, so many opinions on the best way forward! This chapter introduces possible ways of designing collaborative practice research projects aimed at a beneficial outcome for practice. The design phase always follows clear framing of the project that takes into account the various factors impacting on the project and, potentially, the design. As clarified earlier, the research process is made up of certain moments: phases, stages or steps, as proposed by different authors. The five main elements were listed in Chapter Four as: (1) framing; (2) designing; (3) collecting; (4) analysing; and (5) reporting. The second of these moments requires a series of logical arrangements to be developed so to meet the specified research goals, and this is often referred to as designing, research design or research strategy. There are a number of designs that align well with developing and utilising networks in practice research. The aim of this chapter is not to develop a detailed understanding of each of these designs (a single chapter on a number of complex designs can certainly not do any one of them justice) but is, rather, to present design options for collaborative research and to encourage creative exploration of research designs appropriate to your practice context and to the selected topic. As with the framing of the project, designing collaborative research is impacted on by the context and a number of political, ethical and cultural drivers.

There are many ways to investigate the multiplicity of issues in social work practice. It is important that we recognise how these different paths and the choices that we make at every stage of the research process – but most pertinently, in the design phase – may impact on ways of knowing. Werner Heisenberg, in his seminal 1958 publication, *Physics and Philosophy*, stated that we grasp nature only to the extent that our methods of inquiry enable us to do so: 'what we observe is not nature in itself, but nature exposed to our method of questioning' (Heisenberg, 1958, p 57). This statement was made with reference to the natural sciences, but is equally relevant to the social sciences. It is evident that the selection of method will impact on the type of information we get: it will determine the nature of the data, which, in turn, will determine the nature of the findings, and eventually our insights into the problem – not the problem as it is, but the problem as exposed to our method of questioning. At the level of qualitative or quantitative data, for example, a questionnaire may provide information that helps us to develop insight into a broad range of issues from a great many people. How a range of service users from different sectors perceive the role of social workers can be captured in a survey. But if we decide to use a different method of questioning, such as in-depth interviews, this may produce a very different information-richness on the role of social workers from only a handful of service users. As such, we will develop different insights into the role of social workers through our chosen method of questioning. We have options, but the option we select will be an important determinant in the conclusions we make. The task outlined in this chapter is to consider what designs are available and which of those are most likely to meet the purpose of the research. This also includes consideration of the interrelationship between the design and methods of data collection.

In considering a suitable design, this chapter will concentrate on two popular applied design options. Applied designs most often lend themselves either to any one approach or to a combination of quantitative, qualitative and mixed-method strategies and, as such, to any combination of measures to collect qualitative or quantitative data. You may recall that we have defined applied research as research aimed at solving practice problems. There are many design options but, as practice research is very much *within* and *for* practice, this discussion will focus on those most suited to collaboration in this context. The next chapter will continue this logic by exploring various ways of collecting information in practice research, as well as the sampling and feasibility considerations impacting on practice research designs. It is worth noting at this stage that there is a school of thought (not shared by passionate supporters of practice research) that research that is truly applied or knowledge that is generated from and/or by those involved in practice is in some ways less authentic, less rigorous and therefore less significant (discussed by Shaw et al, 2010). Uggerhoj (2011) argues that research that is connected to and influenced by practice can be of equally high quality as research initiated and developed by research institutions. Naturally, both good and robust and weak and unscientific research can be produced by using a range of approaches and methods. The extent of collaboration, as one aspect of quality research, does not make research more or less robust and certainly is not an indicator of its potential authenticity or significance.

The terms used in the research literature to refer to a 'method of questioning' are varied, confusing and inconsistent. In trying to make a decision about a research design, you may think that it is your inexperience as a researcher or your inability to grasp the academic content that causes the confusion. It is not. The confusion lies in the different conceptual schemas used by a great many smart people. We will not explore this in any depth; suffice it to say that what are here presented as applied research

research designs
=
paradigms
strategies
approaches
methodologies

designs (referred to as 'agency research' by Dudley, 2010, p 310, or very appropriately, 'committed research' by Smith, 2009, p 127) are sometimes called paradigms, strategies, approaches or methodologies (Carey, 2012), types of research and even specialised areas of social work research (Dudley, 2010, p 31) by different authors. Some good research sources may not even include these types of research at all, but propose only experimental designs.

To further contribute to this conceptual confusion, the term 'research design' has two meanings in the research literature. It can be rather confusing if you don't understand this dual use when you are trying to form an understanding of the term. Research design can be defined as 'alternative logical arrangements from which one or more can be selected' (Babbie, 2001, p 107) – in other words, a step in the research process where operational decisions are being made. However, research design can also refer to the act of designing the study in its broadest sense – that is, all the decisions made in planning the study, including the framing of the topic, the literature reviews and the operational decision – the step sometimes referred to as research design. For the purpose of this discussion, research design comes after the research problem has been comprehensively formulated, the goals of the study have been clearly specified and an overview of the literature has been completed. Two research designs, the most popular and useful to practice researchers, have been selected for discussion in this chapter: action research (and its various permutations, including participatory-action or community-based participatory research), and evaluation research (including the various forms of formative, process and summative evaluations). However, you are encouraged to explore (in partnership with experienced researchers) other designs and to be innovative in your application of such designs. These include (and this is by no means an exhaustive list): data mining (Epstein, 2010); case studies research (Yin, 2014); intervention research (Fraser et al, 2009); and narrative inquiry (Clandinin and Connelly, 2000) as suitable designs in the context of collaborative practice research.

Reflection exercise 5.1: The method of questioning

According to Heisenberg (1958), we grasp nature only to the extent that our methods of inquiry enable us to do so. In considering how significantly the outcome of research will be impacted on by the way you frame the questioning, what are the core principles that you should keep in mind when making decisions about design?

Action research

The nature of action research

Action research can be regarded as a study with a focus on the involvement and participation of various stakeholders in a particular research project; a single activity that is simultaneously a form of inquiry and a form of practical action. Action research is aimed at assisting a range of people involved in a practice problem to resolve that problem through extending their understanding of a situation. By supporting this goal in an orderly way, by collectively generating new knowledge, both the *research* and *action* aspects of the design will be achieved. Coghlan and Brannick (2005) see the aim of action research as being to contribute simultaneously to basic knowledge in the social sciences and to social action in everyday life. The relevance to practice research is, therefore, very clear.

There are a number of labels associated with action research, including: cooperative inquiry; action inquiry; empowering participation; emancipatory research; service-user research; and ideas -in action. All of these have their origins in the conceptualisation of the researcher as a change agent. Action research became popular during the counter-cultural and activist political movements of the 1960s and 1970s and fits well with feminist and anti-oppressive practices. In action research the knowledge (research) and solutions (action) to practice problems occur simultaneously as opposed to more traditional research, where the findings of an investigation are used to inform action. Action research is often referred to as participatory action research (PAR), and some regard the two terms as synonyms (see Carey, 2012). Those who make a clear distinction between the two obviously place a heavier emphasis on the participatory nature of the design. The term PAR is often used by those who wish to associate themselves explicitly with the more democratic and emancipatory understanding of action research as proposed by the commonly accepted founder of the movement, Kurt Lewin.

According to Carey (2012), the widespread dissemination of action research in diverse contexts has inevitably led to various permutations in its application, some of which have become altered from the original form. This type of research assumes a relationship with community development and organisational learning. Community-based action research is the model aimed at forging community relationships. As Stringer (2007, p 20) notes, 'Community-based action research seeks to change the social and personal dynamics of the research situation so that the research process enhances the lives of all those who participate. It is a collaborative approach to inquiry that seeks to build positive working relationships and productive communication styles.' Community-based participatory research (CBPR) is a similar approach, and refers to research that is based on a commitment to sharing power and resources and working towards beneficial outcomes for all participants, especially 'communities'. Communities refers to groups of people who share something in common – for example, people living in a particular locality (a housing estate, village or urban neighbourhood), or groups based on common identity, interest or practice (such as a lesbian women's group, a black young people's network, an HIV support group or a netball team). CBPR may be led and undertaken by members of community groups and organisations themselves or, more commonly, by community groups working alongside or in partnership with professional researchers (including academics and research students). In recent times, community-based research approaches and the asset-based community development (ABCD) approach have gained momentum and show similar characteristics to those of action research. ABCD is at the centre of a large and growing movement that considers local assets as the primary building blocks of sustainable community development. Building on the skills of local residents, the power of local associations and the supportive functions of local institutions, ABCD draws upon existing community strengths to build stronger, more sustainable communities (see http://www.abcdinstitute.org/).

Designing action research projects

This type of research, whatever label it may carry, involves collective tasks and roles in a cycle of action and investigation. The phases in the process of action research discussed by various authors are varied, but share a similarity as follows.

1. 'Setting the stage' refers to the preliminary activities leading into the project. This phase involves negotiating entry into the community and establishing a positive climate of interaction. A crucial task includes the establishing of roles and identification of stakeholder groups. Respective roles and time commitments are clarified from the outset, with the researcher retaining final decision-making power over focus, method and management. It is a crucial component of the success of these projects that community partners are consulted initially and throughout the project, so as to ensure that the research remains relevant to community needs. This arrangement also avoids unreasonable demands on consumers' or professionals' scarce time, while the researcher's clear leadership enhances the likelihood that the work will be taken seriously by funding bodies and the scholarly community. Naturally, robust existing partnerships and relationships make this phase much more effective and efficient and are often the determining factor for

practitioners with already well-established and developed networks in selecting action research as a preferred design. This is indeed the most common start for action research projects: having been immersed in a community with existing relationships where action research seems a logical choice to advance understanding of a particular problem. Reason and Bradbury (2008) suggest that those who lead or generate action research are very often those who have experienced it and understand its potential impact. The most common mode for action researchers is to start alone or initially to work in small teams and to convene a team of co-inquirers later on in the research.

2. 'Building the picture' refers to the phase of problem identification and goal formulation. This phase comprises the gathering of information and the development of a descriptive account of the problem and the context. Formulating a collaborative account of the situation serves to frame the project and to develop shared insights into the nature of the problem. The process is not significantly different to framing any other research project, but the focus here is on the capability for the project to deliver change. Explanations are constructed as to *what* is happening and *how* this is happening. This action naturally involves the potential for different accounts of reality and the challenge of vocal views and opposing realities. As highlighted above, co-design from the very beginning isn't always realistic, and Reason and Bradbury (2008) encourage leadership that facilitates the emergence of participative inquiry – which challenges the skills of the action researcher and the core team.

3. 'Resolving the problem' refers to the planning, implementation and analysis phase. This phase comprises setting priorities and defining tasks (why? what? how? who? where? when?), with supporting activities implemented to ensure the accomplishment of these tasks. These actions are closely linked to decisions on method(s) of data collection and on sampling techniques (see more discussion of this in the next chapter). Core activities relate to adequate resourcing, effective coordination and skilled facilitation of people and processes. Reason and Bradbury (2008) suggest that, as a rule, the size and nature of the team are determined by the degree of impact required from the action research; 'co-design is limited to those stakeholders who can carry the work into the larger system' (p 437). As such, this phase of deciding *what* needs to change will affect a range of important decisions, as the larger the impact is in terms of scope, the smaller the proportion of co-inquirers involved as co-designers. The level of impact refers to the place in a system where the impact will be felt: individual, small group, organisation, community or society.

4. 'Disseminating insights' refers to the phase where collective decisions on the research outcome are made, progress is reported on actions achieved and opportunities are provided for critical reflection. Progress is reviewed and the project is evaluated. This phase therefore involves more than mere reporting, as this collaborative reflection is closely interwoven with the action part of the project. Reason and Bradbury (2008) remind us that in action research the 'instrument of inquiry' is the action researcher and that taking time to also reflect on 'self' is crucial. It might be seen as 'equivalent to updating lab instrumentation in the natural sciences' (Reason and Bradbury, 2008, p 437). Here, reflections are not only on impact made, but also on secondary benefits achieved – and these are usually significant, including leaving the co-inquirers stronger than when the research started.

It is most important to understand that effective implementation of these phases requires an advanced skillset, including skills in negotiation and facilitation, in managing large teams of people with varying agendas and egos (and the associated dynamics) and in managing the dynamics of conducting insider research, which is common in action research projects. In this model of research practice, the uses of research are always of major importance and the questions of ownership and control need to be addressed openly (Smith, 2009). A robust discussion of the skills required for action research is offered in the book by Reason and Bradbury (2008) (see further reading list at the end of this chapter). This publication emphasises 'practice and life experiences' and 'the web of relationships, events, influences, role models and experiences' which underpin action researchers' practice as particularly significant (Wicks et al, 2008, p 15). It is widely accepted that the best way of understanding action research is to be immersed in a project. So if you are interested, get yourself into a community of practice that includes action research experience!

Example 5.1: Action research to solve a community problem

A successful mining company has operated in a particular area for years, with the inevitable consequence of a waste site in the community. The company had at some stage experienced an increase in calls to its 'complaints line', which consumed more time and resources than originally anticipated, but also saw a growing trend that was not evident in previous months. This trend involved an increase in calls from health professionals and community workers on behalf of people in the community who were experiencing health problems, and a perceived link with the mining operations. The mining company was dependent on community support and employed a large percentage of local residents at the mine. It wisely decided, rather than to continue with a complaints line and contentious meetings with the community, to contract a researcher to 'get to the bottom of what is really going on'. The researchers decided that practical action was needed just as much as an inquiry and they decided on an action research design. The first stage involved setting the scene by identifying all of the stakeholder groups at the mine and in the community. Representatives from these groups were invited to participate as a team of co-inquirers and were responsible for keeping their stakeholders updated throughout the process. The community workers were very active in this process. The second phase centred on the development of a descriptive account of the problem, facilitated by the co-inquirers. Through many community forums, meetings, group discussions, submissions and reports by various stakeholders (including community workers, health professionals, engineers, concerned parents and mine management), shared insights were developed into the nature of the problem. This was a fascinating process where every assumption was challenged and insight into the reasoning and decision-making processes was developed. Lay people and professionals alike got to understand the engineering processes involved in a waste site, and also the causes and development of respiratory disease. Professionals were challenged with information outside their comfort zones and levels of expertise, and in the process all stakeholders were active participants in gathering knowledge for and against various arguments. The researchers managed this as a robust and scientific process of inquiry – thus, as a research process. The other stakeholders regarded this as a problem-solving exercise – therefore, as action in practice for the researchers involved in the process. Naturally there were some tense discussions, and the skilled facilitation of the process by the action researchers was instrumental in ensuring that the process continued amicably. This enabled strong relationships to develop that were carried into the third phase: setting priorities and defining tasks. In this phase it was decided to propose certain changes to the management of the mining company for how the waste water was managed. This proposal was developed by the co-inquirers with evidence from the medical staff and engineers and a consideration of resourcing implications, developed in consultation with experts. Similarly, a change to the 'complaints line' was suggested, including renaming it as a 'community response service' and introducing a process whereby responses were managed by a team of people that included members from the community (also concerned parents, community workers and health professionals). This phase was intertwined with the final phase of action research, in which insights were disseminated to various stakeholders and a formal review of the process was undertaken. This action research project enabled both the staff of the mining company and members of the community to resolve the problem by extending their understanding of the situation.

Benefits and challenges to action research in practice

There are multiple benefits in using this type of research to design a project – especially in so far as making a difference in practice is concerned. As opposed to more conventional research designs, action research is as bringing about action in a community without the necessity for an additional translational phase comprising the dissemination of findings; the process, not only the outcome, effects change. All participants are educated/empowered with knowledge, experience and skills and a multi-disciplinary approach is encouraged. As will be clear from the nature of the action research highlighted in Example 5.1 the major benefit of this type of research is that it is aimed at practice change through collaborative efforts by and with practitioners. The central focus on partnership with communities in defining, planning and carrying out research relevant to community problems is highly compatible with social work values. In a research project aimed at finding solutions to the tension between a mining company and the neighbouring community over the challenges and benefits of a waste dump site, action research principles proved to be very successful. The involvement and participation of community leaders and mining company employees in a project was simultaneously a form of knowledge generation (that is, understanding the experiences and the intricacies of those experiences, on both sides, in a systematic and orderly process) and a form of practical action (by using the information to find practical solutions). Rather than conducting an exploratory study or collating information by means of a survey, it involved people in a process of change through extending their understanding of their situation. Core to the process were social work-compatible values such as understanding, empathy, trust, honesty, respect and compassion.

However, there are a number of disadvantages to designing a study using action research. Practitioners and community groups may hesitate to engage because of past research experiences that provided them few benefits. Or, at the other end of the scale, low familiarity with this type of research may result in an initial lack of trust. Participation in and commitment to research processes by all participants may be difficult; tension can arise in managing research and community priorities, diverse agendas and varying types of expertise. Having mining company executives and mothers concerned about the health of their children around one table, for instance, is not an easy way to find a solution to the presence of a waste site. Difficulties in terms of the dominant values and culture of the initiatives are legion. As action research encourages researchers and participants to question their roles in the project, this raises a number of concerns from critics, including that action research is open to influence by a number of agendas that may affect the level of control and rigour that can be exercised. Some critics also question the scientific merits of this design, stating that findings cannot easily be generalised. As Somekh (2006, p 31) writes: 'because action research is a methodology that closely involves participants in a social situation it is necessarily strongly influenced by their values and culture'. This also raises issues regarding ethics. Ethical conduct of collaborative research has been previously discussed in some detail and this won't be repeated here, but suffice it to say that a host of issues need to be carefully negotiated in action research, including the ways in which power and control are negotiated, how people's very personal experiences are shared and made public and how the different needs and expectations of the participants are balanced in the design of the research process. There can be significant challenges in ensuring that action research is ethically sound, due to its unpredictability and essentially politicised nature. A very useful guide to ethical principles and practices in community-based participatory research has been published in the UK by the National Co-ordinating Centre for Public Engagement (2012). This resource (and many others on this organisation's very useful website) focuses on the lessons learned by people working intensively in this area and provides links to websites and web-based resources for anyone interested in developing more participatory approaches to their research (see further reading list at the end of this chapter). Most importantly, however, for the purposes of a collaborative effort, action research is a time-consuming and labour-intensive process and demands commitment; this discourages students and others who are required to fit their work into a specific timeline from undertaking this type of research. Both academics and agency partners can be concerned about the slow pace required for successful collaboration, given the competition between pressure for quick results and constraints on time and resources.

One possible way of coping with time constraints is to be selective in the implementation of the process or core aspects of the design. This type of research involves managing power, role and resource differences, while ensuring that time commitments are realistic for all partners. The interactive nature of these factors can give rise to tensions in such a research project, and these can be compounded by issues of power and trust. In a meta-analysis on the commonalities of successful community action projects, conducted by Greenaway and Witten (2006), it became evident that effective community action requires: building skilled leadership; accessing adequate resources; enabling infrastructural development; creating committed strategic support and advocacy from both government agencies and community organisations; enabling effective coordination; vision building; skilled facilitation of people and processes; networking to build relationships, communication and knowledge; accessing mentors; effective planning; and making opportunities for critical reflection. These elements clearly relate to the value of partnerships and networks, as highlighted in earlier chapters.

Collaborative research can narrow the gap between research and practice while circumventing some of the usual obstacles to practice research. It is designed to encourage power sharing and mutual learning, through respecting and mobilising the different kinds of knowledge contributed by scholars, practitioners and consumers, without negating real power and role differences. This type of collaboration has potential benefits for social work researchers and practitioners alike. It offers an opportunity for social work scholars to strengthen their community visibility and their connection to practice. This type of hands-on community research can attract graduate students, increasing their motivation and lasting commitment to integrating research into practice. Community partners can have a rare opportunity to create new programmes and service delivery models and to monitor their effectiveness. This type of research fosters the recognition and mobilisation of forgotten knowledge and skills, which may lead to further practitioner learning and involvement in research-related activity. Lykes and Mallona (2008, p 106) consider action research as having 'liberatory and transformational potential', but also highlight the inherent challenges and contradictions of engaging in this type of research – especially from the base of university systems of power and privilege. Smith (2009, p 130) reminds us that with this type of research an 'uncomfortable ride' might be an indicator of the success of this method, rather than an indication of failure or loss of control.

Reflection exercise 5.2: The value of action research

Have you or your organisation participated in action-based research?

1   If yes, what were some of the most noticeable benefits to the organisation or the clients? Were there any specific challenges?
2   If no, why do you think your organisation has not yet been able to engage in action-based research? What is needed to enable the development of an action research project?

Evaluation research

The nature of evaluation research

The concept of evaluation is not foreign to professions tasked with social service delivery. Analysing the effectiveness of programmes and services or practice interventions has become an increasingly important activity for human service professionals over the last decade. In an age of accountability, managers, funders and even clients demand that some evidence is provided in terms of 'what works', 'how does it work?' or 'how can it be made to work better?' From the early 1990s onwards, there has been a strong global push for formalised evaluation of public as well as private investments, processes, practices and programmes. According to Weinbach (2005) there has been no single impetus for this push, but it is more a result of a combination of overlapping and mutually supportive developments during the later 20th century, including political events, social work critics and on-going efficiency concerns. Since the late 1990s, high-quality evidence has increasingly underpinned decisions on expenditure priorities, with evaluation often being commissioned during a budgeting process and linked to the funding of new policies and programmes (Lunt et al, 2003). Key drivers for evaluation research currently seem to focus on value for money, allocation of scarce resources, accountability and improved service delivery. Evaluation research applies to programmes of varying size and scope. Practice researchers will usually be interested in programmes implemented in a particular context by a particular social service agency or department for a target group served by the agency (even if this takes place across different sites), rather than in national or international programmes. As such, the focus of the discussion here will be on these small-scale, context-specific evaluation activities.

Of all the types of research, evaluation research is probably the one best understood in practice; everyone knows what 'evaluate' means. Paradoxically, it is also the most misunderstood research of all. The term 'evaluation research' is somewhat misleading in that there is not a separate set of research techniques that are distinctly applied for this single purpose (Monette et al, 2008). The definitions of evaluation are varied. Weinbach (2005, p 2) defines evaluation research as 'the systematic use of research methods to make judgments about the effectiveness and the overall merit, worth, or value of some form of ... practice'. According to Dudley (2010), evaluation research is a type of agency research (by being concerned with the practical needs of an agency) that focuses on how programmes and interventions are planned, implemented and ultimately tested for effectiveness. It is an activity undertaken to assess, compare or contrast the value of something. 'Evaluation is the process by which we examine, assess and make judgements about the relative or absolute value of an action, a process, a practice or an investment' (Saville-Smith, in Lunt et al, 2003, p 16). Although there is widespread consensus about the elements of this definition, there is considerable variety in the terms people use when talking about aspects of evaluation. This activity happens in the context of what 'is' and what 'ought' to be – that is, weighing it against something that we already value, expect or want. We cannot 'evaluate' something unless we know what the best or the worst of that particular evaluation should look like. Sportsmen have bad games and good games; chefs taste food to ensure it is just right; we promote coffee shops based on the availability of good coffee. How do we know what constitutes the better option? How will we know that a cup of coffee is 'good', or 'excellent' or 'terrible'? Other than a subjective appraisal of something we enjoy or not, we will have a 'list' of factors/ indicators for what constitutes a good or a bad cup of coffee. It may have to do with temperature, sweetness, strength or the type of coffee beans. Or there may be extraneous factors such as atmosphere, smell and presentation that matter. This is true for the evaluation of programmes or interventions as well. What do we expect this programme to be/do if it is to be judged as 'effective'?

Calls to demonstrate programme effectiveness are often silent about who should participate in or control the evaluation process. Who decides 'what works'? In conceptualising evaluation research as a type of applied research aimed at solving practice problems and well suited to collaboration, this tension is best managed within the context of partnerships and nurtured relationships. In some forms of evaluation research, it is expected that the evaluation will be conducted by an outsider – an evaluator – or at the very least, if it is conducted internally, that the person will 'switch hats', leaving the role of practitioner behind so as to conduct an evaluation as objectively as possible (Weinbach, 2005). In fact, according to Gibbs (2001), agency-based research agendas are often situated in research offices separated from practitioners and the 'coalface' of practice. But evaluation research can (and in some instances should) also very effectively be undertaken as a collaborative, practice research activity.

Designing evaluation research projects

All research is about answering questions, and evaluation research is no exception. Posavac (2011) states that, although there are a range of models for evaluation that seem to differ greatly, all evaluations depend in part on the characteristics and expectations of the stakeholders involved. The purpose of an evaluation can be three-fold, aiming to gather information for improving the design, development, formation and implementation of a programme (formative evaluation); describe the process of a programme as it is being developed (process evaluation); or assess the impact, outcome or worth of a programme (summative evaluation) (Scriven, 1999; Duignan, 2002; Hall, 2008). Programme evaluation was originally focused on measuring the attainment of goals and objectives, that is, finding out if a programme 'works'. This has come to be called summative evaluation, which originally relied heavily on experimental designs and quantitative measurement of outcomes. In recent years, programme improvement (formative) evaluation has become at least as important and pervasive as summative evaluation (Patton, 2002). To ensure that the matters of greatest significance are covered in the evaluation design, the project focus is best formulated through interaction and negotiation with the evaluation sponsors and other stakeholders or with those distinctly positioned in relation to decision making. This is the value of a well-designed collaborative practice evaluation: that the design meets the evaluation needs, but also enables the joint endeavours of critical objective questioning and practice-relevant focus that will ensure that the findings will make a difference in practice. The different types of programme evaluation will be present across the programme life cycle. This may happen intentionally over a predetermined period of time or over a number of years at different times in the life of a programme and be performed by different evaluators, independently of previous evaluation efforts. The different types of evaluation across a programme's life cycle can be visually presented as in Figure 5.1.

Figure 5.1: The varied purposes of evaluation research

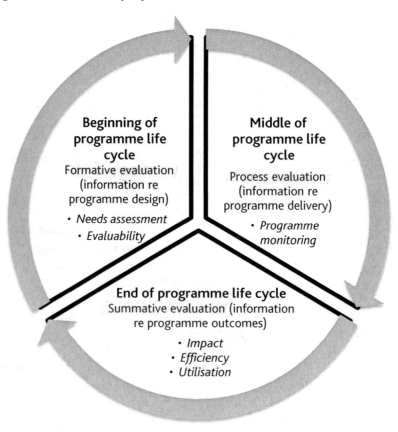

Many authors regard formative evaluations as activities directed at improving a programme's design, planning development and implementation (Weinbach, 2005; Yegidis and Weinbach, 2009; Hall, 2008). The term designates the meaning: this kind of evaluation 'forms' the programme, that is, it helps to improve it at those points where the programme does not seem to meet the criteria originally set by its initiator(s). Weinbach (2005) does acknowledge that the distinction between formative evaluation and programme monitoring (sometimes regarded as synonymous with process evaluation) is blurred at times. There is also some disagreement as to whether a formative evaluation and a process evaluation are indeed different, or whether these are just different labels for the same type of research (like outcome evaluation and summative evaluation). Some authors attempt a fine distinction between formative evaluation and process evaluation (Duignan 2002; Kreuger and Neuman, 2006) by defining formative evaluation as the activities aimed at ensuring a programme is well constructed, as opposed to process evaluation as those activities aimed at describing what actually happened in the context or course of a programme. A certain amount of overlap between process evaluation, programme monitoring and formative evaluation is inevitable, given their shared primary purpose of programme improvement. The logic of programme evaluation builds upward from careful description of the social problem that the programme is expected to ameliorate (needs assessment), through decisions as to whether the programme has the necessary preconditions to allow it to be evaluated, or to what extent these must be incorporated into the design of the programme (evaluability assessment) in the beginning phases of a programme. During the middle phases of the programme life cycle, the focus changes to what was done in the implementation of the intervention, service or programme; the problems that arose; and the solutions that were adopted (programme monitoring). The end phase comprises decisions about the programme's effectiveness (impact and outcome evaluation), efficiency (efficiency assessments) and use (utilisation assessments). This full evaluation cycle is often implemented with national, well-funded and resources programmes, but for the most part practice researchers will find themselves involved in some of these phases at different times and with different programmes; that is the reality of the social services sector. As mentioned earlier, the aim of this discussion is not to develop a detailed understanding of each of these evaluation options – as this chapter can certainly not do justice to any single one – but, rather, to encourage creative exploration of collaborative options for designing evaluative research projects (see the further reading section for more information).

Formative evaluation

There are two activities in formative evaluation, namely, needs assessment and evaluability assessment. Needs assessments can assist programme stakeholders to determine whether an envisaged programme should be initiated at all. If the outcome of the needs assessment points to a lack of interest or need, the funds available can be utilised in good time in an area where a need does exist. However, most often in social services organisations, a needs assessment is conducted on existing programmes, in that a programme has been offered to a particular population for a certain period and has come under scrutiny, with questions being asked about its on-going relevance. Some of these questions can be answered only by a summative evaluation (as will soon become clearer), but a formative evaluation can determine the extent to which needs are being met. In fact, without a proper understanding of the needs that a programme is designed to meet, it is unlikely that a summative evaluation will be effectively conducted and/or its effectiveness potentially determined. It is unlikely that you can determine if a programme is effective if you don't have a strong sense of what it is supposed to achieve! According to Posavac (2011), inadequate assessment of need commonly impacts on whether programmes and services can be determined as efficient or effective. If we return to the example of indicators in appraising a cup of coffee – say temperature, sweetness or strength – these may well be needs expressed by only a subgroup of coffee drinkers. What about coffee producers or coffee-bean growers? Would they look at other criteria? Do we want to consider their views in our evaluation or are they not important? It is only once we have agreement on the different needs that the product/service aims to satisfy that we can focus on the evaluation.

It is important to acknowledge the different types of need that are widely discussed in the literature. Needs can be determined through the expert opinion of experienced practitioners about what ought to be (referred to as normative need); through expressed preference or actual use by a particular population (expressed need); or through determining the lack of availability of a service or product to a particular population in comparison with other populations (comparative need). Dodd and Epstein (2012) warn that it is important to make a distinction between the needs (services) requested by service users (such as what adolescents want to talk about with mental health practitioners) and those needs as expressed by professionals (such as what mental health professionals think adolescents need to talk about) and to ensure a balance where neither is considered of lesser importance. There are a range of methods one can use to obtain information about needs, and these will be highlighted in the next chapter. Here it is important to note that designing an evaluation research project entails a consideration of need from various stakeholders, and this effectively lends itself to a collaborative exercise for the purposes of practice research. Royse et al (2009, p 37) actively encourage a team approach, both for the purpose of making the assessment more 'targeted, appropriate and maximally informative', with feedback from a panel of experts, and also for the purpose of shared recognition and buy-in. They propose the team to include, among others, heads of agencies, politicians, clergy, physicians, judges and university faculty, as appropriate.

Evaluability assessments are usually formative in nature, in that a programme meeting a need or needs would not be discontinued simply because it was difficult to evaluate. Some authors do not refer to evaluability assessment per se, but emphasise the importance of carefully planning an evaluation (Posavac, 2011) or developing a logic model (Yegidis and Weinbach, 2009; Posavac, 2011). They do, by implication, encourage evaluators to consider if all measures have been put into place to ensure that evaluation data can be effectively captured and that a summative assessment will be possible. This is the focus of an evaluability assessment. Hall (2008) suggests that the objective of an evaluability assessment is to determine whether the programme goals and objectives are well defined and plausible; the data on programme outcomes are available and adequate; and the intended users of the programme are in agreement on how the evaluation information will be used. This will ensure that the programme is ready for a formal evaluation. Yegidis and Weinbach (2009) state similar objectives for a logic model, suggesting that it is both a description of the programme and a management tool to display what the programme is about; what it hopes to accomplish; how it hopes to accomplish it; and how it will determine if its purpose has been accomplished. Conducting an evaluability assessment will obviously, therefore, involve working closely with programme stakeholders and is thus a popular practice research option.

Example 5.2: Evaluability assessment

A community agency received funding to pilot a parenting programme for the parents of children diagnosed with behavioural difficulties. The understanding was that the effectiveness of the pilot study would determine future funding. The professionals involved in the delivery of the programme were convinced that they were making a difference and participants often commented on the value of the programme. They reported to the funder exciting statistics related to the growing numbers of attendees and the increase in fathers as participants. However, the funder requested additional evidence that the programme was meeting its intended outcomes and the agency felt challenged in its capability to produce this. In partnership with researchers from a university, service users who had previously completed the programme and all those involved in the administration and implementation of the programme, it was decided to develop a logic model to assess the programme's evaluability and to ensure the programme did meet the need. Multiple sessions allowed for the designers of the programme to articulate their intentions of what an effective programme should achieve, namely a reduction in the number of incidents when the children acted out in public and a reduction in the severity of acting out at home. However, it was accepted that these were the normative and comparative needs as defined by the professionals. A formative evaluation of the programme was proposed and included an assessment of the needs of the parents and the children. This not only enhanced the credibility of the programme but allowed for additional outcomes to be identified, including parents' self-confidence; intermediate outcomes such as the transfer of new parenting skills to other contexts; and the value of building relationships with parents in similar situations. In the assessment of its evaluability, a full description of the programme highlighted the resources allocated to the programme; the activities offered to achieve the programme goals; the measures to capture the profile of participants; and the measures to capture the intended effects of the programme – originally a measure of the frequency and intensity of the children's behaviours. New measures were developed based on this evaluability assessment, including a scale of self-confidence; a self-report sheet for recording number of engagements with other parents on topics of shared interest; and formal interviews focusing on the transferability of parenting skills developed in the programme to other contexts.

Process evaluation

Process evaluation assesses problems in implementation and performance and is also known as process monitoring or programme monitoring. Some process evaluation activities may seem unnecessary – and in some cases they may well be so. But a common problem with the evaluation of programmes is that some are not implemented as intended, and it is important that for some programmes this is monitored properly. Posavac (2011) warns that there are many examples of programmes that, although funded, were never even put into practice – sometimes for fraudulent reasons, but often due to poor planning or a misunderstanding of the needs of the target population that may result in the programme being underutilised. In our coffee example, you can hardly come to conclusions about the quality of a cup of coffee if it has been produced by an inexperienced person or has been standing on a counter for a long time before the evaluation is done. Likewise with social service programmes: the first level of process monitoring is to ensure that the resources are utilised as intended and that the programme activities are implemented as planned. This is best done in a collaborative way, and practice research partnerships lend themselves well to doing this.

Moreover, a process evaluation also allows for the reporting of outputs – something that social service agencies are most familiar with. This entails documenting the extent to which implementation has taken place, the profile of the people served, the activities making up the programme and even data about people who are not using the service. Mostly, if proper administrative processes support the implementation of programmes, this information is readily available. But sometimes it is recorded in ways that make it difficult to access or analyse. A proper evaluability assessment would take this into account, but often programmes are implemented without such an assessment, and the implications are discovered only once a process evaluation is considered.

Example 5.3: Recording and reporting data

The community agency piloting a parenting programme for the parents of children diagnosed with behavioural difficulties (see Example 5.2 above) initially captured information on programme participants in a way that enabled output data to describe the profiles of attendees and of those dropping out of the programme; the number and nature of programme activities undertaken; and reasons for non-participation. After the completion of the evaluability assessment, improvements were made to the forms on which the information was recorded and to the way data was captured, so as to allow for even more interpretations of the process to be available in future, as well as to capture information about the facilitators and resources used to implement the programme.

Summative evaluation

Summative evaluation is utilised when the overall purpose of the evaluation is to determine whether a programme should be continued or, if it has been concluded, whether it has been successful (Hall, 2008). This evaluation is aimed at measuring effectiveness (impact and outcome evaluation), efficiency (efficiency assessments) and use (utilisation assessments). Outcome evaluations are the best-known form of evaluation research: most people would think of evaluation as an assessment of whether the programme was good or effective. Even so, outcome evaluations are less often considered and implemented by practice researchers, as these evaluations present numerous challenges. Practice-based programmes have long time frames and take place in communities where many other programmes are running at the same time, often with the same goals. Practitioners know very well that this makes it difficult to isolate the benefits of any one programme. In fact, most practice-based programmes aim to complement other programmes in the community so as to ensure maximum benefit for service users. Utilisation evaluations are equally challenging: it is not easy to access populations *not* using a programme, nor to estimate the size of an unknown population that can benefit from a particular programme for the purposes of an utilisation assessment. This presents interesting tensions for summative evaluation. Similarly, efficiency assessments are not at all common in social service agencies, partly due to the fact that the question of costs really becomes crucial only when the effectiveness of a programme has been determined. Moreover, efficiency is really pertinent only when the continuation of the programme is considered in comparison with other programmes designed to effect similar outcomes. Therefore formative and process evaluation will be more popular within the usually limited resources available to practice researchers, but this is not always the best alternative.

Accountability pressures mean that documentation of outputs (such as how many people were served) is no longer adequate evidence of a programme's success. The focus is on the degree to which a programme has been successful in achieving its objectives at a reasonable cost (Yegidis and Weinbach, 2009). This points to the importance of a summative evaluation and the relevance of the combined expertise of a community of knowing. Programme planners and facilitators, as well as researchers and decision makers, can collectively design an evaluation that can point to the futility of a programme and thus to its demise, or to its success and therefore to its continuation. Summative evaluations hold powerful information. Each of these types of summative evaluation have been discussed in detail in various publications, and practice researchers inclined to undertake such an evaluation are encouraged to identify relevant material; the scope of these cannot be sufficiently covered in a publication such as this.

Example 5.4: Outcome evaluation

As pointed out in the previous examples [5.2 and 5.3] about the parenting programme for parents of children diagnosed with behavioural difficulties, the organisation involved in this programme needed to provide evidence that the programme was meeting its intended outcomes, but felt challenged in its capability to do so. As a good example of the benefits of practice research, an outcome evaluation could be undertaken after several months of collaborative efforts, even though this was originally a challenging task. It was not originally possible to consider an effectiveness assessment, due to a lack of clarity about the needs of the programme, the processes involved in its implementation and the measures used to capture outcomes data. But once the formative and process evaluations had been completed the programme was much better positioned for analysing and reporting the results from the measures of frequency and intensity of behaviour, parental confidence, stronger relationships with other parents and the transferability of parenting skills developed in the programme to other contexts.

Benefits and challenges of evaluation studies to practice research

Despite the significant investment in evaluations, their findings are often underutilised. There are a number of reasons for this state of affairs, but one solution points to the responsibility of the evaluators to make the findings appropriate. People involved in an evaluation are aware that this always entails making a judgement about the value of a given intervention, service or programme. However, they also know that reliable evidence is difficult to develop and that lasting achievements aren't always easily communicated. Thus, it isn't uncommon to discover a fear that an intervention regarded as valuable by many may show up in a bad light during an evaluation, and this fuels the lack of uptake of evaluations and consideration of evaluation findings.

Evaluations can also be threatening to individuals and organisations for other reasons. The fundamental purpose of evaluation is to use measurements of outcome to plan better services for clients. It is not to put individual practitioners 'on the line', or to rate the effectiveness of supervisors, or to reflect how competent management is (although of course indirectly there can be repercussions in these areas). However, in the professional spirit of wanting to give the best possible service to clients, evaluation and measurement can, rather than being threatening, help practitioners, supervisors and management to direct and, if necessary, redirect their efforts to better purpose. To allow this, the use of the data should be agreed upon, clearly and specifically, within the organisation. Careful consideration should also be given to degree of the freedom that stakeholders have to implement changes in response to the evaluation. It is senseless to expend resources on an evaluation if there is little incentive or no permission or resources to address the findings. Duignan (2002) warns that if evaluation is seen as something that is undertaken only by external experts, then there is little reason for internal staff to improve their evaluation skills. This is particularly relevant for cultural and community sector organisations, which often lack access to outside evaluation resources. If internal staff do not develop evaluation skills, not only will they not participate in evaluations, but a range of research-minded thinking will be lost, including the ways that information is captured and analysed, questions are asked and results are interpreted and disseminated. Even if the data is collected for the right reasons, the use of evaluation findings is still disappointingly low. Their non–use or misuse may be intentional in some cases, but mostly, the low uptake of evaluation findings may be due to a lack of understanding of how to interpret and use the findings. It is important that measures are put in place in a timely way so as to ensure adequate, clear and reliable dissemination.

Once again, the collaborative nature of practice research can contribute to mitigating this low uptake. Careful selection of members of the evaluation project and of a community of knowing will potentially include a team member who is politically savvy and who has access to decision makers. Royse et al (2009, p 36) advise that such a person should be a *seasoned pro* whose knowledge of key personalities will determine whom to go to in order to solve problems that may arise. In addition to this person, a willing convenor, a person well–informed about methodologies, a competent assistant and team members who can do the physical work associated with the evaluation, Royse et al (2009) also recommend having a team member who is comfortable with writing the results and an executive summary of the project. The importance of communicating and disseminating findings will be addressed in Chapter Seven.

Reflection exercise 5.3: The value of evaluation research

1   Have you/your organisation participated in evaluation research?
2   If yes, what were some of the most noticeable benefits to the organisation or the clients? Were there any specific challenges?
3   If no, why do you think your organisation has not yet been able to engage in evaluation research? What is needed to enable the development of an evaluation research project?

Conclusion

This chapter identified a number of designs that align well with developing and utilising networks in practice research. The limited scope of the chapter forced a decision on whether to make a brief overview of a range of designs or a more detailed discussion of a few. The option for the latter led to the detailed discussion of two designs popular in practice research. This comprised a discussion of design issues, as well as of the benefits and challenges of utilising the particular design. The chapter has encouraged the creative exploration of other research designs appropriate to a particular practice context and topic. Action research maintains a focus on the involvement of various stakeholders in a particular research project, with the aim of resolving problems through extending understanding of the situation. Evaluation research does not hold the same focus on a single project, but is regarded as a type of agency research that focuses on how programmes and interventions are planned, implemented and tested for effectiveness. Insights into different practice research designs position us well for a consideration of the most appropriate methods of data collection, to be addressed in the next chapter.

Further reading and resources

Action research

Reason, P. and Bradbury, H. (eds) (2008) *Handbook of action research: Participative inquiry and practice*, London: Sage.

This publication is an important point of reference for anyone thinking about or doing action research. It comprises four sections: the first on the theoretical underpinnings of action research; the second on the practice of action research; followed by a section with 12 international exemplars of action research projects; and concluding with a section on core skills for conducting action research. It is well worth reading and is a useful resource to explore in a community of knowing.

National Co-ordinating Centre for Public Engagement. (2012) *Community-based participatory research: A guide to ethical principles and practice*, http://www.publicengagement.ac.uk/how-we-help/our-publications/community-based-participatory-research-guide-to-ethical-principle.

This guide focuses on the lessons learned by people working in this area and is a useful resource for anyone interested in developing more participatory approaches to their research. It was developed during 2012 as part of a collaborative research project. In addition to gathering feedback at several workshops, two rounds of national consultations took place on earlier drafts of the document. Respondents included community researchers, academic, third sector and public sector researchers, research managers and funders. This is a very useful resource on the ethical challenges of collaborative research and includes many links to other websites and resources.

Evaluation research

Posavac, E.J. (2011) *Program evaluation: Methods and case studies*, Boston: Pearson Education.

This book is a dense text, but with lots of useful material on different types of evaluations, as well as practical applications and considerations, including ethics and tips on common practice problems in evaluation. You may not want to read this book from cover to cover, but you will find different chapters exceptionally useful at different times in the evaluation cycle. You will learn a great deal about practice evaluations if you engage with this text.

Community Sustainability Engagement Evaluation Toolbox, http://evaluationtoolbox. net.au.

This is an extremely useful resource for practice researchers to access material on evaluation in a user-friendly, how-to format. It also contains useful information about innovative methods for data collection, to be addressed in Chapter Six.

Readings on other practice research designs

Clandinin, D.J. and Connelly, F.M. (2000) *Narrative inquiry: Experience and story in qualitative research*, San Francisco: Jossey-Bass.

Epstein, I. (2010) *Clinical data-mining: Integrating practice and research*, New York: Oxford University Press.

Fraser, M.W., Richman, J.M., Galinsky, M.J. and Day, S.H. (2009) *Intervention research: Developing social programs*, New York: Oxford University Press.

Yin, R.K. (2014) *Case study research: Design and methods* (5th edn), London: Sage.

Useful websites

Asset-based community development, http://www.abcdinstitute.org/.

Community-based participatory research and public engagement in general, http:// www.publicengagement.ac.uk/.

An overview of evaluation methods and procedures that practice researchers may find useful can be accessed at: http://www.wmich.edu/evalctr/checklists/.

A good description of a study aimed at measuring the effectiveness and cost-effectiveness of social care for adults and the measures that can be used in quantitative analysis of such an evaluation, including the challenges in defining and measuring outcomes, can be found in a report by Netton (2011), accessible at: http://www.lse. ac.uk/LSEHealthAndSocialCare/pdf/SSCR%20Methods%20Review_6_web_2.pdf.

6

Data collection and analysis in practice research

Introduction

What are the best ways to obtain data? Who will be the people to target for this information? Where will I find them? How many responses do I need? This chapter continues to consider aspects of the practice research process by focusing on data collection as one of the five main moments of the research process, preceded by framing and designing and succeeded by analysis and reporting. Methods of collecting data cannot be considered in isolation, though; supporting decisions regarding issues of sampling, as well as techniques for analysing data and ethical and logistical considerations will need to be made, and will therefore also be considered in this chapter.

The previous chapter considered two popular applied design options: action research and evaluation research. These designs, and all the others listed as useful practice research designs, are suitable for qualitative, quantitative or mixed-methods research. This chapter will explore various ways of collecting data for practice research projects – using any suitable practice research design. The ways of collecting data are generally referred to as 'methods', although some authors use this term to refer to a range of research approaches and also refer to methods as 'procedures' or 'measures'. Hall (2008) brings clarity to these terms by distinguishing between constructing the instruments for collecting data (such as questionnaires, scales and protocols) and the procedures for obtaining it, such as interviews or observations. These data-collection methods can be used alone or in combination with others. Although the combining of different data sources and types can be contentious (as highlighted in the discussion of mixed methods), there are benefits to a combined dataset and it is a popular option for pragmatic practice researchers. As the focus of this book is on advancing collaborative practice research, the aim of this chapter is to explore data-collection methods used in both qualitative and quantitative research, but always aligned to developing networks and to making a difference to practice.

There are many traditional methods of collecting data, including individual and group interviews, surveys and more contemporary methods such as photovoice and social networking that are becoming increasingly popular among both researchers and potential respondents. There is no one best method to obtain data, each of them has strengths and weaknesses, depending on the context and the nature of the data to be collected. Each method will require the selection of instruments or tools for collecting data and comprises particular techniques of analysis. Table 6.1 provides an outline of data collection methods and the related instruments for obtaining data. The techniques for analysis will not be discussed in any depth in this chapter, as there are numerous research texts available that eloquently unpack the intricacies of these techniques. And hopefully, by this stage the partnerships for the research will have been sufficiently established that the expertise required for data analysis will be exist within the practice research community. But it is important for all members of the team to understand the relationship to analysis when selecting the data-collection method.

In considering the best method for collecting data for your particular practice research project it is, furthermore, important to remember the integrated nature of research; that is, that the nature of the research questions and the type of design will point towards the most appropriate data-collection method. For instance, if your research objectives have moved you to adopt an *action research* approach, then community forums, group discussions and templates for submissions can be regarded as most useful (Reason and Bradbury, 2008). Similarly, there is a range of methods suitable for collecting data for different types of evaluation research, if that is your preferred design. For a *needs assessment*, focus groups, community forums and surveys tend to be popular, while secondary data is also increasingly considered an unobtrusive and informative method (Royse et al, 2009). *Outcomes evaluations* will be best served by data collected through questionnaires, scales, self-report sheets, or interviews. Secondary data, in the form of routinely available records about service recipients, interventions and outcomes, is also considered crucial for a *data-mining approach*, where charts, diaries, logs and case notes allow for the extraction of both quantitative and qualitative data (Epstein, 2010). *Case study* research encourages the use of a range of 'sources of evidence' (Yin, 2014, p 105), including documentation and archival records about the selected case, interviews and direct and participant observations.

All these methods allow for choices between utilising existing data and generating new data and for consideration of the benefits of qualitative vs quantitative data in the context of practice research. Social work researchers and practitioners tend to routinely collate copious amounts of practice data, but somehow consider it important to collect new data for the purposes of research. Likewise, social work has always had a stronger focus on qualitative research and probably will maintain that in future; it makes sense, as there is a natural affinity between practice activities and qualitative research. But the need for quantitative data remains high and unfulfilled. Shaw (2003) links this state of affairs partly to the risks of routinisation and dilution:

the tendency whereby popular methods such as focus groups become the 'uncritical method of choice' and whereby research studies display an absence of methodological imagination.

Powell and Ramos (2010) encourage creative use of existing methods, alongside the development of innovative approaches to data collection and alternative ways of involving previously excluded groups. To this end, this chapter will not be organised along the usual lines of methods for qualitative and quantitative research, respectively, but will discuss both traditional methods (with suggestions for how these can be used more and/or more creatively) and contemporary methods (for which limited examples are available in social work practice research and the innovative use of which is encouraged). There are a range of contemporary data-collection methods available that suit collaborative practice research efforts within social work. These methods can also be regarded as alternative ways of involving previously excluded groups by helping to empower marginalised groups and bridging cultural differences (Huss, 2012). Each method has its own benefits and challenges, as will be illustrated below. It goes without saying that before you initiate the process of data collection you should know what it is that you are trying to measure and what purpose the data will serve. Careful consideration of the suitability of each method for the population under study will clarify that it is more relevant or less relevant for any one study. Dodd and Epstein (2012) suggest that, as a guiding principle, the data-collection strategy for any practice research project that involves original data collection should have both a practice and a research purpose.

Data-collection methods

Individual interviews

Although interviews do not naturally lend themselves to participatory or collaborative approaches, they are probably one of the most common and widely known methods of data collection – especially in disciplines such as social work, where they are closely related to the values and skillset of practitioners. Moriaty (2011) reminds us that interviewing is a familiar and flexible way of asking people about their opinions and experiences, and that a considerable amount of data can be generated from an interview lasting one or two hours. As such, it will inevitably be considered in practice research. Interviews can vary considerably in terms of mode (face to face or telephone), structure (unstructured, semi-structured or structured) and number of participants (individuals or groups). These have been discussed so many times in so many contexts that some level of existing knowledge is assumed and the basic discussions about the nature, advantages and disadvantages of this method won't be repeated here.

Table 6.1: Methods and instruments for data collection

Methods (or procedures) for obtaining data	Modes for obtaining data	Instruments (or techniques) for obtaining data
Interviews (individual, group or focus group)	Face to face Telephone Skype™ or Facetime™ World Café Community forum Most Significant Change method (MSC)	Unstructured interview schedule Semi-structured interview schedule Structured interview schedule Critical conversational questions
Surveys	Computer-assisted personal interviewing (CAPI) Computer-assisted self-interviewing (CASI) Computer-assisted telephone interviewing (CATI) Interactive voice response	Questionnaires Standardised scales Indexes Checklists Report sheets Templates
Online research	E-mail or web surveys Weblogs and chat rooms Social networking sites	Web-based questionnaires
Observation	Participate as observer Observe as participant Observer only Covert participant	Unstructured observation guide Semi-structured observation guide Structured observation guide Checklists Report sheets Templates (recording frequencies, intervals, duration or time periods)
Documentation and secondary data	Publicly available documents (newspapers, magazines, books, historical records, government statistical publications, minutes of meetings, parliamentary legislation, reports of inquiries) Personal documents (e-mails, diaries, case notes) Administrative records (proposals, progress reports, electronic records)	Template and protocol for data extraction
Visual arts	Creative works of expression Visual storytelling Photos Videos	Template and protocol for data extraction Unstructured observation guide Semi-structured observation guide Structured observation guide Checklists

Technological developments have opened up opportunities for the creative use of this method via other means such as Skype™ or Facetime™, allowing affordable options for interviewing across geographical boundaries. Increased accessibility to video conferencing likewise creates opportunities for group interviews (to be explored next) that previously would not have been affordable. Of course, access to and the capacity to successfully use these technologies will determine their relevance for a particular population group, and due care should be taken that their use does not introduce a bias (such as age and social class) into the findings (Dodd and Epstein, 2012). If feasible, temporary access to the required technology may be arranged for the purpose of the research, especially in view of the portability of devices that incorporate webcams, such as tablets. The impact of this technology in conducting interviews has not been researched intensively but it does seem to have some negative effect on rapport and on the richness of the interview. But the benefits of having data, for instance, from international key informants that in the past would have been nearly impossible to obtain would outweigh any drawbacks. Sheppard (2004) reminds us that evaluation studies also rely increasingly on qualitative data through client-perspective or service-user studies. Individual interviews are regarded as a particularly useful method for obtaining information about participants' lived experiences, although group interviews (discussed below) are growing in popularity. Naturally, a combination of these interview types can be considered and might prove to be a useful solution to manage disadvantages of any single method. Case studies, in particular, depend on 'a variety of documentary, interactive and observational material, which offers a series of internal checks and balances and mitigates the possibility of relying on partial views or selective recollections' (Smith, 2009, p 121). This may well be true for a range of other designs and studies, and you are encouraged to consider this in your own practice research context.

Example 6.1: Extending the methods of data collection

A study was undertaken that aimed to investigate the elements that make up an effective client-focused dementia day programme and the methods employed by organisations to measure the quality of outcomes of day programmes. Participants included multiple stakeholders. The project initially focused on data collection via traditional means, namely individual interviews and an online survey in a mixed-methods approach. A discussion at a practice research team meeting revealed the opportunity for access to alternative data sources, including the people living with dementia and their caregivers, as well as the health records of subjects and notes by health professionals available to the agencies. An attempt to move beyond the traditional methods led to the additional inclusion of document analysis, focus group interviews, site observations and a photovoice exercise. Some of the findings confirmed results from other data sources and some were rather contradictory. This enabled a critical discussion and analysis of the elements that make up an effective client-focused dementia day programme from the perspectives of various stakeholders.

The instrument required to conduct an interview (individual or group) is often referred to as an interview guide or schedule. These instruments can range from an unstructured schedule, with only a few questions to guide the conversation, to a structured schedule with a list of consecutive questions to manage the discussion. Most often, a semi-structured interview schedule seems to be favoured, where the interviewers ensure that all interviewees are asked to respond to the same set of questions but that these questions don't guide the interview in terms of structure. A semi-structured schedule allows a natural flow to the interview, while serving as a reference point for consistency across interviews. Many useful guides exist on the development of an interview schedule. See also the discussion of questionnaire design below.

Group interviews

Interviewing respondents in groups is another well-known and commonly used data-collection method. Obviously the greatest incentive for using group interviews is that they increase the number of research participants significantly and may additionally enable respondents to feel more comfortable exploring issues relevant to shared identities (Smith, 2009), thereby cost-effectively generating a huge amount of very useful data in a short period of time. For practice researchers, their real benefit lies in the opportunity to involve the voices of various stakeholders. Smith (2009) encourages the consideration of trade-offs between existing groups with their own internal dynamics, such as families, colleagues or group members involved in a particular programme, and newly established groups, whose members may be less comfortable with each other. Depending on the topic being researched, group interviews may be advantageous or a hindrance. You may not necessarily want to have the managers and service users of a youth group in the same group interview, even though they may know each other well; but interviewing all the managers of various programmes together – even though they may never have met one another – may generate quality data for an evaluation of the programme.

When you consider the creative use of this method, alternatives normally confined to a particular design may appear to have wider use. In an action research or needs assessment project a practice research team may readily consider a community forum for data collection, but this method is relatively underutilised in other designs. Community forums are public meetings or hearings where members of a community state their preferences or present their demands (Royse et al, 2009). Even though those who attend may not be representative of the community or its views, and some vocal participants may use the meeting to air complaints or disagreements (Royse et al, 2009), this method may yield valuable information that is not accessible by other means.

Preparation and purpose are key considerations for group interviews, and the ethical considerations should be managed in advance. Participants should know what will be recorded and how it will be used. Group interviews have the capacity to be culturally appropriate (especially in oral cultures) in situations where vulnerable or marginalised groups may feel more comfortable to express their views in a more natural way than in a one-to-one context with a stranger. Such discussions have the benefit of flowing more freely and representing more closely what participants think rather than what they think the researcher wants to hear – or shouldn't hear (Smith, 2009). But group discussions (especially public ones on topics of political concern) may also become a source of frustration, as individuals may use them as a forum to serve their own agendas. While group interviews may lose the voice of individual contributors, they may be beneficial in getting a sense of the extent to which a range of people agree or disagree about a point (Dodd and Epstein, 2012).

Group interviews can include focus group interviews as a method. Even though these are often positioned in practice as the same thing, there is a distinct difference in the nature of focus-group interviews as opposed to group interviews. The purpose of a focus group is to create an interactive and dynamic process where the focus of data collection is on the interactions and collective dynamics, rather than on the experiences or views of a group of individuals. McLaughlin (2012) considers one of the advantages of a focus group interview to be the rich data that is generated when participants present and defend their own views, while challenging the views of others. They also allow for new insights to develop, such as when a needs assessment is being undertaken. The method may prove very useful for creating a dialogue and soliciting more than participants' individual views. Having various stakeholders in a focus-group interview helps to solicit expert opinion on the normative need (of what ought to be), the comparative need (through determining the lack of availability of a service in comparison to other populations) and the expressed need (expressed preference or actual use by a particular population). Linhorst, in Smith (2009, p 118) reports that focus-group methods are intrinsically empowering for vulnerable populations in that they promote ownership of the research and improve commitment and participation levels, while intra-group dynamics may provide additional data for the researcher.

There are various other, innovative ways of collecting data that can be classified as 'group' interviews, but these are essentially methods in their own right. The scope of this chapter does not allow for a full discussion of these, but two examples will be highlighted briefly and you are encouraged to explore these and others, as appropriate. The most significant change (MSC) technique is an innovative way of gathering participants' stories as data. It lends itself well to any participatory processes, as a range of stakeholders are expected to be involved both in deciding the sorts of change to be recorded and in analysing the data. The process involves the collection of significant change stories from the field under study and the systematic selection of the most significant of these stories by panels of designated stakeholders. When the stories are read for the first time, dominant themes are recorded, similar themes are grouped and the top themes are chosen for reporting. The stories can then be regrouped into these themes (Davies and Dart, 2004, p 8). According to Davies and Dart, when the technique is implemented successfully whole teams of people begin to focus their attention on programme impact.

Another form of data collection in a group setting is the World Café. The aroma of coffee or herbal teas, calming music and cafe-styled table settings are not ordinarily associated with research or, for that matter, with social work practice. A cafe-style setting is, however, reasonably familiar to most researchers, social workers and a large section of the population in general and combines a series of social norms. This method enables a conversational process that helps groups to engage in constructive dialogue around critical questions, to build personal relationships and to foster collaborative learning (Brown and Isaacs, 2005). Depending on the time frame and objectives, a World Café may explore a single question or use several conversational rounds to explore multi-layered questions. Facilitating conversational rounds and asking people to change tables between rounds allows for a web of discussions. In some instances, it may be helpful to have one person remain at a table to act as the table host both to summarise the conversation of the previous round for the newcomers and to invite them to share the essence from the previous round (Fouché and Light, 2011).

What makes this method particularly powerful in terms of the iterative building of ideas is the café-style social context, which allows the sharing of information in an equitable and non-threatening manner. Such a method provides space for people to join conversations and make impromptu connections. This method also allows for creativity in terms of cultural relevance, where the beverage served and the nature of the 'cafe' can be adapted to any context and the tables can be 'waited' on by the cafe hosts, allowing for a cross-pollination of ideas and social connectedness.

Unlike other small-group discussions, where a moderator uses the group process with a small number of participants to stimulate discussion (as outlined under group interviews above), the World Café enables groups of all sizes to participate in evolving rounds of dialogue with a few others, while remaining part of a single, larger connected conversation. This allows for small, intimate conversations to link with and build on others, as the World Café is facilitated to allow people to move between groups and discover new insights into issues. As Brown and Isaacs write, 'people often move rapidly from ordinary conversations ... toward conversations that matter' (Brown and Isaacs, 2005, p 4).

Reflection exercise 6.1: The use of interviews as a data-collection method

Recall one of the most data-rich interviews you have conducted.

1   What made this interview successful?
2   Why do you think these aspects were crucial?

Surveys

Surveys are frequently used to obtain a snapshot of attitudes, beliefs or behaviours for a particular group of respondents at a certain point in time. There are a number of instruments that can be considered for collecting survey data, based on the topic under study and the design selected. These include questionnaires, standardised scales, indexes, checklists, report sheets or templates. Questionnaires can range in complexity from 'home-grown' types, designed by the practice research team for a particular context, to those that are standardised and have previously been validated (Royse et al, 2009). Practitioners sometimes refrain from using questionnaires, as they feel obliged to use standardised measures to obtain useful data. However, this is not necessarily so; it depends on the scope of the project and the availability of resources. Home-grown questionnaires can provide valuable quantitative data either on their own or supplemented by data from another method of data collection, such as interviews. In some studies, for instance, it is useful to have baseline data to measure change over time. A scale or questionnaire may be administered at the beginning of an intervention and again at the end – especially if an impact evaluation is anticipated. If, however, the aim is to monitor the implementation of a programme, checklists may be useful at different times throughout the project. On a basic level, a 'faces' scale (happy face indicating enjoyment or agreement, to sad face indicating displeasure or dissatisfaction, with a neutral face indicating an 'OK' response) can deliver useful results in a context where no measurement is taking place. It is crucial to select data-collection methods that serve the needs of the project.

For quantitative studies, standardised instruments (sometimes called scales or indexes) are preferred, as these bring with them explicit instructions on how to administer, score and interpret data. Consequently, the scores will be comparable when used with different populations; for instance, to measure resilience in adolescent populations – such as those transitioning from care to independence, those experiencing grief and loss and those in gifted-and-talented programmes. It is amazing that very useful and easily accessible scales are still underutilised in some practice contexts. Similarly, if an action research project needs participants' opinions on a range of predetermined issues, a one-off, self-designed questionnaire with targeted questions related to the project will be needed. A major factor will be the sampling frame and strategy (see later in this chapter).

The administration of surveys was traditionally done by mail or telephone or was interviewer assisted. According to Groves et al (2009), the computer revolution has not only altered the traditional methods but has added new ones to the mix, which now includes computer-assisted personal interviewing (CAPI); computer-assisted self-interviewing (CASI); computer-assisted telephone interviewing (CATI); interactive voice response; and the more popular and accessible e-mail or web surveys (discussed below as online research). All these alternative methods have their roots in the traditional modes mentioned above. The computer-assisted methods enable administrators to contact participants nationally and internationally and to enter responses into a data file as they assist respondents to complete the questionnaire (Cooper and Schindler, 2011). Telephone-administered surveys have the advantage of covering large geographical areas, potentially in a very short time. This is especially useful in agencies that have ethical means of access to the contact information of potential participants.

Surveys are most popular due to their cost-effectiveness, the speed associated with their implementation and the fact that they can cover large samples (Cooper and Schindler, 2011). A weakness of this method is that the accuracy of the data may be affected by the participants' understanding and interpretation of the questions, which cannot be clarified as easily as in an interview situation. This is where computer-assisted methods or mixed-method designs are often considered useful, in that qualitative data may add insights to the responses obtained through a quantitative survey. Practice researchers should also be aware of the challenges of instrument construction. This book does not allow for an in-depth discussion of these challenges, but it is best to discuss these in the research team and to have a timely consultation with the person who will assist with the analysis of data. Many publications go into some depth on the principles of question wording, formulating response categories, the use of rating scales and so on (see Hall, 2008). The design, administration and analysis of instruments for a survey can be a useful collaborative exercise for a practice research team, with various stakeholders, including service users, begin given the opportunity to contribute.

Online research

The internet is widely used for social work research, including for recruiting participants (such as former service users) through social networking sites (Masson et al, 2013); for obtaining consent, collecting data and disseminating findings (Weeden, 2012); as a replacement for hard-copy versions of questionnaires; and to use public forums as a method for collating opinions about services (Denscombe, 2009). The advantages of using online research appear obvious and include reduced costs and the increased freedom for participants to start or terminate a study at their leisure. It also affords increased access to marginalised groups (Nosek et al, 2002; Stern, 2003; McDermott et al, 2013).

In web surveys, the respondent interacts with the survey instrument via the internet, using their own hardware (computer and modem) and software (internet service provider and internet browser) (Groves et al, 2009). An important aspect of web surveys is that various options are available for obtaining responses from participants. Software tools for surveys are varied, ranging from desktop applications to complex web systems for monitoring consumer behaviour. SurveyMonkey and SurveyGizmo have become very popular with social service organisations. If you have not yet explored these options, you should, but you are advised to consider reviews of the various software tools so as to find the one(s) that will best suit your needs. Advantages such as the ability to reach a large number of potential participants, the ability to incorporate multi-media and the low cost as compared to other survey methods bring web-administered surveys within the reach of social service agencies. Other noticeable advantages are the speed with which results can be made available, as well as the possibility of doing multiple surveys within a short time frame at a relatively low cost (Cooper and Schindler, 2011). However, despite the proliferation of web-based surveys and the initial prediction that this method will replace other communication-approach surveys, a declining response rate has been observed (Couper and Miller, 2008). Since contact lists may not be as readily available as for other survey methods, the ethical recruitment of participants may be problematic. Questionnaires online still seem to elicit a higher response rate than do hard-copy questionnaires, and a huge consideration is that their use contribute to the empowerment of marginalised populations (Denscombe, 2009). The availability of internet access, the potential technical difficulties associated with large web–based surveys (such as bandwidth and hardware platforms) and confidentiality concerns should, however, be taken into account.

Weblogs, more commonly known as blogs, are similar to diary research as a way to collect data, but offer more benefit for the researcher, such as cost-efficacy, the vast amount of data presented in writing and the anonymity of the online context – resulting in unselfconscious expression by participants (Hookway, 2008). There are also advantages for the participant, such as the perceived anonymity and the possibility of self-reflection (Hookway, 2008; Hickson, 2012). One aspect of using blogs within research that may affect their validity as data is the influence of the potential reader, as the blog is typically written for an audience. Bloggers may portray themselves as highly moral, although the anonymous positioning of blogs may prevent this. Another validity-related aspect of blogs is their trustworthiness (Hookway, 2008). The main issues with online research relate to matters of privacy and respect. Public forums, such as blogs and chat rooms, may seem to be anonymous, which stimulates self-disclosure, but are in fact publicly accessible. This duality of anonymity and public access may cause stress to participants (Weeden, 2012) and impact on the reliability of data. As technology is evolving constantly, there is a lack of evaluation of the long-term consequences of online research with human participants (McCleary, 2007). Additionally, data obtained through the internet without personal contact with the participants increases the risk of misinterpreting data (Sixsmith and Murray, 2001; Elgesem, 2002). Rather than seeing this as a reason to be cautious, you are encouraged to explore this method and evaluate its efficacy for practice research in social work to make a difference in practice.

Example 6.2: Generating qualitative data from online surveys

A study aimed at investigating the elements that make up an effective client-focused dementia day programme (see Example 6.1), included an online survey. This enabled caregivers to voice their opinions at a time that was convenient to them. Open-ended questions in this survey and in a similar survey with the partners of people living with later stages of Alzheimer's also allowed for responses that were outside the scope of researcher-initiated questions and might not have been solicited in any other method of data collection. Long and revealing accounts of people's experiences were recorded via this means, enabling a subset of qualitative data to be generated. This prompted the practice research team to enable self-written, electronically submitted responses for other populations. Populations particularly used to web-based interactions, such as teenagers, members of virtual teams and transnational families, have been particularly responsive to web-based surveys and in providing electronic feedback to open-ended questions. Once the access to hidden and hard-to-reach populations can be overcome and the availability of a web-based questionnaire is known, populations such as people living with HIV, gang members, child prostitutes and abused women can also effectively be reached this way.

Observation

In a review of services for people with learning disabilities Mansell (2011, p iii) states that, 'Given evidence that measures of process and care standards often do not adequately reflect the lived experience of people using care, researchers should include observation as one of the data–collection methods in routine use in social care research.' Participant observation has been used extensively over the years in studies about prostitutes, teenage gangs and drug dealers, some of these enabling theorising and classification of issues for the first time – such as the study by Bourgois (2003). Observation is also closely related to the values and skillset of practitioners – which is why social workers value home visits! This may lead some to assume that practice researchers can undertake observation with relative ease, but McLaughlin (2012) warns that this method is probably one of the most personally demanding and analytically difficult methods to undertake in research. This may partly explain the lack of its application in practice research studies, even though it lends itself to gathering informative data not necessarily obtainable through other methods. However, social work practitioners have a natural skillset for managing this, and the benefits should be explored. Remember that some observations may be totally unobtrusive and easy to analyse, such as counting the number of children being dropped off for school at a particular intersection, or the number of times telephone calls to a particular service go unanswered. This will require a template or observation sheet. Observational research is particularly useful where people using services are unable to answer interviews or questionnaires about their experiences, and where respondents' articulated views may be regarded as insufficiently accurate sources of data (Mansell, 2011, p 6).

Example 6.3: Insights gained from observational study

In the previously highlighted study on the parenting programme for parents of children diagnosed with behavioural difficulties (see Example 5.2 in Chapter Five), a self-report sheet and formal interviews were used for recording incidents of positive relationships with other parents and the transferability of parenting skills developed in the programme. In considering the results of this study with key stakeholders, it was agreed that an observational study may have enhanced insights on the actual depth and nuances of the programme's implementation and the actual level of change effected in the lives of the parents and children.

Depending on the topic under study and the selected design, the nature of the observation can differ significantly: it may take place in natural settings (sometimes referred to as field research or ethnographic study); or in a controlled environment, as in an experiment (Hall, 2008); it may be utilised for collecting both qualitative data through unstructured recording, and quantitative data through the use of structured schedules (recording frequencies, intervals, duration, time periods and so on); it may comprise unobtrusive observations made without the knowledge of those being observed; or observations done where active participation from the respondents is sought. Ethnographic studies, where the researcher observes society from the point of view of the subject of study, uses observation as a method in a particular way (Van Maanen, 2011).

In whatever way it is done, this method requires the researcher to define their role (Hall, 2008) and needs detailed planning of the purpose and procedures for data collection. A considerable degree of rigour is required, including a 'rationale for the choice of setting', 'clear parameters of time and space', mechanisms and processes for undertaking 'thorough analysis of copious amounts of raw material' (Smith, 2009, p 114), as well as decisions on how many people will be included in the study and how observers will be recruited and trained (Mansell, 2011). This naturally links to wider concerns about reactivity (where those who are being observed have a reaction that causes them to change their behaviour); the accuracy of information captured (as the observer may be reliant on memory); and how power is exercised and imbalances in status and authority are acknowledged. Some authors propose a balanced view on this, suggesting that change due to reactivity is not always a bad thing in studies, especially when those observed are requesting assistance and where practice researchers can make a difference to practice (Dodd and Epstein, 2012), or where power imbalances can be acknowledged and positively incorporated into a participatory framework (Healy, 2001). Similarly, with technological advances and developments in research-minded practice contexts (where permission is obtained for the routine recording of activities in certain contexts and for the use of such data for research purposes – providing that privacy is respected), this method may increasingly allow for creativity in practice research. See also the discussion of the use of secondary data as a source for data collection. While it will always be a time- and resource-intensive exercise, it is a method the practice researcher should consider in situations where observations are possible.

The collaborative nature of practice research suggests that a combination of appropriate methods will mitigate some of the challenges.

Documentation and secondary data

Hall (2008, p 207) lists a range of documents that can be regarded as records of social activity and can potentially be useful for practice research, including 'newspapers, magazines, books, historical records, government statistical publications, minutes of meetings, parliamentary legislation and reports of inquiries'. Yin (2014) expands these to include personal documents such as e-mails, diaries and notes (which, for some social service agencies, may include case notes) and administrative records such as proposals, progress reports and internal records (which for some social service agencies could include clients' electronic records). For some research studies, mainly those about the history of an organisation, programme or event, these can be regarded as primary data sources, but most often these documents are regarded as secondary data, since they won't have been collected for the purposes of the research and were already in existence before the start of the research. Epstein (2010) regards all available agency data as secondary data, since the primary purpose of this information will be to inform clinical, programmatic or administrative decision making, and it will not originally have been generated for research purposes.

For the purposes of data mining, Epstein (2010) regards secondary data as any data stored in personal diaries, filing cabinets, personal computers and clinical/management information systems. He usefully categorises it for the purposes of practice research as data 'about clients, about interventions and about outcomes' (p 77). This may include huge administrative datasets; data that was collected without directly surveying individuals. This is the main distinction between the use of secondary data and secondary analysis – where the latter relies on data originally generated for research purposes and being reused for purposes other than those for which it was originally collected. There is an increasing interest in making use of such administrative datasets for research purposes, as they have many benefits, including virtually no missing data, the possibility of tracking trends over long periods and access to very large samples. Analysis within and across these datasets will unearth interesting patterns and trends and allow for comparisons, randomised sampling and experimental designs, which are potentially not feasible with primary data.

As with all other data-collection methods, the nature of the research and the topic under discussion will determine the suitability of certain documents. Needs-assessment studies routinely use secondary data, as do researchers using case studies. Some types of action research also depend on previously submitted material. For most practice research projects, existing documents may provide additional insights alongside other data-collection methods such as interviews, observation or questionnaires. Dodd and Epstein (2012) remind us that document analysis or secondary data analysis can be useful for both qualitative and quantitative studies. Some practice research studies may use quantitative data (client characteristics) to do a quantitative analysis and qualitative data (case notes) to do a qualitative analysis. But it is also possible to quantify qualitative data by, for instance, counting the number of times a particular referral is made or an incident is reported across a number of cases.

According to Yin (2014), the strengths of documentary research are based on the assumption that the data is stable and specific, in that it can be reviewed repeatedly and contains exact details, and that the method is unobtrusive. It can also cover a broad span of time, events and settings, depending on the nature of the documents. As with all methods, there are also a number of pitfalls to consider in using existing material in research. Gaining access is one of the major challenges in that, at times, documents may be unavailable, incomplete or of poor quality, or access to them may be denied (Hall, 2008). Access and retrievability are also raised as concerns by others (Epstein, 2010, Dodd and Epstein, 2012; Yin, 2014). There are many instances where the claim of inaccessibility is made, and yet channels to obtain access and permission to use existing data for research purposes have never been pursued. Most agencies and government departments have protocols and processes for accessing data, and it will be wise to investigate these options before discarding this method. Epstein (2010) suggests that it is important to work through both the political issues of access as well as the technical issues of connectivity. In fact, with the abundance of material publicly available through internet searches and more accessible means of storage, Yin (2014) warns that the opposite may be true: you may become lost in reviewing large quantities of material. Either way, the solution is to be clear about the purpose of the inquiry and the most pertinent information required. Robust instruments to guide the researcher to the information needed are the best way to structure an observation.

Another major concern, sometimes linked to the challenges of being denied access and sometimes to the quality of available data, is the ethical consideration of using data not originally collected for research purposes. The coverage in international media of security breaches and inappropriate use of national data provides justification for concern about the ethics and legitimacy of using existing data. However, the management of most organisations and ethical review committees internationally seem to be reassured when two criteria are met: (1) that the data are de-identified or assigned unique identity numbers that ensure total privacy of individuals – in so far as the material is not already publicly identifiable through other means (such as court reports or organisational reviews); and (2) that the individuals have given permission for their information to be used for research purposes. Regarding the latter, though, this may be debatable, as the focus of some studies may involve monitoring of practice or quality assurance – in which case permission from service users will not be required. It seems once again that these sorts of decisions are better managed by a practice research team where service users, managers, funders and practitioners share the focus of the project and the decisions on accessing information. The additional benefits offered by such documentary studies or analysis of secondary data may well be a convincing consideration too, as is clear from the example of a community-based provider discussed below.

Example 6.4: Secondary benefits of documentary research

A community-based provider of a long-term therapy programme for people with sexually abusive behaviours wanted to explore what factors influence non-completion of adult and youth programmes. A practice research team conducted an analysis of over 500 client files. The results highlighted the major reasons for non-completion, but the research also generated secondary benefits. Issues relating to the impact of mandated versus non-mandated treatment and referrer issues were highlighted, and these could be addressed to improve services. Furthermore, not all the files clearly and consistently documented completion details, which led to the development of consensus among team members on best recording practices. As with all practice research projects, this team also discovered the benefit of the opportunity to develop cross-team relationships, as the projects had to involve representatives from different services within the organisation, including managerial and administrative staff. This allowed them to spend time together for which they would otherwise not have had the opportunity in their day-to-day work.

The use of secondary data for qualitative and quantitative studies, including evaluation studies, is discussed in some depth by Epstein (2010) in his book titled *Clinical data mining*. A number of useful examples and procedures for data extraction and collection are included too. If this appears to be a useful method for your organisation, you are encouraged to explore it more in the above-mentioned and related publications. As with other methods, proper planning and a clear strategy concerning why the data is needed and how it will be used and disseminated is crucial for the effective use of documentation in practice research.

Reflection exercise 6.2: The use of existing data

What are the types of data regularly collected in your agency?

1   Which of these types of data do you consider to be particularly
     information rich?
2   How can you use them to develop insights into your practice?

Visual arts

Elaborating on empowerment, Huss (2012) argues that in diverse
marginalised groups the use of images and visual arts can serve as a means
of collecting data. This method has enabled participants (such as heart attack
survivors and Bedouin women, in the examples used by Huss) to overcome
language barriers, express cultural differences and address sensitive issues
and has even given access to unconscious levels of information (Hocoy,
2002; Huss, 2007). By allowing this type of expression, stigmatisation can
be reduced (Hocoy, 2002; Huss and Cwikel, 2005; Huss, 2007). The use
of visuals to obtain information in social work is not new, if one thinks of
interventions such as play therapy and the use of art in discussing traumatic
events. Creative works of expression allow insight into the world of the
participant or group under study. A more experimental method that
incorporates creations by participants is the use of Lego models (Gauntlett,
2007). This type of expression often unlocks information that may not be
found in other methods of data collection, such as an interview, where the
information is produced in response to the correct questions.

   The most common instruments for collecting data by visual means are
through the use of photos and videos. These tools for data collection offer
a range of possibilities, including photovoice, photo-elicitation, visual
storytelling and participatory videos. Although originally developed for
health-promotion strategies (Wang et al, 1998), photovoice has been
used successfully in varying contexts, including research targeting young
people (Bolton et al, 2001; Streng et al, 2004; Epstein et al, 2006), with
marginalised groups such as homeless people (Wang et al, 2000) and with
individuals directly impacted on by tuberculosis (Moya, 2010). Photovoice
incorporates everyday photos of individual participants to promote a greater
understanding of community issues and to promote change by influencing
policies (Wang, 1999). It is an excellent method for collaborative practice
research, as photographs are shared with all the participants, who will jointly
create titles or descriptions for the photos (Wang et al, 2000; Streng et al,
2004; Carlson et al, 2006) and decide on the narrative to be shared. Photo-
elicitation also uses photographs, but focuses on the verbal data elicited by

means of the photos rather than on the visual data itself (Harper, 2002; Fleury et al, 2009). Participants talk about the photographs and this becomes the focus of data analysis. Visual storytelling draws upon photovoice and photo-elicitation. This method appears to engage young people, particularly, with the research process (Drew et al, 2010). Visual storytelling entails creating descriptions for the photographs via a group process or by a series of in-depth individual interviews, thereby making it suitable also for discussing sensitive issues (Drew et al, 2010). Participatory video as a method is very similar to visual storytelling, but allows the participants to weave the image with the story. Prior to filming, participants learn as a group how to use video cameras, how to film, direct and edit the videos collaboratively (Sitter, 2012). According to White (2003), participatory videos are powerful tools for fostering positive change, and these videos can also contribute to the creation of conceptual frameworks and provide guidelines for other researchers. In some instances this method has value outside of the research focus, as demonstrated in the following project.

Example 6.5: Using photovoice

In the study on elements that make up an effective client-focused dementia day programme [see Examples 6.1 and 6.2], there was a real commitment by the research team to finding ways to capture the experiences of those living with dementia. Photovoice appeared to be a potentially useful method. This method requires clear instructions to participants on the number of photos to be captured during a specified period of time and on the purpose of the images. A photovoice pack, which contained all the resources needed to take part in the photovoice exercise, was distributed to participants: researchers' contact details; a disposable camera; participant information sheets and consent forms; and instructions for participating in the photovoice exercise. These instructions outlined 10 photographic situations that the researchers wanted to be captured throughout the day: at home (before and after attending the day programme); with the driver (going to the venue and home again); and at the day programme. Consideration was given to the clients taking photos themselves, but it was decided that it was too much to ask of them. However, in hindsight it was thought that those clients with early-onset dementia could be asked in the future, as there was evidence of them positively engaging with the photographic situations. Critical dialogue by the team informed a thematic analysis of the photos and notes from participants. The themes from the photovoice, combined with findings from the interview data, indicated that the photos were regarded as an innovative way to document the daily learning of the participants and the way that various activities are used to both enhance learning and generate feelings of success. In response to the photovoice exercise, caregivers reported that the photos had additional benefits in that these helped them to know more about the programme and the activities their loved one was involved in, as the usual discussion of daily activities is not possible with this population.

Some of the barriers to using images for collecting data include the difficulty of analysing visual arts: how to access and interpret the data in a valid manner. Creative solutions include team analysis, the use of templates and combining this method with others so as to mitigate potential criticism of validity. Another disadvantage of using images as a data–collection method consists in issues of ownership, privacy and future use of the images (Huss, 2012), and these should be discussed with participants prior to implementation of the method. The collaborative nature of these methods allows for team analysis and the possibility of comparing and validating insights. These methods can be implemented by deciding on who takes the photos or videos and this, too, will impact on analysis. In some instances the fact that the researcher, rather than the participants, may take the photos or videos may introduce a bias, or it may well enable focused discussion of targeted photo opportunities. It is well known that reactivity can influence the natural course of behaviour as a result of being observed, but allowing time for the observations and permitting the participants to acclimatise to the observer and to each other may prevent this. Although photography enables a unique analysis of social issues, it has certain drawbacks, including access to technology and the management of loan equipment. The time required for continuous coaching to complete tasks, especially with some populations, may also be a consideration for some projects (Bolton et al, 2001; Drew et al, 2010).

Reflection exercise 6.3: The creative use of data-collection methods in practice

1   Which of the data-collection methods discussed in this chapter will best serve the needs of your organisation?
2   How can you use these methods more creatively to ensure a participatory approach with the population you serve and the involvement of previously excluded groups?

Sampling

Grappling with the question of who can provide the required information and how many should be included is a very common moment in research.

Sometimes the answers are obvious and easily provided, but other times the total number of individuals who are potentially eligible either is too high or cannot be determined and a decision needs to be made about how many would constitute an adequate sample. A population is the entire group that the findings from the data are expected to present, whereas a sample frame constitutes the selected group (or subset) of the larger group (population) from which the target group (sample) will be selected (Royse et al, 2009). Sampling aims to target a group within a population in such a way that reliable findings will be produced, and at the same time aims to lower the cost of the research, increase the accuracy of the results, increase the speed of data collection and improve the availability of respondents for the planned research (Groves et al, 2009).

Mostly, sample size depends on what you want to know, the purpose of the inquiry and what is at stake. Sampling strategies are generally grouped into probability and non-probability sampling strategies (Cooper and Schindler, 2011). Non-probability sampling strategies are used when the required sample is easily available or accessible and, as such, are less likely to produce a representative sample. The most popular types of non-probability sampling are accidental sampling (selecting eligible participants that happen to be available), purposive sampling (selecting eligible participants that have been identified as able to provide the richest data) and snowball sampling (seeking information from eligible participants to identify other participants), and they are more prevalent in qualitative research (Hall, 2008). Probability sampling strategies are used when it is impractical or impossible to access the whole population and yet some conclusions need to be made about it. This sampling strategy is more prevalent in quantitative research, as greater confidence can be placed in the representativeness of such a sample. The most popular types of probability sampling include simple random sampling (numbering each eligible case and selecting the required number of cases from any random table of numbers), systematic sampling (randomly selecting the first case and then selecting further cases according to a particular interval) and stratified sampling (proportionally selecting a predetermined number of participants from subsections of the population) (Hall, 2008). These types will not be discussed here, as detailed descriptions can be found in most research texts.

One of the most important aspects to grasp before making a decision on sampling is the principle of representativeness. When a qualitative data-collection method is selected, the basic principle of representativeness falls away and is replaced by sufficiency and saturation: how many interviews are needed to get the research questions answered satisfactorily? This inevitably leads to the practicality that only non-probability sampling is necessary in qualitative research. The principle of sufficiency asks whether there are sufficient numbers of participants to reflect the range of participants and sites that make up the population, so that others outside the sample might have a chance to connect to the experience of those within it. Saturation is reached at that point in the study where the researcher begins to hear the same information repeatedly being reported and no longer learns anything new. The rule of thumb that seems to work with practice researchers is an 'educated guess' as to the size of the population and a calculation of about 5 to 10% of that number to determine the number of participants to interview. Within these broad guidelines the sample size can then be either stretched or shrunk according to the principles of sufficiency and saturation. This is not a very scientific formula, but it tends to be a more acceptable procedure than merely to interview 15 or 30 people, as some researchers do.

When quantitative data-collection methods are employed it is highly important to know how representative is one's sample of the population under inspection, in order to draw valid conclusions about the population. Sampling thus occurs only subsequently to the broad planning of the study. There are many tables and guidelines available to help determine the size of the sample and, if a representative sample is important for the study you are undertaking, you should familiarise yourself with these tables and their use. If the sampling strategy is flawed and the sample is not representative of the larger population, this is considered as sampling bias (Royse et al, 2009).

Reflection exercise 6.4: Sampling in practice research

1   Do you need to accurately determine the size of the population you aim to research, or will an educated guess be adequate?
2   How important is a representative sample for the purpose of your study?
3   How will you go about deciding on the best sample size for the investigation?

Data analysis and interpretation

Data analysis is the process of relating the information that we have collected to the research question(s), with the aim of reaching informed conclusions and recommendations. Although data analysis is most often presented as a separate stage in research, the ways that data will be analysed require consideration throughout the research process and are determined by the research question, design, data-collection methods and sampling strategies. There are countless publications on techniques for data analysis, ranging from highly complex statistical techniques for analysing quantitative data, through commonly accepted procedures for analysing qualitative data and explaining various computer software options to facilitate these processes (Bazeley, 2007; Acton and Miller, 2009).

Creswell (2003, p 190) considers qualitative analysis as 'an ongoing process involving continual reflection about the data, asking analytic questions, and writing memos throughout the study'. For some inexperienced researchers this seems vague and potentially unscientific. However, alongside these informal and individualised ways in which researchers order, sort, systematise and make sense of the materials they have collected are more formal strategies that have been developed over the years and include specific procedures related to a chosen qualitative design or strategy. In the field of applied research, various research designs or strategies have their own set of processes for data analysis, such as the iterative coding processes for narrative inquiry (Clandinin and Connelly, 2000), the analytic techniques for case study evidence (Yin, 2014) or the steps involved in conducting a data-mining study (Epstein, 2010). The analysis of data for the various data–collection methods is equally guided, in that analyses of interview data, observation data, photovoice data or data from scales and questionnaires all need to follow a robust, scientific process that will engender confidence in the findings.

Quantitative techniques of analysis fall into four main categories, according to Blaikie (2010), namely description, association, causation and inference. Descriptive statistics are procedures that describe numerical data in that they assist in organising, summarising and interpreting sample data (Monette, Sullivan and DeJong, 2008). Descriptive scoring is shorthand for describing the population of the study and is the type of analysis most used in practice research studies. It comprises knowledge of basic techniques such as calculating frequencies and percentages. Inferential statistics, on the other hand, use probability theory to test hypotheses, permit inferences from a sample to a population and test whether descriptive results are likely to be due to random factors or to a real relationship (Kreuger and Neuman, 2006). The mechanics of causation and inference requires a background in statistics and should best be pursued in consultation with and preferably in collaboration with partners experienced in quantitative analysis.

It is not surprising that the phase of data analysis can seem daunting to some practitioners; statistical formulae and the mechanics of causation and inference are not everyone's language. However, once a project has been properly planned and there has been adequate consultation to formulate decisions on data collection, the phase of data analysis becomes a pretty mundane affair. Mostly, data are analysed by the person in the team (or contracted to the team, if resources allow) who is most experienced and most appropriately informed to undertake this task, with the others being consulted on the interpretation of the findings; and for practitioners interpretation is indeed the exciting and manageable part of data analysis! It is not uncommon for researchers experienced in advanced techniques of analysis to happily conduct the analysis in their own time and then to seek an opportunity to discuss the potential anomalies and areas for further analysis with people close to practice. It is naturally a bonus if these competencies reside in the same person, but this is not often the case. Herein lies the joy of practice research partnerships; trusting relationships and close ways of working will have been developed at this stage and will allow for effective and robust analysis between people with skills in data analysis and those able to interpret the discoveries for practice. You are encouraged to work in partnership with other members of the research team to locate books that will provide a detailed explanation of the techniques for data analysis that best fit your particular method of data collection and will be at a level of explanation that will serve your purpose.

This does not mean, though, that practitioners are 'off the hook' as far as analysis is concerned, or that statisticians have sole responsibility for analysis. Statistical literacy is important to enable an understanding not only of the collected data but also of the findings reported in other relevant research reports. Similarly, literacy in qualitative reporting will ensure robust reporting and a grasp of the quality of other reports – as has been alluded to in the discussion of critical appraisal in Chapter Four. An understanding of how the findings were derived is equally crucial in the dissemination phase, as will be discussed in the next chapter. There are commonly accepted procedures for analysing both quantitative and qualitative data that could be regarded as core knowledge for practice research. Coding practices are most commonly used for classifying qualitative data, but because there are few limitations as to what may constitute qualitative data (as has been outlined in the various methods above), data analysis techniques are as varied as the methods used. General thematic analysis is an important skill, and some understanding of this and a general inductive approach to analysis (Thomas, 2006) is crucial, as this is generic to a number of qualitative analytical techniques. This is also true for quantitative data analysis, where, depending on the purpose of the research and the nature of data collected, a range of methods of analysis might be available, but skills in at least basic descriptive analysis are important, as this is generic to a number of quantitative analytical techniques.

One of the most important innovations in recent years to facilitate the ordering and categorising of data has been computer-assisted qualitative and quantitative data analysis software, by means of which researchers can creatively manage and make sense of their data. Computer-assisted qualitative data analysis software (popularly referred to as CAQDAS), has been a growth area in terms of both the range of programs available and the numbers of people using them. The most popular CAQDAS options include NVivo and ATLAS.ti. Quantitative data analysis software options are extensive and their number is overwhelming, as statistical packages have become a growing commercial enterprise. SPSS is the commercial package used widely by researchers, but a range of open source options are also available. Competent use of commercial software such as Microexcel is a relatively affordable option for quantitative data analysis. Even though practice researchers may resist mastering the software, the advantages of using data analysis software include time saving in managing huge amounts of qualitative data and increased flexibility in data analysis and presentation. Monette, Sullivan and DeJong (2008) warn that computer software does not do the researcher's work – it simply assists the researcher in doing many of the tasks related to data analysis. It is worth exploring the possibilities, though!

Reflection exercise 6.5: Data analysis in practice research

1   Are you familiar with the techniques you plan to use to analyse the data that will be collected via your preferred data-collection method?
2   If not, where will you obtain this expertise *prior* to data collection?

Ethical and logistical considerations

The very nature of practice research implies a range of ethical and logistical challenges to be managed. Chapter Two focused on the various political, ethical and cultural drivers that shape the social work research landscape and those issues won't be reiterated here. Suffice it to say that they are particularly important in the phases of data collection, sampling and recruitment. Moreover, the nature of all the relationships and permutations of relationships created by practice research collaborations carries various obligations, including ethical ones, and these have been addressed in Chapter Three. Similarly, this complexity will not be considered here, but the strategies to manage it, as discussed in Chapter Three, should be revisited. A number of key ethical issues associated with practice research at different phases in the project are proposed by McLaughlin (2012, pp 56–71) and are summarised here.

Ethical issues to be considered before the research commences:

■ research governance framework
■ informed consent
■ use of covert methods
■ anonymity and confidentiality.

Ethical issues to be considered during the research:

- right of respondents to end their involvement
- protecting participants from harm
- protection of researchers from harm.

Ethical issues to be considered after the data collection has been completed:

- sharing the data
- publication of the research results
- authorship
- confidentiality and publication.

Social work researchers may not be involved in medical interventions that may cause bodily harm, but their actions can still result in harm, albeit less obvious to the observer. The point in a practice research project where decisions are being made about the best ways to obtain data, and the people to be targeted for this information, is a good time to stand back and reflect on the ethical responsibility to avoid harm. Steyaert et al (2001) offer a few examples from different professions and times, illustrating that even well-meant interventions can carry the risk of adverse effects. Moreover, the impact of mismanaging the logistical details of a research project should not be underestimated in the ethical conduct of research. By and large, project management skills are needed, and if you are aware that you don't have these, you are advised to surround yourself with others who do! You need to be able to provide detailed answers to a range of project questions, such as those listed in Table 6.2.

Table 6.2: Considerations in project management

Collection procedures	Who will be mainly responsible for collecting the data? If more than one person, have they been briefed/trained so as to ensure consistency between and across collection points?
Information storage	How will data be stored for analysis? Is the plan to enter data into a spreadsheet or computer database? Who will do this and how will confidentiality be maintained?
Timing of implementation	When will you collect information? Why? Are there any issues in terms of the timing of the research that should be considered? Do you need to be sensitive to the order of collecting information or the order existing data have been collected?
Risk factors	What problems are likely to arise that could be detrimental to the project? Can you plan for eventualities such as sickness?

Conclusion

As stated many times, a practice research project mirrors social work practice, and the in the same way that you would ensure that you draw on networks and resources in the best interests of a client, so you are encouraged to draw on multiple resources and skills to best serve the research project. Smith (2009, p 161) captures this very eloquently with the following analogy: 'Research is like decorating. A considerable part of the task involves preparation; it will probably not be seen (although it may be reported), but if done well, it ensures that the finished product is more easily accomplished.' This chapter has focused on data collection methods most suitable to collaborative practice research projects. We have considered decisions regarding sampling and techniques for analysing data. It has become evident that a number of ethical and logistical considerations in the process of data collection can have a significant impact on the project. With the foregoing in mind, we can now turn to the importance and dynamics of making research available, when we consider the elements of dissemination and utilisation in Chapter Seven.

Further reading and resources

Moriaty, J. (2011) *Qualitative methods overview*, London: School for Social Care Research, http://www.sscr.nihr.ac.uk/methodsreviews.php.

This publication is an extremely useful resource for practice researchers contemplating the most appropriate method of data collection. The advantages and disadvantages of a number of methods of data collection used most frequently in qualitative research are discussed, including in-depth interviews, focus groups and observation.

Mansell, J. (2011) *Structured observational research in services for people with learning disabilities*, London: School for Social Care Research, http://www.lse.ac.uk/LSEHealthAndSocialCare/pdf/SSCR_Methods_review_10_web.pdf.

As with the publication by Moriaty, this review is an extremely useful resource for practice researchers contemplating the benefits and challenges of observation as a data-collection method. It deals with the methodological issues that arise in using this approach, and with issues of sampling in order to obtain representative information; and considers the practical steps that have to be taken in order to make observations.

Resource PCMH Research Methods Series: http://pcmh.ahrq.gov/page/evidence-and-evaluation.

This website contains mountains of useful information on a range of under-utilised methods of data collection. Each of the briefs describes a method; discusses how researchers have used it or could use it; outlines advantages and limitations of the method; and provides resources for researchers to learn more about the method.

Community Sustainability Engagement Evaluation Toolbox: http://evaluationtoolbox. net.au.

As highlighted in Chapter Five, this is a useful resource for practice researchers to access evaluation material, but it is worth repeating here, as it contains particularly useful information about innovative methods for data collection, including the most significant change (MSC) method.

Part Three
Nurturing networks

7

Dissemination and utilisation

Introduction

Would you expect your doctor to keep up with developments in their profession? How about your pharmacist, dentist or physiotherapist? And is this important for your personal trainer, hairdresser or plumber? Clients receiving a service may expect to be dealing with a well-informed social work practitioner. This may include: new interventions for mental well-being among older adults or for managing problem gambling; effective assessments for intimate-partner violence or cyber bullying; innovations in child protection or for preventing human trafficking. The question is: can you confidently say that you are keeping up with developments in your field? A full response to this question has two parts. On the one hand, social workers are encouraged to be research minded and consider their professional and ethical obligation to be consumers of research; generators of research questions; and collaborators in the design or implementation phases of research as active practitioner-researchers conducting relatively small-scale projects in the workplace or as contributors to research-related activities. Mostly, as we have seen in previous chapters, this has to be balanced with front-line demands and often comes a fair way down the list of priorities. On the other hand, though, researchers need to be practice minded so as to ensure that the findings of research have practice relevance and can be easily accessed by practitioners. This is not to suggest that practitioners are reluctant to fulfil their evidence-informed and research-minded obligations. Doing this just has to be possible within the demands of practice. If this is not the case, the blame cannot solely be placed on the social work practitioner. Making a positive difference in practice – one that is based on recent evidence and well-informed practice – relies on research-minded practitioners and practice-minded researchers. Steyaert et al (2011, p 137) very eloquently state: 'Just as some characteristics of social work practice make it more or less research oriented, characteristics of research make it more or less outreaching to practice.' The focus of this chapter is on the importance and dynamics of making research available so as to ensure that we can keep up with developments in our field of practice. Disseminating research is posed as part of the research process, but also, more importantly, as a product of and influence on networks.

Discussions on the reporting of research often focus on the end phase of the research process: on whether the outcomes are used in practice and on whether users have access to and read journals where research findings are published. This is the logical progression of a scientific process, and the last of the five main moments of the research process, preceded by framing and designing of the project and data collection and analysis. However, this end phase should not be the first time that the reporting of research is considered by practitioners. In fact, this phase in the research process is arguably the most important and the one that should be the main focus of the research from step one. Smith (2009) regards this as the critical phase whereby substance is given to initial ideas and turned into credible and valuable observations on key aspects of the social work terrain. For Engel and Schutt (2013, p 412), the success of the research depends on the effectiveness of this dissemination phase: 'if the intended audience for the research comprehends the results and learns from them, the research can be judged a success. If the intended audience does not learn about the study's results, the research should be judged a failure.' As such, in considering the utilisation of research in practice, the focus should really be on the research question; this parallels social work practice, where the intervention really is where substance is given to the problem initially posed. For example, if the guiding question relates to concerns about the support that older people receive when moving into residential care, dissemination and utilisation will be the phase where the findings are turned into substance through recommendations to clients, families, hospital social workers and managers of residential care facilities. To ensure that recommendations have relevance to stakeholders and are effectively implemented, the research should have been framed in that way from step one. If the question was framed to be practice relevant, the results will be relevant too, and practitioners, managers and policy makers will be interested in reading and implementing the findings. Similarly, if the methodology is practice relevant, the findings will, ideally, be believable and understandable.

Dissemination can broadly be regarded as a process that aims to convey key messages to specific groups via a range of methods, resulting in some reaction, impact or implementation (Scullion, 2002). Planning for the dissemination and utilisation of research findings is as important as planning the actual project. To ensure that the potential audience receives a credible message in the most appropriate format, it is recommended that a dissemination plan be developed (Table 7.1). Many authors offer suggestions for forming such a plan, sometimes called an action plan (CARE [Community Alliance for Research and Engagement], nd; Beddoe, 2007; Wadsworth, 2011) and some also offer templates or checklists to this end. Such a plan will include decisions on the goal or purpose of the dissemination; aspects of credibility in planning for dissemination; the target audience for dissemination; and the relevant medium or types of dissemination for reaching the audience. These elements will be considered next, before the challenges of dissemination will be highlighted.

Table 7.1: Dissemination plan

Purpose	Audience	Credibility	Types
Main message What do you want to communicate and/ or achieve with the dissemination?	*Key stakeholders* Who should be the target of the message and/or needs to know of the recommendations of the research?	*Accessibility* How can you ensure that people will be able to access the findings?	*Format* What is the best way to get the message across?
Timing When should the message be disseminated or the findings released?	*Disseminator* Who is the most appropriate team member or stakeholder to be responsible for the dissemination?	*Quality* What should you include to ensure that findings are presented in a credible manner?	*Strategies* What are the best means to convey the findings?

Purpose of dissemination

There are various reasons why people disseminate the findings of their research. These are most often driven by funding requirements or other compliance goals; linked to professional development goals; or driven by the expectations of an academic qualification. But sometimes these reasons extend to a need to receive feedback on innovative ideas or new interventions or to impact on policy or practice. Postgraduate students are always encouraged by their research supervisors to prepare a more accessible publication from their thesis (which for practice purposes is a highly inaccessible research report), but not all take this task seriously, especially at Master's level. Similarly, funders encourage the accessible dissemination of mandatory reports, but this is often a low priority for busy practitioners or fund managers. What can you do to ensure that dissemination is real and relevant?

Throughout this book, the development of partnerships, networks and knowledge communities has been promoted as a strategy for advancing practice research. Such partnerships will also ensure the effective dissemination and utilisation of research. Decisions about networks, collaborations and learning circles that can be fostered to advance practice research will eventually determine the extent to which a social work practitioner and other stakeholders are informed about and engaged in the implementation of new developments. Practice researchers will therefore have a vested interest in the appropriate dissemination of findings.

An informed decision is required about the main messages to be communicated and the aims to be achieved by the dissemination. You will have made some decisions in this regard when you were framing the project (as discussed in Chapter Four). If the research was aimed at gaining insights into a situation or describing an experience or phenomenon, now is the time to share those insights; if the aim was to test the relationship between variables or explain the cause–effect relationship between variables, now is the time to disseminate the findings about this relationship; or, if the aim was to measure the implementation of social interventions or to develop a new technology, programme or intervention, now is the time to share the evaluation findings or new interventions. But all these aims will have multiple, rich and layered findings and not all of these findings can be communicated at once. Really important decisions are needed about what you want to communicate; what you want the impact to be; and what you want from the people whom you will tell about your findings. Ensure that you consider in this process the potential impact the dissemination can make, the opportunity it will allow for debate and critique and how this will address the ethical commitments you have made in your research.

Potential impact

Inadequate dissemination will minimise the potential impact of the research. It is not possible in the early stages of a project to predict the influence that any research may have, although it is possible to try to create a culture in which research messages may be heard. Collaborative efforts in the earlier stages of practice research will, potentially, enable a culture of effective dissemination and maximise the contribution of research to making a difference in practice. Early relationships with funders, employers, colleagues, participants and/or service users, ethics reviewers or the intended beneficiaries of the research become beneficial when results are due to be published. These stakeholders can help to identify the implications of the research and actions to be taken as a result of the findings. Very often this will involve sensitive discussions about what, when, how and to whom findings will be released. The impact of research may be more powerful when some findings or recommendations are withheld until the political, organisational or financial climate is such that they will be heard – the timing considerations for dissemination are crucial.

Opportunity for debate and critique

A lack of or ineffective dissemination creates a lack of opportunity for debate and critique and limits the transformative power of research. Scullion (2002) advises that the main message should be presented in such a way that the audience may critically consider how it can be used in a particular practice situation. In small–scale research more questions than answers tend to develop, necessitating other, sometimes more advanced research activity. It is crucial that a published document is available for these issues to be raised, so as to ensure iterative knowledge development. This not only ensures more robust evidence, but also helps to build increased confidence in the quality of social work practice. Even the best research does not necessarily change practice. At some times a small study can have effects beyond what could have seemed possible at the outset and at others a large–scale project may not meet its intended purpose. It is only with proper dissemination of the results of the efforts devoted to the various parts of the process that we create a record of research undertaken and ensure that someone will benefit from the learning. If this happens in the course of collaborative work, the players of various roles and a range of potential contributions to research will be identified and this will create a platform for, and indeed expectations of, on–going activity. A focus on the momentum generated by research is essential so as to maximise the real transformative nature thereof.

Ethical commitment

Without proper dissemination of the results, there will be ethical concerns, as dissemination completes the ethical commitments made in the initial stages of the project. A lack of dissemination implies a lack of ethical responsibility to those involved in the research, those who funded or supported the research and those affected by the findings. Ethical considerations in reporting research, according to Engel and Schutt (2013), include an honest accounting of how the research was carried out and acknowledgement of all those who made a contribution. Dissemination enables communication of the findings to the various stakeholders identified and consulted earlier in the research process, including to: participants and/or service users or the intended beneficiaries of the research; employers and colleagues; interest groups; the wider professional community and relevant organisations; and funders. Alston and Bowles (2013) remind us that reporting results to the people who participated in the research is increasingly being acknowledged as also contributing towards the social justice and empowerment agendas of social work research.

Reflection exercise 7.1: The main message(s) for dissemination

1   What was the main impetus for your research; what did you hope to achieve?
2   What are the findings or recommendations you want to disseminate in order to achieve this goal; what is the central argument?
3   Why are your findings a useful or new contribution?
4   What would you want to see happen if you were to tell someone about this?

Audience for dissemination

An equally important and almost simultaneous decision to be made when the main message for dissemination is considered is about the target audience. Once you have decided what you want the impact to be and what you want from the people you will tell about your findings, you will have to decide who 'those people' are. In some instances they may include the general public and academic and practice communities. You will have decided on a central argument; now you need to decide who your audience will be. In some instances you may want to consider whether you have more than one argument for one audience or more than one audience for your central argument. Once again, if stakeholders in the research were identified at the start of the project and have been involved as appropriate in its planning and implementation, you won't need to 'convince' them at this stage of the research to join forces for effective dissemination. They will, hopefully, already be on board – having been consulted – and will understand the project to the extent that approaching them with its findings will not come as a surprise. Not all of these people may have been included in the research project all of the time, but you will have given due consideration all along as to who they are and how they will be able to act upon the findings.

As highlighted above, the impact of research may be more powerful when some findings or recommendations are withheld until the timing is right for the messages to be heard. Furthermore, there may be a greater impact when findings are disseminated or a report is released by a certain person or agency, such as a service user, front-line practitioner or government official, CEO, manager, prominent researcher or media spokesperson. Smith (2009) is of the opinion that the value of practitioners feeding back their findings (positive or not) as practitioners should be acknowledged more widely. At times a presentation by one of the most passionate and articulate members of the team, the one with the 'gift of the gab', may be considered most effective. Smith (2009) also reminds us of the underlying potential of giving service users a voice in the process of dissemination, despite any potential practical challenges. Who is the most appropriate person to engage in dissemination and sometimes, even, who will be the primary author for certain types of dissemination is an important decision to make. Equally, the opportunities that exist for sharing knowledge and ideas through social media should be discussed and the best person for this activity should be identified. This might create tension if now is the first time that these conversations are raised. But if such matters were collectively considered in the planning of the research, even in the broadest terms, they will be less of an issue at this stage of the process.

Credibility of dissemination

There are many different avenues for dissemination, including articles in scholarly journals, research reports or monographs, books, newsletters, social and other media and presentations. Each of these has strengths and weaknesses, will reach a different audience and will potentially meet a different dissemination aim. These will be discussed later, but it is worth noticing in the first instance that the dissemination options available to a practice researcher mirror those sources of existing information accessed earlier in the process of framing the topic. This was discussed at some length in Chapter Four and you may want to revisit that chapter. We learnt there how others disseminate their research, and this may now influence our own decisions in this regard.

Research reports

We have learnt that research reports and monographs often provide readers with a broad-brush description of the results of research and the methodology utilised. These reports are also widely available on publicly accessible websites. To ensure that the totality of your project and the main findings are recorded and widely available you should consider a research report as a 'base' document from which all other types of dissemination can flow. An accessible document, acknowledging the contribution of all stakeholders and capturing the whole of the research journey, can be a very worthwhile product of the research and a source of reference.

'Grey' material

We have also learnt that 'grey' material is valuable to practitioners but difficult to access from outside the organisation. As such, you will not consider agency newsletters, in-house publications or local discussion forums as the best place to reach a wide audience. However, they are a great place to ensure that you make your work known to colleagues and other parties within your organisation. With the advances in storing of electronic material, these publications are increasingly linked to other networks, including professional listservs or other agencies with similar interests, and in this way 'grey' material can reach an even wider, unintended audience. It may be beneficial to have your research announced to other parties within your organisation that do not necessarily access journals in your field of study and it may even be valuable to provide a link to the research report for those interested in further information.

Presentation material

As we have learnt, a large amount of information and knowledge is generated during conferences, symposia and workshops and made available to participants at these events. Other researchers often utilise such information with a critical evaluation of the credibility of the source. As such, to ensure that any oral dissemination of your findings is considered credible, you should include references to other published material (such as a research report or article) on your hand-outs. Alternatively, include clear contact details so that someone interested in following up on the credibility of the material can get in touch with a member of the project team. In addition to successful presentation of your material at a relevant conference, it is beneficial to also see that participants reference your material in their own work or contact you to discuss aspects of the project.

The internet

As previously discussed, a disadvantage of the internet is that there is a lot of unreliable information available, but it is a powerful means of making new and recent information available expeditiously and for finding out who else is interested in your field and for sharing ideas and resources with them. To ensure that others consider your material as reliable and reputable, you may want to explore the option of requesting or negotiating its dissemination on topic- or service-specific portals – some of which also offer automatic e-mail information-alert services. Or you may want to share a link to a research report, article or press release through social media. It is exciting when a targeted group of busy practitioners are alerted to your findings or publication by e-mail or through social media.

Journal articles

We have also learnt that there are numerous search databases or systems to access journal articles, but that it is important to use search terms and search parameters effectively so as to access relevant material. To ensure that others will find your research, it is important to choose a title, write an abstract and carefully consider the choice of keywords that will ensure your work will be identified in a literature search. It is important that your publication is listed in a search when someone is looking for material on a topic related to your research.

Book chapters

It may not be realistic to publish an academic book from your practice research study, although this is quite possible in some instances. But, as we have learnt, edited books bring together experts who write on a particular theme, and these edited texts are often used by researchers in shaping their own studies. To ensure that your research is consulted alongside the work of other known authors in the same field or on the same topic, you may want to approach authors whom you have identified in your own literature search. Published researchers you came across (or worked with in your practice research team) can also be approached to discuss the option of contributing a chapter to an edited book, or even to propose an edited publication. It is an affirmation of the value of your research if a book with diverse angles on a specific topic includes a chapter on your particular project findings.

Just as the dissemination options available to a practice researcher mirror those sources considered earlier in the process, considerations of credibility in reporting the findings from your research mirror the criteria in the critical appraisal of existing information. In Chapter Four we considered three key questions for judging the quality of a publication: who says it? how do they know? does it make sense? These questions will be used to determine the credibility of your work, so it is useful, in preparing for dissemination, to consider how you can ensure that these questions will generate a positive answer. You should ensure that you make it clear who conducted and funded the research, and consider if you should include any disclaimers. As others will judge your research on the quality of the methodology, you should include details on how the information was obtained and analysed, and ensure that arguments are supported by evidence and compared to other publications and research findings.

There are a number of principles core to all data analysis processes that are worth noting during dissemination, as outlined in Figure 7.1. All forms of data reported in any form of dissemination should aim to demonstrate that:

a systematic process of data reduction, organisation and interpretation has been followed in analysing the data; the process used is described in such a way that others are able to follow the logic and replicate it in a future study; the recorded process is comprehensive and takes into account all the data collected – not a convenient subset; and that there is adequate discussion of similarities and differences across and within cases. Communicating findings is about interpreting the story from the data for the reader. These 'stories' are made up of both qualitative and quantitative data and are influenced by the target audience and the type of dissemination, as will be discussed below. You are encouraged to consider how important it is for any particular audience to use numbers (statistics and graphs) or words (stories and quotations) to get the message across.

Figure 7.1: Principles core to all data analysis processes

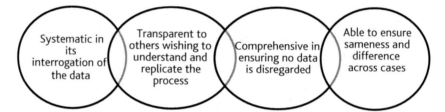

Types of dissemination

In light of the above considerations concerning how others may access and judge what is disseminated, we will now turn to the type of dissemination that will best communicate the main message to the target audience. The format for dissemination may range from very prescriptive in terms of requiring completion of a template or adherence to a specific word count, to more flexible in that a particular argument or series of findings are presented in innovative, informal and creative ways. The format may similarly cover a wide range: face-to-face discussions with individuals, small groups or large forums; via social or other media; circulation by e-mail; access via websites or social networking sites; availability in print or through whatever means seem appropriate. Since a collaborative practice research project will have involved a range of stakeholders, a variety of avenues will be appropriate for dissemination, and in some instances multiple types of dissemination may be needed to get the same message across to the same audience. In this regard, Steyaert et al (2011) suggest that multiple avenues of dissemination can be considered a key element in increasing the 'stickiness' of research results. The 'stickiness' of research is a well-known concept from the field of economic geography and refers to the ability to make research 'stick' to practice. Steyaert et al analysed three international case studies and concluded that where the results of the projects were communicated in a greater variety of ways (including free availability of digital versions of all publications to all those interested in the results) the research results had a higher 'stickiness factor'. Cook et al (2013) list six characteristics of messages that are likely to 'stick': simple, unexpected, concrete, credible, emotional or narrative. Your practice research partners will be able to assist in testing dissemination ideas and sharing the task of dissemination.

Each target audience will require a slightly different message, presented in a different format. Hall (2008) emphasises that flexibility in presenting findings is a necessary quality. Peers, colleagues from relevant organisations, fellow researchers or practitioners, for instance, will benefit most from dissemination in accessible journal articles, organisational newsletters, reports, on websites or in social media or in presentations. In the case of the research on effective day programmes for people living with dementia (see Examples 6.1, 6.2 and 6.5 in Chapter Six), people working in dementia care will be accessing newsletters and reports on websites targeted at this area of work, and these would be appropriate places to publish recommendations on workforce capability. Scientific communities, academics, scholars and researchers, however, will more likely access journal articles, possibly some forms of media such as newspapers or press releases and, if particularly interested, linked sources such as a research report. Discussions about activities aimed at improved the functioning of people living with dementia will potentially best be debated in scholarly articles. Participants in and/ or intended beneficiaries of the research will benefit most from oral presentations, although dissemination via social or other media and websites might be more appropriate for a vulnerable, hidden or marginalised group. In most projects, participants are offered a summary of findings and this should almost always be made available to every participant as a standard form of dissemination, unless the project involved a method that anonymised the data and thus makes access to the participants impossible. In such instances, dissemination of the summary of findings should be through interest groups or forums where people can access a report. This was the case in the dissemination of findings to a group of Black African migrants living with HIV, where the newsletters and websites of community agencies delivering HIV-related support services were utilised for dissemination. Dissemination to funders, government agencies, managers, trustees and senior colleagues will be limited to an executive summary, often accompanied by a brief presentation and optional access to a research report. Let's now consider the various options available for dissemination.

Abstract

An abstract would not, at first, be considered a form of dissemination, and certainly not the first type that comes to mind when considering the circulation of findings. However, an abstract is often the first and sometimes the only piece of writing someone would read to make a decision on whether to access any other material linked to your research. An abstract is required if you express an interest in making a presentation at a conference, or to respond to a call for journal articles or to contribute a book chapter to an edited book. It is also provided as a summary of your work once an article or chapter has been published and is intended as a guide for readers to make a judgement about whether to read further. As a conference abstract, it will be consulted by conference attendees so as to decide whether to attend your presentation. An abstract is a very short overview of what the paper, report, article or presentation is going to cover (topic) and usually includes an introductory sentence that describes the phenomenon (problem); a sentence or two about what has been studied and how (study); a sentence stating the results of the project (findings); and a sentence discussing the findings (implications). It is often limited to 200 words, but may, at times, be limited to as few as 100 words or may generously allow up to 500 words. At times, it can become a really interesting exercise to consider the use of adjectives and to consider sentence construction so as to stay within the word count. Many authors (Alston and Bowles, 2013; Engel and Schutt, 2013) suggest that an abstract should be written last and are in agreement that it is one of the most difficult parts of a report to write. But many times, an abstract is a useful tool to provide you with structure and to organise your thoughts in the initial stages of writing. You are encouraged to discover the value and art of writing a good abstract. The intention to present at a conference is a good incentive for developing an abstract. Remember, though, that you won't be able to get away with producing only one abstract from your research; a generic one may serve various purposes, but each dissemination message, audience and type of dissemination will require its own unique abstract.

Example 7.1: Content and structure for an abstract

There is growing interest in the place of ethical review and broader processes of research governance in practice research. (Topic)

There is a lack of clarity or a common perspective among stakeholders about procedures and practices for practitioners to respond to calls for ethical review. (Problem)

This article reports on a study aimed at exploring the issues of ethical review raised by practitioners and the procedures and practices used for ethical review. (Study)

Almost all of the 285 respondents highly value ethics review, but report a lack of clarity and support in order to carry it out. (Findings)

It is argued that agreement on procedures and practices can ensure that ethical principles are considered while also fostering practitioner research developments. (Implications)

Presentation

A presentation seems the most likely place to start dissemination because, when we are passionate about something, we enjoy talking about it! This is particularly true for social workers. Hosting or presenting at seminars, conferences, workshops or other professional gatherings are common ways to disseminate research findings. It is also useful to attend workshops and seminars so as to learn about the nature of such events for your own future participation. Orme and Shemmings (2010) remind us that a lot can be gained by actually meeting and engaging in debate with the authors of research. Some oral presentations can take the form of a public discussion, community forums or social gatherings. This is particularly popular in certain cultures where service users, participants or communities of interest have a vested interest in the outcomes of a research project. These gatherings often involve food and celebrations, and a full day can be allocated to informing and being informed. Oral presentations can also be made at meetings as an agenda item (such as staff or board meetings). The nature of these events will determine the length of the presentation and how interactive it can be. Mostly, you will be expected to present for 10 to 20 minutes (with or without the use of technology such as Microsoft PowerPoint) and to include time for questions. Public speaking does not come easily to everybody, though, so, as highlighted earlier, you may want to select the member of the team who is best able to do this. Some people may feel comfortable presenting to some audiences (such as peers and participants) but not to others (such as managers or academics).

A poster presentation is not a very common form of presentation, but is gaining popularity at conferences. This is a good way for those unfamiliar with the expectations of national and international conferences to get involved as presenters. You will be expected to produce a poster and discuss its content with interested parties. The benefits of poster presentations are that once you have applied significant time and effort to producing a poster, the product is available for other purposes, not the least of which is to be able to affix it to various noticeboards, doors or walls in corridors, meeting rooms, tearooms and other high-traffic areas! And you will be surprised at the types of conversations generated by questions about a poster. There are various resources to support the development of posters and you are encouraged to consider this form of presentation and to access support for design and production as needed. Delivering either an oral or a poster presentation at conferences is a good way to get feedback on ideas so that you can develop them into an article. Christensen (2012) adds a creative option for verbal dissemination and presentation through an example of research storytelling with indigenous communities. She suggests that storytelling is an effective medium for presenting research findings in a way that is participatory. In a similar vein, Foster (2007) considers how the arts, creativity and imagination can be employed to present research findings in an authentic way. She suggests that stirring the audience's imagination through art and drama is a powerful way of getting a message across. The basic qualities of a good presentation include: a strong start and ending; a clear, central message; appropriate use of humour and anecdotes; more than reading from a paper or from slides; clear and readable presentation material; knowledge about the topic; and delivery within the time limit.

Reflection exercise 7.2: The qualities of a good presentation

What do you regard as your strengths and weaknesses in delivering a public presentation?

Traditional and deconstructed newsletters

A printed, electronic or virtual newsletter is an informal way to disseminate findings to a wider audience and a common form of communication for members of professional associations, or as internal correspondence to a group of people with a shared purpose or interest. These documents tend to have a conversational nature and usually contain various items of information. It is expected that readers will spend only a brief period of time reading any one news item, and then only on those items that draw their interest. It is therefore crucial to attract attention with a catchy title and even visual information about the research. Readers of newsletters will seldom be interested in the science of the research (unless this is the actual focus of the newsletter) but will be particularly interested in the main findings and implications or recommendations. Traditional newsletters sometimes find their way onto websites and social media, so you may want to provide a hyperlink to a research report, article or other information, as appropriate. Do not, however, rely on people accessing additional material; the item in the newsletter should be a stand-alone piece able to introduce the research and succinctly communicate a core finding.

The development of text and visual material (including photos) for a newsletter will also enable you to produce material appropriate for social media as well as for various websites and media releases. Naturally, the pace and innovation of technology have seen a growing diversity of options for making announcements or sharing newsworthy information. Sharing on social media can be regarded as a form of newsletter, but the material becomes deconstructed and interactive; it allows for snippets of information to be shared and immediate feedback to be received but also, unlike traditional newsletters, the potential generation of new content. The reach of a single posting about a research project on Twitter, Facebook, Instagram or any similar platform can be far and wide, it can be resent to a great many people across the globe and it can be added to and critiqued. This enables dissemination that is wider than the scope of any traditional newsletter. According to Allen et al (2013), dissemination of research via social media has the additional benefit that end-users do not have to search for, or 'pull', relevant information, but the social media instead 'pushes' relevant knowledge to the end-user.

A deconstructed newsletter has its obvious downsides in that discipline-specific language needs to be avoided so as to reach people unfamiliar with your discipline. In some respects this may be regarded as a dilution of scientific information, but by this means the information may reach audiences never before accessible through traditional newsletters, such as young adults. The warning by Ruckdeschel and Chambon (2010) about the difference between knowledge and information is relevant in this context. It is the task of the practice researcher to distinguish between disseminating knowledge that can be useful to policy and practice, and disseminating information that might enable a better understanding and appreciation of the findings or of social work practice generally.

Reflection exercise 7.3: Developing text for a deconstructed newsletter

Consider one of the main findings from your research.

1   What will be a catchy headline (no more than five words) to attract attention to this finding?
2   How should the content of your abstract be changed to enable sharing with students from various disciplines on social media?

Full reports and research summaries

A practice or research report is written for a different audience than are many other forms of dissemination, but can serve many purposes. Reporting on a research project in the form of a complete report enables you to pull all the parts of the research together in a communicable whole: the justification for undertaking the project in the first instance; the goal of the research; the existing knowledge on the topic; the design, methods of data collection and sampling; and the analysis and interpretation of the data. The whole report can be prepared well in advance of this final stage of the journey; much of the writing of the report can (and should) begin early and progress throughout the project so as to ensure that a draft is in place by the time the analysis is completed. This is important, as it assists the reliability of the reporting and eliminates the daunting prospect of having to 'write up' the project in the final stages when the energy and incentive for staying involved with the almost-completed project become limited. This is often the point, however, where some practice research projects fail, in that the project has been done and everyone is perceived to be informed about the findings and nobody feels obliged to put hand to paper (or keyboard). You are advised to start the writing process early so as to keep up the momentum and maintain enthusiasm. If the report is a joint effort, it is most useful to decide on a structure and headings for the report and to task one person to pull the various parts together. Plan the use of tables, photos, diagrams and other visual material and get organised early so as to ensure these are sourced or developed well ahead of time. A report creates a clear record of the project and can be a useful point of departure for other forms of dissemination and a document to refer to in other publications. Sometimes the report can be used to provide a broad, descriptive overview so that particular aspects can be presented more succinctly in several journal articles, presentations or newsletters. It is also a useful way to enable co-authorship and shared ownership and to mark the contribution of all stakeholders, irrespective of subsequent publications. Greene and Ruane (2011) offer practical tips for such writing collaboration through use of 'the cloud'. These authors consider the emerging technologies extremely useful for both the storage and dissemination of research, despite the risks associated with cloud computing.

A report can be designed as a glossy document with input from individuals or organisations with specialised skills in design and marketing, if that would serve a purpose. At its most basic, a report can simply be created as a word processing document, properly formatted with a title page, table of contents, appropriate headings, maybe colourful graphics and made available in PDF format. It is crucial to include basic referencing information in such a report, including the date and place of publication and, of course, the names of the authors. It is really frustrating when one consults a report on an interesting practice research study but is unable to reference it because these details have not been provided. You are encouraged to consider applying for an International Standard Book Number (ISBN) if the report is significant in nature and scope. The ISBN is a unique numeric commercial book identifier. The process for obtaining an ISBN is country specific; in some countries a nominal fee is charged, while in others it may be free; in some, the registration of ISBNs is based in national libraries or within government ministries, while in others it is handled by organisations that are not government funded Mostly, it is not an onerous process to obtain an ISBN and the benefits include having the report listed and available in a public international database.

Many useful publications are available on writing a research report, especially on presenting qualitative and quantitative findings, and this will not be discussed in any detail here. All reports generally include basic sections comprising: an abstract or summary; a review of the literature; guiding questions or goals of the research; methodology, including ethics, sampling and data collection methods; a discussion of findings; and a section on implications and recommendations. Various templates for research reports are available and vary in the level of technical information and practice relevance required.

Reflection exercise 7.4: A research report

Recall a time when you had to read a research report (or obtain one if you have not read one recently).

1   What did you find most accessible about the report?
2   What hindered its readability and/or your understanding?

For many audiences, including service users, participants, managers and government officials, a full report is unsuitable, and in such instances you should consider the use of a summary report. An executive summary or a summary of findings is a hugely useful form of dissemination for audiences that are unlikely to read a full report. In essence, an executive summary serves the same purpose as an abstract, but naturally is more substantial in length and contains more detail. A summary of findings is similar in this regard, but its nature is very different. A summary of findings, as the name suggests, contains limited technical information about the project and the scientific process, minimal discussion of aspects of credibility and techniques of data analysis, but focuses on the findings and the implications thereof. Some very useful examples of a summary of findings (or research briefs) are accessible at http://care.yale.edu/index.aspx. If you want to provide more detailed information to your audience, key findings can be expanded as fact sheets, typically in no more than a half to one full page, with graphic images to illustrate a point (CARE, nd).

Journal articles

Scholarly dissemination favours journal articles. The reasons for this are multiple, but mostly related to universities' expectations of their staff to publish in prestigious journals. In Chapter Two we considered the context, including the political context, of practice research. There it was made clear that tertiary education institutions are funded for their research activities and such funding depends on the quantity and quality of staff publications. Steyaert et al (2011) make mention of a standing joke among academic researchers that it is not important how much funding a research proposal generates or how relevant it is to the progress of our understanding, but how many publication opportunities it affords. However cynical this may be, pressure to publish is a reality for most academics and has implications for the financial survival of universities. As such, any collaborative research endeavour will have to take cognisance of this expectation and include opportunities for this type of scholarly dissemination.

Naturally, this is only one part of the picture. Scholarly articles are important in contributing to our collective knowledge; they are the way that academic researchers communicate with each other about research in their respective fields and a way to debate and critique issues of importance to the profession. This type of dissemination is therefore particularly relevant and useful for other scholars and academics and focuses mostly on a targeted aspect of the research that lends itself to academic debate. This does not mean that practitioners won't also access and contribute to scholarly articles. On the contrary, in collaborative practice research, hopefully, practitioners will increasingly be seen as co-authors. The introduction of open access journals has changed the views of and access to journal articles and in the future the impact of these journals on the writing and reading of articles is likely to be increasingly important. The rapid expansion of social media and free access to scientific information have also raised practitioners' awareness of the importance and availability of scholarly articles. The problem starts when highly academic journal articles are the only – and inaccessible – form of dissemination of research.

Preparing a manuscript for a journal requires attention to a few core aspects and it is useful to bear in mind that, in writing a journal article, you will first and foremost write to editors and reviewers, as without their acceptance of the manuscript there will be no publication. There is a surprisingly rich list of journals directly and indirectly related to social work. It is best to obtain the advice of an academic on journal options, as the selection of a journal can be a particularly difficult decision and significantly impact on success in getting published. Guidelines for contributors are usually printed in the back of a hard-copy issue of a journal or available on the journal's website. It is crucial, once you have decided on the most appropriate journal(s) for dissemination, to consider these guidelines carefully and ensure that you stick to them religiously! They will contain information on the recommended word length for an abstract (usually 100–200 words), word limit for the manuscript (4,000–7,000 words) and style of referencing and layout. They may also highlight the different types of submissions accepted, such as articles reflecting the practitioner's voice or articles based on postgraduate research. Before selecting a journal it is good practice to read a few articles from a recent issue to see what the journal focuses on and the type of articles it accepts.

The most prestigious international journals follow a system of peer review (where all manuscripts received are sent for review) or double peer review (in that two reviewers offer comments on changes needed before publication). In most instances blind review is carried out where the author does not know the identity of the reviewer(s). A major part of submitting a journal article is dealing with the review process. If you haven't done this before, it will be wise to attempt your first journal publication with an experienced co-author, as many manuscripts end up unpublished because authors were unwilling to respond to, or inexperienced in dealing with, the comments from reviewers. Revision and resubmission of articles is a part of the publication process and ensures the quality and credibility of the publication. Very few authors will be able to get an article published without some revisions. Do not allow (even nasty) comments from reviewers to deter you from revising and resubmitting your work – albeit sometimes to a different journal. Generally, reviewers will expect: a strong, clear, focused introduction that hooks the reader; a central argument; strong integration of recent and relevant literature; clear scientific methodology; a message to the readers of the particular journal. Most prestigious journals are assigned an impact factor, which is a measure reflecting the average number of citations of recent articles published in the journal and thus reflects the relative importance of that journal within its field. Publications in journals with higher impact factors are more helpful for scholarly careers. Practice researchers are advised to aim initially for less-prestigious, lower-ranked journals and those with a local or regional audience. Not only will it be easier to get published, but the publication may also be more accessible to practitioners, if these happen to be the target audience.

Reflection exercise 7.5: Writing an article

Which of the following tips for writing an article would you find challenging? Where will you find support to raise your competency in this regard?

1   Decide on your audience and choose a journal to match.
2   Read article(s) in that journal and consult the guidelines for authors.
3   Choose one or two main messages for your chosen audience and clearly state (preferably in one sentence) the aim of the article.
4   Structure your article with the help of an abstract.
5   Demonstrate the significance of the research from what is known (integrate recent literature on your topic, including relevant articles previously published in your chosen journal).
6   Report on the project: what you did and how you did it.
7   Report on the findings.
8   Discuss the implications of the findings, as appropriate for the audience of the journal. This should link back to your main message and the reason for writing the article.
9   Check all in-text citations and reference list.

Media interviews, articles and press releases

A press release is a useful way to attract media attention to research findings and to increase the possibility of an invitation for a media interview which, in turn, will initiate discussion and generate interest. Alston and Bowles (2013) remind us that interviews on radio and television reach a wide audience and can bring the results of research to the notice of policy makers and decision makers. Dealing with the media requires a particular skill, and even though you won't necessarily be expected to draft the press release or write an article for dissemination in the media, you will have to be interviewed so as to provide sufficient material to be reworked into the proper format. Ensure that you have a number of well-formulated, considered and clearly articulated arguments, devoid of technical language, prepared for such an interview. Timing of press releases must also be carefully orchestrated (CARE, nd). A press release template and a form that can be used to prepare a press release are available in the document developed by the Community Alliance for Research and Engagement (CARE, nd) (see also the further reading list at the end of this chapter). The CARE document also encourages thinking about the main message and the target audience. Most organisations will have a media spokesperson or access to a consultant or an individual with journalistic skills and you would be wise to develop a rapport with this person in the interests of the research and the research team if your research may (or should) attract media attention. A good media release should be a good story, well told, leaving the journalists to whom you've sent it wanting more.

> **Reflection exercise 7.6: The most appropriate type of dissemination**
>
> You have earlier considered the purpose of dissemination of your research.
>
> 1 Consider the most appropriate audience to whom to communicate findings and recommendations from the research and the most appropriate way to do this.
> 2 Are there any sensitivities in terms of the best timing of an approach to any of these audiences and the best person or agency to perform the dissemination?

Research utilisation

Practice research is primarily concerned with the impact of the research, and dissemination is therefore intricately linked to the goal of seeing recommendations implemented and research evidence utilised. Dissemination has little value unless individual practitioners and agencies can be encouraged to utilise research findings. Furthermore, due to the collaborative nature of practice research, expectations may have been raised about a project and its potential impact, and the utilisation of the research may well become a moral obligation.

Ruckdeschel and Chambon (2010) encourage discussions about research utilisation in social work research and propose that research utilisation should take into account the immediate environment, while not losing sight of broader systemic issues. According to these authors, research use should be tied to practice communities and clearly connected to modes and platforms of dissemination. The case was made earlier that dissemination should be a strategic exercise in consultation with (and with the support of) key stakeholders and an activity anticipated from the beginning so as to allow for the development of core relationships. The support of decision makers is crucial to effective research utilisation. Communication failures about the core messages or forum for dissemination between researchers, policy makers and practitioners are regarded as an important factor in the under-utilisation of research, according to Hall (2008). Similarly, the traditional view that a researcher need not have a role in the implementation of findings and that practitioners are unable or unwilling to engage with research findings, also contribute to the under-utilisation of research findings.

In this context, over the last few years increased attention has been given to translational research, which aims to make use of the findings of scientific research in practical applications – originally within healthcare and increasingly in the social sciences. Translational research had two distinct domains, according to Woolf (2008): the 'bench-to-bedside' enterprise of harnessing knowledge from the basic sciences for the development of new treatments; and the translation of findings from clinical trials into everyday practice to ensure that new treatments and research knowledge reach the patients or populations for whom they are intended. The impetus for translational research will potentially increase in years to come as policy makers and funders show a growing interest in the utilisation of research. Several mechanisms have been progressively developed in different contexts to increase the practical relevance of research findings (Orme and Shemmings, 2010). One example of such a mechanism is the Institute for Research and Innovation in Social Services (IRISS) in Scotland. This institute aims to 'promote positive outcomes for the people who use Scotland's social services by enhancing the capacity and capability of the social services workforce to access and make use of knowledge and research for service innovation and improvement' (http://www.iriss.org.uk/about). Another example is the Social Care Institute for Excellence (SCIE) in England. This institute claims to 'gather and analyse knowledge about what works and translate that knowledge into practical resources, learning materials and services' (http://www.scie.org.uk/Index.aspx). However, the origins of effective utilisation of practice research findings are with well-developed and nurtured networks.

Challenges of dissemination

Confidential or controversial findings

Practice research projects conducted in a specific context may have commercial or other sensitivities and the reports from such research can be expected to be treated as confidential. Dissemination through a variety of channels is then not possible. Hall (2008) reminds us that negotiation of intellectual property rights needs to be conducted before the research is undertaken so that disputes over publication of findings are avoided. With some projects, it is useful to consider how the main findings have relevance to broader audiences and how the message can be disseminated without making the identity of the provider or organisation known. In other instances it may, on the contrary, be expected to make the identities of participants or organisations known, as this may be the way to acknowledge the uniqueness of their contribution and to establish ownership of their knowledge or information.

It is also possible that the research findings may indicate that a particular intervention or project is ineffective or doing harm, whereas the future funding and livelihoods of many may depend on the intervention continuing. Hall (2008) acknowledges that such problems are common in applied research and that researchers may experience pressure to suppress or alter findings. This should be anticipated in framing the study, as mentioned earlier. Engel and Schutt (2013) warn that conflict and controversy are unavoidable in research on sensitive issues. Despite the best intentions to communicate important findings, different agendas drive people's reaction to and re-reporting thereof, and you can expect that attention will sometimes turn to less important but controversial aspects of the research – controversy is newsworthy. Some principles for engaging with the media, as discussed above, can go some way to mitigating these tensions, but mostly good partnerships based upon a degree of reciprocity can address many such tensions in practice research.

The voice of participants

It is important to include the voice of participants in the dissemination of findings, through the integration of qualitative data. But it is equally important to ensure that participants are protected in the process. Orme and Shemmings (2010) make us aware that indigenous groups and particular groups of service users may feel that some knowledge belongs to individuals, tribes and communities and is not to be shared without agreement. Members of these communities may have particular views on what, how, when and where knowledge collected during the course of the research may be shared. As mentioned above, ownership is an important part of this, but once ownership has been clarified, it is important to honour the voices of participants as to how the data is presented. If an individual participant, a group of participants or an organisation consented to be identified in the research, it is critical that all content attributed to them be cleared in advance of any dissemination. If, however, the intention was for the participants to remain anonymous, this too should be honoured. This does not only mean that no identifying information should be released, but also that care should be taken to ensure that no participant is identifiable through a particular quote, or reference to a particular incident or case, or inadvertently when URLs are included in referencing. In a report on the views of key informants involved with a work programme for refugees, for example, it was made clear that only two centre managers were interviewed, one male and one female. In the discussion of findings, quotes from centre managers were included and reference was made to 'her controversial statement'. It wasn't too difficult for any stakeholder in the field to determine the identity of the person who had made the controversial statement. Such oversights not only do harm to the individual concerned and the integrity of the project but will also undermine assertions of confidentiality in future projects. Where findings could be construed as unfavourable or even damaging to a cultural group or organisation and its reputation, their dissemination should be dealt with very carefully.

Conclusion

This chapter has focused on the importance of making research available and has encouraged consideration of the dynamics involved in the utilisation and dissemination of findings. Planning for dissemination is an essential element of effective dissemination. The elements of such a plan were discussed and comprise consideration of: the purpose of the dissemination; the target audience; aspects of credibility in planning for dissemination; and the relevant medium or types of dissemination for reaching the target audience. The strengths and weaknesses of different avenues for dissemination were highlighted. The development and nurturing of partnerships, networks and knowledge communities is seen as important to ensure effective dissemination and will eventually also determine the extent in which a social work practitioner and other stakeholders are informed about and engaged in the implementation of new developments.

Further reading and resources

Institute for Research and Innovation in Social Services (IRISS) in Scotland, http://www. iriss.org.uk/about; and the Social Care Institute for Excellence (SCIE) in England, http:// www.scie.org.uk/Index.aspx.

Both these institutes have extensive evidence-based resources for various stakeholders on a range of topics. They are accessible and robust and should be one of the first places to search and access information that may be relevant and useful to your own areas of interest. Both these sites also link to other useful sites.

CARE (Community Alliance for Research and Engagement) (nd) *Beyond specific publication: strategies for disseminating research findings*, http://care.yale.edu/index.aspx.

This publication is an extremely useful resource for practice researchers contemplating dissemination of their research findings. It comprises a number of templates that can be used for various purposes during the dissemination planning process.

Research mentoring relationships

8

Introduction

Who are the people that supported you in developing practice competence in your field of expertise? I assume that you will be able to name a few! It is extremely rare for anyone, on receiving an award or accolade for an achievement, not to acknowledge others who have made the achievement possible. Mostly, the acknowledgement will be extended to support networks, but there may also frequently be mention of a mentor or coach. In fact, career development initiatives are based on the notion that coaching and mentoring will enable a person to achieve greater heights (Connor and Pokora, 2012). Research is traditionally viewed as a solo exercise, mostly undertaken towards a higher qualification or by academic researchers. This is sometimes true, but certainly not in the case of applied, practice research. In Chapter Three we considered the nature of relationships in research and concluded that social research is about people. A Maori proverb, very well known to most social workers and widely used in New Zealand, seems particularly relevant in this context: *He aha te mea nui o te ao? He tangata! He tangata! He tangata!* What is the most important thing in the world? It is people! It is people! It is people! This is true also of the aspirations for collaborative research shared in this book.

It is easy to envisage the permutations of capabilities and complexities that collaboration brings. Think about all the collaborative relationships we have explored so far, and then consider the possibilities that some individuals in these networks are in need of mentoring on any particular aspects of practice research, and others are in a position to provide that advice. In the discussion of practice research relationships in Chapter Three, we encouraged dialogue about strategies and models whereby networks are utilised, and consideration of the use of inter-organisational networks for learning and knowledge development. We considered the definition by Wenger et al (2002) of communities of practice as groups of people who share a concern, a set of problems or a passion about a topic and who deepen their knowledge and expertise in this area by interacting on an on-going basis. It is in this 'interacting on an on-going basis' where the rich possibilities for mentoring originate. You may want to consult Chapter Three again, as those earlier discussions will not be revisited here. But this chapter can be considered as another piece of the debates addressed there. Here we want to focus on the subtle expectations of mentoring (among other dynamics) when working relationships, collaboration and partnership are considered.

Wilson (2014), writing on partnerships between universities and employer organisations in social work education, states that such partnerships have many advantages, but warns that the task of bringing together a wide range of stakeholder interests is not easy and presents challenges that may engender disadvantages. He emphasises that specific collaborative arrangements are required to facilitate efficient working relationships. Huxham and Vangen (2013) write extensively on the nature of collaboration and on collaborative advantage, and suggest that one of the common bases of most collaborative partnerships includes opportunities for mutual learning. Managing collaborative networks in practice research parallels social work practice, and it follows logically that supervisory and mentoring relationships will develop in the management of research networks. It is not realistic to expect that mentoring relationships will develop between everyone on the practice research team who has something to offer and those eager to receive, or that mentoring is the only or most important part in a complex process of partnership working. Yet, in considering the potential that mentoring can add to on-going research activity in practice and to keeping up the momentum generated by research, mentoring can be regarded as a key feature for realising the potential of practice research.

Reflection exercise 8.1: Mentoring relationships

Recall a mentoring relationship where you were either the mentor or mentee.

1   Was the relationship hierarchical and supervisory, or collaborative and mutually beneficial?
2   What were the advantages and disadvantages of your particular model of mentoring, for both parties?
3   How would such a relationship benefit you if you were to participate in a practice research initiative?

Models of mentoring

Mentoring has become a worldwide phenomenon in a number of contexts, including health and social services (Byrne and Keefe, 2002; Pololi et al, 2002), education (Pololi et al, 2002; Clarke, 2004) and business (Rymer, 2002). Connor and Pokora (2012) define mentoring as learning relationships that help people to take charge of their own development, to release their potential and to achieve results that they value. However, the definitions of mentoring are many and varied and this results in confusion about the nature of mentoring relationships. Traditional mentoring models tend to be criticised for power imbalances and for the controlling nature thereof when driven by institutional goals (Darwin, 2000; Colley, 2001). Darwin (2000, p 198) argues that 'traditionally the mentoring relationship has been framed in a language of paternalism and dependency and stems from a power-dependent hierarchical relationship aimed at maintaining the status quo'. Recent developments point to a change in this traditional, expert–pupil relationship.

Chaudhuri and Ghosh (2012) raise the notion of 'reverse mentoring' as an inverted type of mentoring relationship whereby older or more experienced colleagues learn from younger or less experienced colleagues. Younger colleagues are seen as being more self-directed, resourceful, more accepting of diversity and masters of technology. The more experienced colleagues, usually also in the older age groups, are seen as thriving on work challenges, valuing personal growth and as believers in lifetime employment and company loyalty, and are often viewed as workaholics. Having people in a genuine mentoring relationship where the sharing of experiences across the intergenerational gap is seen to be worthwhile may have benefits for both the individuals and the organisation.

An alternative model of mentoring is based explicitly on non–hierarchical and collaborative partnerships, which have been termed by some as co-mentoring (Kochan and Trimble, 2000; Rymer, 2002; Clarke, 2004). This terminology recognises that co-mentoring is based on collaboration and shared decision making (Kochan and Trimble, 2000), with a key aspect being that the relationship is of mutual benefit to all involved (Kochan and Pascarelli, 2003; Clarke, 2004). The roles are seen as supportive, rather than supervisory, and responsive to queries or concerns raised by both parties. In reflecting on a unique, long-term co-mentoring relationship, Jipson and Paley (2000) present co-mentoring as a safe space within which to encourage, support and critique the trying-out of ideas and exploring feelings and actions. These authors offer four metaphors that have emerged from their co-mentoring relationship and discuss how these analogies have informed their professional conduct, while acknowledging tensions, frustration and disappointment as part of the journey. This is worth exploring in your own context (see the further reading section at the end of this chapter), as it resonates with the close relationships in practice between colleagues and the potential for co-mentoring to enable research activity that otherwise might not be possible.

Fouché and Lunt (2010) report on innovative approaches to mentoring in practice research and indicate that, if various permutations of co-mentoring are allowed, different networks of mentoring may develop. They refer to these relationships as 'nested' mentoring. Nested mentoring is regarded as a commitment to process, underpinned by a view of changed relations and a rethinking of power relationships, workplace culture and purpose. Fouché and Lunt (2010) argue for a nested mentoring approach consisting of a reciprocated process of communication that is multiple (allowing a range of mentoring relationships to develop), malleable (allowing mentor relations to be steered or reworked if their particular development and operation is proving problematic), contingent (accepting that what happens within particular settings cannot be anticipated) and dynamic (will undergo constant development and reworking).

It seems that, if we are committed to advancing practice research and the culture of practitioner enquiry through mentoring relationships, we need to be bold enough to allow mentoring relations that go beyond vertical relationships and explore alternative models of mentoring related to co-mentoring, reversed mentoring and nested mentoring practices.

Example 8.1: Mentoring relationships in the GRIP project

In an initiative aimed at assisting the development of a research culture in social services agencies, mentoring formed a crucial part of the process. This initiative, referred to as Growing Research in Practice (GRIP), and highlighted in earlier chapters (see Examples 2.2 and 3.2), brought together academics, practitioners, agencies and funding bodies through a number of core partnerships. Four academic partners and a project manager worked with nine selected social service agencies practice teams to explore research questions of immediate concern to them. A series of resources and strategies supported the initiative, including the provision of workshops and academic and peer mentoring. The mentoring relationships envisaged as part of the initiative initially included (a) academic mentors and practice teams and (b) peer mentoring taking place between the practice teams at workshops, where topic experts presented. It soon became clear, however, that many different networks of mentoring started to develop that were never anticipated, nor would have been possible to orchestrate. This was allowed and encouraged. Meetings with practice teams about their projects were directed at their learning, and insights were shared between the academic partners, the project manager and the practitioners, in effect each mentoring and being mentored by the other. The same pattern soon emerged within the various practice teams.

Practice teams acted as co-mentors and availed themselves of appropriate forms of support from within their groups. Groups needed to also seek support and approval for their projects within their employing organisations and, as such, developed partnerships with their managers and knowledgeable colleagues, including those mandated to advise on protocol. Projects were discussed and methodologies considered that enabled skills, knowledge and cultural competence to be shared within groups and organisations that made for new forms of mentoring. In this emergence of mentoring relationships the experience was not just one of more mentor connections being made between mentors and mentees. Rather, it was a process whereby new relationships helped to modify existing ones. It was not simply that the quantity of relationships increased, but the range and nature of all relationships changed as a result of the within-group mentoring.

Another set of mentoring relationships developed at workshops where practice teams shared with one another, as envisaged, in a peer-mentoring model. But, in addition, the invited presenters engaged in a mentoring-type relationship with the practice teams by contributing sessions at the workshops on methodologies, data collection, data analysis, presentation of results and cultural expertise. In addition, individual and team skills and experiences were also shared with the presenters, who had been challenged and enlightened on the complexity of the practice projects and the relevance of the presented material to the practice context. In summary, we saw the emergence of sets of co-mentoring: (a) between the academic partners and practice teams; (b) between the various practice teams; (c) within the practice teams and their agency networks; and (d) between the workshop presenters and the practice teams. This went beyond a co-mentoring model to become a nested and reversed mentoring approach.

Certainly not all contexts will allow for this to happen successfully and in some of the practice teams these nested mentoring relationships worked better than in others. They were affected by different personalities, group dynamics and, in two instances, by mentors occupying more than one role (this barrier to mentoring will be discussed further below). Group dynamics obviously enable richness in learning and sharing, but the diversity also poses challenges in terms of managing strengths, perspectives and deficits.

The characteristics of mentoring relationships will be discussed next, before our attention turns to the importance of mentoring infrastructure.

Research mentoring relationships

Within the vast pool of mentoring research, literature on research mentoring tends to focus on the academic mentoring of postgraduate students, or the mentoring of academic staff to support the development and retention of productive, satisfied, collegial and socially responsible staff (see for example Fleming et al, 2012; Barratt-Pugh, 2012; Ripley and Yarhouse, 2012; Straus et al, 2014). The focus on mentoring *practice* research, and on developing research capacity outside the specific goals of the university system, is limited. Practice research mentoring seems to fall between the two areas of general mentoring practices and academic research mentoring. Learning about mentoring relationships across the various sectors and in a range of contexts may have relevance for research mentoring, but Fletcher (2012) warns that it shouldn't be assumed that the techniques successful in one context will be successful in another. According to Barratt-Pugh (2012), mentoring practitioner–research capability builds on considerable and diverse practitioner knowledge bases and has considerable challenges in terms of the selection and adaptation of methods for multiple and diverse contexts. A number of key features, benefits and barriers to effective mentoring are relevant.

Key features of effective mentoring

The key factor influencing the success of mentoring practices seems to be the quality of the mentoring relationship. High-quality relationships are characterised primarily by trust. Many authors identify mutual respect, trust and shared values as important features for effective mentoring. Klasen and Clutterbuck (2002) note the importance of a close, developmental relationship based on mutual trust. Zerwekh and Claborn (2006), in the context of nursing, maintain that trust and caring are hallmarks of the bonding that occurs between mentor and mentee. Straus et al (2014) identify key features of a successful mentoring relationship, including mutual respect and shared values, but also consider bonding to be important, adding personal connection and reciprocity to the list. A willingness to participate in a mentoring relationship contributes to its success, and outcomes tend to be more positive when mentees want to be in the relationship and value their mentor's intervention (Klasen and Clutterbuck, 2002).

One of the key features highlighted by Straus et al (2014) is clear expectations. Connor and Pokora (2012) highlight the same aspect by stating that all good mentoring starts with clear expectations and a working agreement, on-going review and well-prepared endings. Connor and Pokora (2012) remind us however, that clear expectations do not imply rigidity. They warn that effective mentoring models should merely provide a sense of direction, but be fluid enough to accommodate varying needs. Clarke (2004) also emphasises the need for flexibility and notes that mentoring is not a linear process, as is sometimes portrayed, but one of overlapping layers. According to Clarke (2004, p 131), 'within mentoring relationships

… the skills of each of the participants complements and enhances the skills of others in the relationship'. This seems to be particularly pertinent in the context of collaborative practice research relationships. According to Kochan and Trimble (2000), discussing the status of the mentoring relationship on a consistent basis can be beneficial in maintaining, transforming or dissolving the relationship as appropriate. This links to the notion of nested mentoring, where rich interactions are allowed to develop.

Effective mentoring further depends on the qualities of the mentor and the mentee. According to Connor and Pokora (2012), a good mentor facilitates learning: they understand that the mentee will have to do things between sessions and that mentoring is only a catalyst for learning and action. The mentor uses a repertoire of skills, tools and techniques appropriately to develop insight and release potential. The qualities of the mentor enable, affirm and sustain the mentee. Good mentors communicate care, respect and empathy. A quality mentee, on the other hand, can be regarded as resourceful: they have a purpose for the learning relationship and a focus to identify and use resources. The outcome of such a mentoring relationship is change and action: the mentee achieves something that they care about and that makes a positive difference, and the mentor is able to act as the catalyst.

Benefits of effective mentoring

A number of benefits of mentoring relationships have been outlined in the literature, including providing sociological and emotional support (Campbell and Campbell, 2000, cited in Kochan and Pascarelli, 2003) and fostering career advancement (Gardiner et al, 2000, cited in Kochan and Pascarelli, 2003). Practice research teams can become resilient (sometimes against organisational odds) not only through logistical support but also through the emotional support of colleagues, managers and others. According to Fleming et al (2012), an effective research mentoring relationship serves a career function where the mentee learns how to become a productive researcher. Career advancement can range from having an abstract from a practice project accepted at a conference to pursuing advanced qualifications (Katz and Coleman, 2001). This signals an important message in the practice research context. Members of the practice research team may be inexperienced or reluctant researchers in need of developing research as part of their careers. One of the experienced researchers in the team could be tasked with the mentoring responsibility to assist these colleagues to become productive researchers. Barratt-Pugh (2012) suggests that the practice researcher, by being engaged in the mentoring relationship, may not only gain knowledge about management of the project but also experience socialisation in a community of practice researchers.

Another related and more obvious benefit can be regarded as enhancing skills and professional growth (Alexander, 2002, cited in Kochan and Pascarelli, 2003). Professional growth is often attributed to the practitioners in the team – that they develop research competence. But this is equally true for other members of the team; academic partners may develop increased understanding of the hurdles faced by practitioners and of the extent of high staff turnover and the consequent impact on practice research. If this potential for professional growth is recognised and embraced, there are several possible advantages to the quality of conversations and learning.

Fleming et al (2012) further note that the outcome of a relationship that accomplishes these functions also prepares the mentee to eventually mentor others. Building mentoring capacity is important in the context of practice research. This does not refer only to providing mentoring, however, but also to receiving mentoring. As with professional supervision relationships (Davys and Beddoe, 2010), there is an expectation that mentoring will be more successful if the mentee is prepared for and engaged in the relationship. As such, the experience of receiving mentoring will also impact on the capacity to provide mentoring in the future. Fletcher (2012) refers to this as 'generative' research mentoring, where research mentees emerge to become research mentors for others.

Barriers to effective mentoring

Despite the fact that there is a substantial amount of literature on the benefits of mentoring relationships, there is an increasing amount being written about barriers to effective mentoring practices. One of these is mentors occupying more than one role. In discussing the research context, for example, Shamoo and Resnik (2003, p 60) describe mentors as 'advisors, counsellors and friends', while at the same time they may be employers and supervisors. They argue that this conflict of interests affects the quality of the mentoring relationship. In practice research teams, supervisors and practitioners in a subordinate position may participate as co-mentors and there is thus a real possibility for such a conflict to arise. This is further discussed by Klasen and Clutterbuck (2002), who maintain that, in such situations, mentoring is less likely to be a power-free, two-way, mutually beneficial learning situation where the mentor provides guidance and shares experiences in a low-pressure, self-discovery approach. This is not to say that a multiplicity of relationships is not beneficial. In practice research teams where the stakeholders include managers or supervisors there is usually strong leadership, accompanied by timelines, scheduled meetings and steady progress (Fouché and Lunt, 2010). While it is never possible to dissolve the power context within which practice research activities take place, a nested mentoring approach offers some insurance against this being unrestrained.

Another barrier to effective mentoring includes previous experiences of mentoring. The fact that individuals have experienced mentoring relationships may affect their willingness to engage in further mentoring – especially if those relationships were not experienced as positive. In their review of the literature Hansford et al (2003) found that poor mentoring experiences resulted from lack of support; ineffective or inappropriate advice; personal or professional incompatibility between mentors and mentees; a lack of partnership; and differing expectations. It is envisaged that other mentoring relationships, including openness to nested mentoring, might be impacted by this experience. For nested mentoring to work, groups must be open to non-linear relationships and must be given the authority to work within the learning set. This may involve dispensing with what they have learnt previously.

Reflection exercise 8.2: Research mentoring

You are encouraged to consider mentoring needs and opportunities in practice research.

1   What would you want to know as the mentee?
2   What would you be able to offer as a mentor?
3   What is your greatest hesitation in committing to a mentoring relationship?

Facilitating nested mentoring in a framework of opportunity

Cooke (2005, p 3) provides a useful reflective model of research capacity building with social care practitioners. This author indicates that building research capacity requires attention to four structural levels: individual, team, organisational and network. Cooke's model has been adapted by Barratt-Pugh (2012, p 19) and continues to promote the need for a collaborative community of practice so as to allow effective mentoring relationships. This aligns with previous discussions about the collaborative nature of practice research and the notion of learning organisations. At its core, it implies that mentoring can be really effective only if it is supported by an infrastructure that will enable and support the mentoring. To this end, this chapter concludes with a description of and reflection on two examples of mentoring that were implemented through the use of a structured approach to advancing practice research (for more information see; Lunt, Fouché and Yates, 2008; Lunt, Shaw and Mitchell, 2009; and Fouché and Lunt, 2010, 2011). Central to this reflection is how a structured partnership approach may enhance the process and outcomes of practitioner research. The two practitioner research initiatives illustrate the value of the innovative use of a structured approach that has a time-limited focus, a shared vision, a work breakdown structure and cohort membership. You may recall that we have referred to these examples in previous chapters too. In this context, they demonstrate the application of unusual mentoring relationships. Mentoring and tutoring were perhaps the two most valued elements of all within the two initiatives.

Example 8.2: Structured approaches to practice research

Two practitioner research initiatives were implemented independently of each other in two different countries at different times (Auckland, New Zealand, 2005–07 and Scotland, 2006–09). Both initiatives involved individuals or groups of practitioners in conceptualising, designing, undertaking and disseminating their own research and both were developed through a structured partnership approach. The first initiative (Growing Research in Practice, or GRIP), with which you are familiar by now (from Examples 2.2, 3.2 and 8.1), aimed to strengthen research-mindedness and research activity in social service settings by working with social service agencies to explore research questions that were of immediate concern to practitioners. This programme was time limited to 15 months and culminated in a practice symposium. Groups of practitioners across a range of fields of practice were required to conduct their own research with workshop support, mentoring support and peer support from methods experts, mentors and peers. Mentoring support responsive to the queries or concerns raised by the practitioners was provided by paired mentors via e-mail and face to face. Mentors encouraged the teams to create a timeline for their project and to assign tasks within and set goals for small components to be completed. Oral progress reports were obtained at each mentoring session. These activities were all integrated into a funded programme that set a framework and a timeline for achieving the outcomes.

The second initiative, a practitioner initiative of CHILDREN 1st (a large voluntary agency in Scotland) and the Glasgow School of Social Work, aimed at supporting individual practitioners to develop and undertake their own small-scale research projects focused on children and family support. The programme aimed to promote reflective and investigative practice among practitioners, to aid their professional development and to contribute towards an evidence base. It intended to influence practice at three levels: individual team, and organisation. Two cohorts of practitioners were recruited, with each cohort taking one to two years to complete their projects. Individual practitioners were selected from the agency's multiple sites. The entire fieldwork, analysis and writing up for each individual study were conducted by the individual practitioners. Support to this end consisted of a series of structured, face-to-face training days with topic experts from within the university delivering frequent workshops. This was supplemented with on-going one-to-one support throughout the research process provided by an academic tutor via contact by telephone and e-mail. These activities were all integrated into a funded programme that set a time framework of 12 months.

The use of a structured approach to facilitating practice research – in what is called 'a framework of opportunity' – contributed to the management of obstacles and opportunities and eventually to the success of the initiatives. As outlined above, the structured approach displayed the following characteristics.

- A time-limited focus: operating with predictable expectations allowed best use of limited time and an opportunity to plan other commitments within the set parameters. For many front-line practitioners, activities that have a beginning, an end and clear parameters allow personal and professional management of the nature and extent of outputs and enable decisions on commitment to the activity. Both initiatives were able to offer 'customised' mentoring to practice groups as a way of addressing the diverse range of interests present within the workshops.
- A shared vision: part of the success of the initiatives aimed at facilitating practitioner research lay in their ability to harness practitioners' enthusiasm. Findings from the projects suggested that a sense of passion for the topic and a commitment to change practice for the better kept the projects alive – even amid serious adverse conditions in some instances. Getting the practitioners to enter into a partnership and to recognise their own resources and expertise to produce findings that would change practice for the better facilitated task identity and task significance and allowed them to forge ahead with their work and maintain a belief that what they were doing had value.
- Work breakdown structure: in the context of the practitioner initiatives, this implied the delivery of workshops, mentoring and resources to enable the practitioners within their own projects to implement those projects and disseminate the findings by submitting reports and making presentations at the end-of-project conferences (CHILDREN 1st) or the final symposium (GRIP). Being held to account for these deliverables and tasks added another layer of deadlines over and above the deadlines for the research projects. To this end, project teams came together for

their own project meetings, during mentoring/tutoring sessions or at workshops. At these times, ideas were shared and progress was noted. The workshops or training seminars were seen by the practitioners as being the most important part of the network activities.

- Cohort membership: peers from within the cohorts or project teams played a role in support and completion. Team members provided, among other resources, motivation, organisational ability, particular research skills and presentation skills to the research process and to team deliberations. The practitioners worked together as cohorts or practice teams until the end of the programme, despite changes in membership due to staff turnover and practice obstacles – even geographical obstacles in the case of CHILDREN 1st. A major outcome of this cohort membership was the amount of learning, support and camaraderie that occurred throughout the process. Practice teams and cohorts were acting as co-mentors and also availing themselves of appropriate forms of support from within their groups. Projects were discussed and methodologies considered, enabling skills, knowledge and cultural competence to be shared within groups and organisations.

Barriers to practitioner research are of three kinds: resource-based (demands on time, workload pressures and difficulties in obtaining assistance to hone research knowledge and skills); those arising from professional roles and identity construction (social workers viewing themselves as helpers rather than intellectuals, and research being regarded as an add-on or luxury to 'real' social work); and broader organisational and cultural constraints (the workings of organisational systems and the cultures and power structures that pervade them). While not discounting the barriers and difficulties that practitioners often face in conducting research, the success of mentoring relationships within a structured initiative suggests that, under particular circumstances, these can be surmounted.

Conclusion

In our consideration of collaborative research and the development of practice research partnerships throughout this text, we have addressed the benefits and challenges of complex relationships. This chapter has focused on a different and more subtle aspect of these relationships, namely mentoring. Different models of mentoring and aspects of effective mentoring relationships have been considered. The benefits of facilitating nested mentoring relationships in a structured 'framework of opportunity' have been discussed and promoted. Mentoring contributes to maintaining the momentum generated by practice research and to the potential of practice research partnerships.

Further reading and resources

Huxham, C. and Vangen, S. (2013) *Managing to collaborate: The theory and practice of collaborative advantage*, New York: Routledge.

This book extensively covers debates on the nature of collaboration and on collaborative advantage. The authors suggest one of the common bases to most collaborative partnerships includes opportunities for mutual learning. As such, this book also addresses mentoring as a dimension of collaboration and is worthy of attention.

Jipson, J. and Paley, N. (2000) 'Because no-one gets there alone: collaboration as co-mentoring', *Theory into Practice*, vol 39, no 1, pp 36–42.

This article captures the encounter of two friends and colleagues over a long period, working together, 'serious, committed, helping each other figure it out' (p 36). It is an easy read with a lot of food for thought on the nature of co-mentoring. The authors reflect on the similarities and differences, and the complexities and intensities that laid the foundations for their co-mentoring experience.

9

The full cycle

Introduction

Can you remember where this journey started? In Chapter One we considered the question of why you do what you do. We discovered that the effectiveness of social work practice is a principal concern of the profession and cannot be ignored. In Chapter Two we contemplated the frustrations of knowing what to do to deliver an effective service but not being able to act on our insights for lack of authority or resources, or because of the challenges of professional boundaries, or for reasons of job security. We discussed the dynamics that we have to consider and the relationships to negotiate in order to make a difference in practice. Chapter Three challenged our beliefs in the value of relationships and our commitment to developing those for the purposes of social research, which often involves a focus on vulnerable or marginalised individuals or groups, and scarce organisational resources. Turning to Chapter Four, we explored what it is that we want to achieve when we 'research' and came to understand that a project will stand or fall by the way it is framed. We also considered the benefits of developing partnerships at this stage. Chapter Five queried the best ways to implement such a project, once properly framed. We focused on the many ways to investigate the multiplicity of issues in social work practice and the importance of recognising how these different paths and the choices we make at every stage of the research process may impact on ways of knowing. We carefully considered two popular designs for collaborative practice research. Chapter Six challenged our thinking about the best ways to obtain data. We considered various collaborative methods of collecting data and the issues involved in sampling and data analysis. Chapter Seven focused on aspects of the dissemination and utilisation of research findings. We learnt that making a difference in practice relies on research-minded practitioners and practice-minded researchers. In Chapter Eight we considered the place of others in developing practice competence and turned to the subtle expectations of mentoring in collaborative research. And now we return to the original question, asking 'Why do you do what you do?' We need to consider not only our commitment to effective social work practice but also our commitment to collaboration in social work practice research as a strategy to realise this, and our subsequent commitment to developing capacity for practice research partnerships.

Reflection exercise 9.1: Practice research

1   Is the effectiveness of social work practice a principal concern for you?
2   Are you prepared to contribute to practice evidence?
3   What are the main insights you have gained from this book to enable that?

The commitment to effective social work practice

Research in the social sciences has seen major transformation in recent years and social work is increasingly part of this landscape. Traditional ways of doing research are still prominent, but more emphasis is placed on the social aspects of research, with acknowledgement that a variety of stakeholders with diverse competencies and skills are needed to generate and disseminate new knowledge. As such, research activities are increasingly developed by different people, from different institutions and different walks of life, who at some times compete with each other and at other times collaborate for the achievement of a common objective. And this brings with it a level of complexity that requires clear strategies in order for research to flourish. On-going collaboration, throughout the entire process of developing practice knowledge, is one strategy for securing evidence-based relevance in demonstrating the effectiveness of social work practice. This strategy is impeded by logistical considerations, organisational resources and cultural, ethical and political constraints. And also, unfortunately, by professional identity: the will and intention to be identified as a practitioner committed to practice effectiveness.

There are on-going debates about the appropriate relationship of social work and research and, indeed, the best research model to follow so as to advance this, as we discussed in Chapter One. In moving from these debates and into practice, there is always the danger that rhetoric around practice research outruns the reality. Indeed, as Mullen and colleagues (2005) note: 'The social work profession, then, is in danger of thinking that, because we are defining, writing about, and teaching evidence-based practice, it really exists in the field' (p 63). We still have some way to go to ensure significant, demonstrable commitment to effective social work practice.

The commitment to collaboration in social work practice research

If on-going collaboration is accepted as a strategy in demonstrating the effectiveness of social work practice, careful consideration should be given to the nature of engagement. Himmelman (2001) proposes a four-level model that comprises a continuum of engagement that occurs between partnering organisations: networking, coordinating, cooperating and collaborating. According to this model, when moving from networking to collaborating, the degree of time involvement, commitment, risk, interdependence, power and trust, as well as a willingness to share territory, increases. Cautionary tales abound of best practice going bad, and warnings for effective collaboration include patience, perseverance and flexibility. Engaging indigenous communities of interest brings with it particular challenges that can easily be under-estimated in discussions about collaboration. It can be assumed that strong collaborative relationships will take time to develop and will grow from networks and a commitment to coordinate activities and to cooperate to achieve a collective goal. This continuum of engagement can visually be presented as in Figure 9.1. Once we acknowledge the different roles involved with regard to practice research, the transforming potential of networking becomes clear.

Figure 9.1: Levels of engagement in developing partnerships

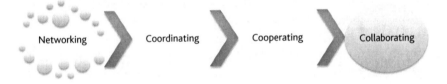

The commitment to developing capacity for practice research partnerships

Engaging for the benefit of social work practice research can provide advantages that extend beyond the project's purpose and content. This provides further support for the value of committing resources and developing infrastructure to supporting practice research. Many authors have written about these secondary benefits, which are usefully summarised by Yawn et al (2010). According to these authors, the secondary benefits of collaboration include: a more systematic practice style; more effective teamwork; practice adaptation and extension of the study tools; increased professional self-worth and community recognition; opportunity and support for staff members 'stretching' into new roles; and increased research literacy within the practice. These authors realised in their practice-based research study that networks became 'common laboratories for translational and clinical research, moving from ... observational studies to clinical trials and translational projects' (Yawn et al, 2010, p 455).

According to Cooke (2005), research capacity building can be seen as a means to an end (the end being research that informs practice), or an end in itself (emphasising developments in skills and structures enabling research to take place). Over and above the requirement to address the structural levels, she also promotes six principles for increased capacity building, namely: building skills and confidence; developing linkages and partnerships; ensuring that the research is 'close to practice'; developing appropriate dissemination; investments in infrastructure; and building elements of sustainability and continuity. Greenaway and Witten (2006) report on a meta-analysis of 10 community action projects aimed at identifying commonalities in structures and processes that enhanced or impeded the projects in meeting their goals for social change. The analysis revealed that the recognition of power dynamics between stakeholders and the transformation of relationships between individuals, groups and organisations are critical to the development of effective community action projects. Creating structures for collaborative action and learning, along with power sharing and fostering of developmental practices, created the conditions within which change could occur. We have considered several examples throughout this book where structures and practices for collaborative action and learning not only realised practice research outcomes but also delivered secondary benefits. Active attention to the development of such structural and practice capacity is regarded as a major hurdle in many practice contexts. McRoy et al (2012) advanced this argument with strategies for building research capacity in social work education programmes and research administration, and a consideration of the role of funders. Even though the focus of the book is different in terms of advancing academic research and the productivity of university staff members, it suggests the need for effective interdisciplinary, cross-university and community collaborations and a focus on sustaining infrastructure.

Example 9.1: Partnering to make a difference

Stakeholder commitment can be illustrated through an initiative launched by a philanthropic funder. This funder wanted to ensure that the reporting of data by grant holders is more robust, and that there is increasing evidence that the money allocated makes a difference to practice. This commitment to effective social work practice informed discussions about how best to support agencies to enable such reporting. A training institution was contracted to assist 39 agencies that had received grants from the funder to develop competency in creating evaluation plans and reporting against their evaluation goals. Three workshops over a three-month period supported individual representatives from agencies to consider their evaluation aspirations for a particular project. They were challenged to consider how these aspirations aligned with their strategic plans and other programmes or activities in their agency. This required them to discuss their plans with other role-players not involved in the workshops and ensured wide dissemination of learning and discussion of ideas. Thirty-two of these agencies took up the challenge; another great illustration of commitment to practice effectiveness.

The partnership between the funder, the training institution and the agencies (mostly managers or CEOs) enabled increased robust reporting against the evaluation plan. The funder received reports highlighting outputs, outcomes, innovative ways of collecting evaluation data and insights into the bigger evaluation plan for the agency. It will be interesting to see how the quality of reporting changes in future. This exercise required decisions about the need for (and in some instances success in) partnering to enable baseline data collection. For instance, one agency CEO negotiated with a food bank (as a referring service to the agency) and a budgeting service (as a service to where it refers clients) about ways to obtain data that will illustrate the effectiveness of its service. In another instance, plans for another such collaboration for data collection across service providers were proposed. This necessitated the increased involvement of other colleagues, other agencies delivering similar services, researchers and even students and is a good illustration of commitment to collaboration as a strategy for realising the practice research aspirations.

A request for on-going training was supported by the funder, and this initiative has now seen more agencies becoming involved in developing evaluation plans and partnerships to enable robust evaluation data. Within a 'framework of opportunity', a commitment to developing capacity for practice research partnerships is demonstrated. All this evolved organically with the original commitment by one funder to ensure that practice effectiveness is demonstrated. Imagine what could be achieved if we had more stakeholders committed to such practices!

Conclusion

The chapters of this book have collectively aimed to demonstrate the need for both practice research and a range of strategies to develop partnerships to enable this. The discussions have spanned: contextual issues of practice research (Part One), where we considered the dynamic relationship between practice and research; the research process (Part Two), where the pragmatics of designing and implementing a collaborative practice research project were explored; and the benefits and responsibilities of collaborative research (Part Three), where we highlighted activities to maximise use of the findings from collaborative research and strategies to sustain the momentum. We have unequivocally privileged a particular approach to research – that of an applied focus that is of benefit to a practice context. This does not to undersell the value of basic research and the 'scientific studies' aimed at the development of knowledge that may have a more indirect value and implication for practice. In the preference for the former, we have not focused on a range of valuable and valid ways of sampling, data collection, analysis and dissemination –due only to their limited value for application to and for practice, which is at the heart of this book. Basic research is hugely important for social work – not only because it contributes to the conceptual advancement of knowledge of and about practice, but also because this is the way that social work can hold its ground among other academic disciplines.

The research process is not a linear process of sequential steps, even though it is often and unavoidably presented as such. Similarly, the development and maintenance of practice–research partnerships to make a difference in practice is not a neat, tidy and straightforward process. But then, neither is social work or human interaction! Research, like social work, is a social activity, highly contested and contextual and fraught with political, ethical and cultural debates. There are certainly unanswered questions and grey areas open for interpretation and negotiation throughout this book.

Perhaps in completing the full cycle, from considering the context of practice research, through the process to designing and implementing a collaborative practice research project, to the benefits and responsibilities of collaborative research, it is most helpful to consider two things: the importance of research, and the implications for practice when we lack evidence; and the importance of collaboration, and the implications for practice when we lack partnerships. We cannot serve the aims of social work and social justice without research. But for practice research to have value, it must be properly framed, ethically conducted and effectively disseminated. To ensure that research is used and the implications for practice are considered, commitment is needed from key stakeholders, including educators, practice managers, practitioners, postgraduate students and organisations. For most, this requires changes in culture and in the way that research is encouraged, understood and supported. We have limited success stories of this happening and, to make a difference, we need to find new ways of doing research the social work way – using social work values and embracing the importance of relationships. There is growing evidence of the value of communities of practice – here presented as communities of knowing – as a means of bringing about change for effective partnerships between various stakeholders. I will leave you with a few final questions: what is your commitment to effective social work practice, to collaboration in social work practice research and to developing capacity for practice research partnerships? What will you do to advance communities of knowing and practice research partnerships?

Further reading and resources

McRoy, R.G., Flanzer, J.P. and Zlotnik, J.L. (2012) *Building culture and infrastructure*, New York: Oxford University Press.

This book captures a range of strategies for educational institutions and funders to support practice research and may have limited value to some readers, but is hugely valuable to educators.

References

Acton, C. and Miller, R. (2009) *SPSS for social scientists* (2nd edn), Basingstoke: Palgrave Macmillan.

Allee, V. (2000) 'Knowledge networks and communities of practice', *OD Practitioner Online*, vol 32, no 4, 1–15, accessed at www.vernaallee.com/images/VAA-KnowledgeNetworksAndCommunitiesOfPractice.pdf.

Allen, H.G., Stanton, T.R., Di Pietro, F. and Moseley, G.L. (2013) 'Social media release increases dissemination of original articles in the clinical pain sciences', *PloS One*, vol 8, no 7, e68914, accessed at www.plosone.org.ezproxy.auckland.ac.nz/article/info%3Adoi%2F10.1371%2Fjournal.pone.0068914.

Alston, M. and Bowles, W. (2013) *Research for social workers* (3rd edn), Oxon: Routledge.

Amabile, T.M., Patterson, C., Mueller, J., Wojcik, T., Odomirok, P.W., Marsh, M. and Kramer, S.J. (2001) 'Academic–practitioner collaboration in management research: a case of cross-profession collaboration', *The Academy of Management Journal*, vol 44, no 2, pp 418–31.

American Evaluation Association (2011) *Statement on cultural competence in evaluation*, accessed at www.eval.org/p/cm/ld/fid=92.

Anghel, R. and Ramon, S. (2009) 'Service user and carers' involvement in social work education: lessons from an English case study', *European Journal of Social Work*, vol 12, no 2, pp 185–99.

Babbie, E. (2001) *The practice of social research*, Belmont, CA: Wadsworth.

Babbie, E. (2007) *The practice of social research* (11th edn), Belmont, CA: Wadsworth.

Babbie, E. and Mouton, J. (2001) *The practice of social research*, London: Oxford University Press.

Barker, R.L. (2003) *The social work dictionary* (5th edn), Washington: NASW Press.

Barratt-Pugh, L. (2012) 'Mentoring the next researcher generation: reflections on three years of building VET research capacity and infrastructure', *International Journal of Training Research*, vol 10, no 1, pp 6–22.

Bazeley, P. (2007) *Qualitative data analysis with NVivo*, London: Sage.

Becker, H.S. (1967) 'Whose side are we on?' *Social Problems*, vol 14, no 3, pp 239–47.

Beddoe, L. (2007) 'Writing and dissemination', in C.B. Fouché, N. Lunt and D. Yates (eds) *Growing research in practice: A collection of resources*, Auckland, New Zealand: Massey University Press, pp 57–68.

Benson-Rea, M. and Wilson, H. (2003) 'Networks, learning and the lifecycle', *European Management Journal*, vol 21, no 5, 588–97.

Bessant, J. and Tsekouras, G. (2001) 'Developing learning networks', *AI & Society*, vol 15, no 1–2, pp 82–98.

Blaikie, N. (2010) *Designing social research,* Cambridge: Polity Press.

Bloom, M., Fischer, J. and Orme, J.G. (1999) *Evaluating practice: Guidelines for the accountable professional*, London: Allyn & Bacon.

Boland, R.J. and Tenkasi, R.V. (1995) 'Perspective making and perspective taking in communities of knowing', *Organization Science*, vol 6, no 4, pp 350–72.

Bolton, A., Pole, C. and Mizen, P. (2001) 'Picture this: researching child workers', *Sociology*, vol 35, no 2, pp 501–18.

Botkin, J. (1999) *Smart business: How knowledge communities can revolutionize your company*, New York: The Free Press.

Bourgois, P. (2003) *In search of respect: Selling crack in El Barrio* (2nd edn), Cambridge: Cambridge University Press.

Brannick, T. and Coghlan, D. (2007) 'In defense of being "native": the case for insider academic research', *Organizational Research Methods*, vol 10, no 1, pp 59–74.

Brehaut, J.C. and Eva, K.W. (2012) 'Building theories of knowledge translation interventions: use the entire menu of constructs', *Implementation Science*, vol 7, pp 114–24.

Broad, B. (ed) (1999) *The politics of social work research and evaluation,* Birmingham: Venture Press.

Brown, J. and Isaacs, D. (2005) *The world café*, San-Francisco, CA: Berrett-Koehler Publishers.

Bryman, A. (2012) *Social research methods*, New York: Oxford University Press.

Byrne, M.W. and Keefe, M.R. (2002) 'Building research competence in nursing through mentoring', *Journal of Nursing Scholarship*, vol 34, no 4, pp 391–6.

Campbell, L. and Fouché, C. (2008) 'Research in social work', in M. Connolly and L. Harms (eds), *Social work: Contexts and practice* (2nd edn), London: Oxford University Press, pp 393–409.

Carey, M. (2012) *Qualitative research skills for social work: Theory and practice,* Aldershot: Ashgate Publishing.

Carlson, E.D., Engebretson, J. and Chamberlain, R.M. (2006) 'Photovoice as a social process of critical consciousness', *Qualitative Health Research,* vol 16, no 6, pp 836–52.

Carroll, L. (1920) *Alice's adventures in wonderland*, London: Macmillan.

Chaudhuri, S. and Ghosh, R. (2012) 'Reverse mentoring: a social exchange tool for keeping the boomers engaged and millennials committed', *Human Resource Development Review*, vol 11, no 1, pp 55–76.

Christensen, J. (2012) 'Telling stories: exploring research storytelling as a meaningful approach to knowledge mobilisation with indigenous research collaborators and diverse audiences in community-based participatory research', *Canadian Geographer*, vol 56, no 2, pp 231–42.

Clandinin, D.J. and Connelly, F.M. (2000) *Narrative inquiry: Experience and story in qualitative research*, San Francisco, CA: Jossey-Bass.

Clarke, M. (2004) 'Reconceptualising mentoring: reflections by an early career researcher', *Issues in Educational Research*, vol 14, no 2, pp 121–43.

Coakes, E. and Clarke, S. (eds) (2006) *Encyclopedia of communities of practice in information and knowledge management*, Hershey, PA: IGI Global.

Cochran-Smith, M. (2005) 'Teacher educators as researchers: multiple perspectives', *Teaching and Teacher Education: An International Journal of Research and Studies*, vol 21, no 2, pp 219–25.

Coghlan, D. and Brannick, T. (2005) *Doing action research in your own organisation*, London: Sage.

Colley, H. (2001) 'Righting rewritings of the myth of mentor: a critical perspective on career guidance mentoring', *British Journal of Guidance and Counselling*, vol 29, no 2, pp 177–97.

Collins, S. (2008) 'Statutory social workers: stress, job satisfaction, coping, social support and individual differences', *British Journal of Social Work*, vol 38, no 6, pp 1173–93.

CARE (Community Alliance for Research and Engagement) (nd) *Beyond specific publication: Strategies for disseminating research findings*, New Haven, CT: Yale Center for Clinical Investigation, accessed at http://care.yale.edu/index.aspx.

Connor, M. and Pokora, J. (2012) *Coaching and mentoring at work: Developing effective practice* (2nd edn), Berkshire, England: McGraw-Hill.

Cook, B.G., Cook, L. and Landrum, T.J. (2013) 'Moving research into practice: can we make dissemination stick?' *Exceptional Children*, vol 79, no 2, pp 163–80.

Cook-Craig, P.G. and Sabah, Y. (2009) 'The role of virtual communities of practice in supporting collaborative learning among social workers', *British Journal of Social Work*, vol 39, no 4, pp 725–39.

Cooke, J. (2005) 'A framework to evaluate research capacity building in health care', *Bio Medical Central Family Practice*, vol 6, no 44, pp 1–11.

Cooper, D.R. and Schindler, P.S. (2011) *Business research methods* (11th edn), Boston, MA: McGraw-Hill.

Corby, B. (2006) *Applying research in social work practice*, London: Open University Press.

Cordoba, J. and Robson, W. (2006) 'Understanding communities of practice to support collaborative research', in E. Coakes and S. Clarke (eds) *Encyclopedia of communities of practice in information and knowledge management*, Hershey, PA: IGI Global, Chapter 93, pp 558–64.

Couper, M.P. and Miller, P.V. (2008) 'Web survey methods', *Public Opinion Quarterly*, vol 72, no 5, pp 831–5.

Coy, M. (2006) 'This morning I'm a researcher, this afternoon I'm an outreach worker: ethical dilemmas in practitioner research', *International Journal of Social Research Methodology*, vol 9, no 5, pp 419–31.

Cree, V.E. and Davis, A. (2007) *Social work: Voices from the inside*, Oxon: Routledge.

Creswell, J. (2003) *Research design: Qualitative, quantitative and mixed methods approaches*, London: Sage.

Creswell, J. and Plano Clark, V. (2011) *Designing and conducting mixed methods research*, Thousand Oaks, CA: Sage.

Darwin, A. (2000) 'Critical reflections on mentoring in work settings', *Adult Education Quarterly*, vol 50, pp 197–211.

Davidson, C. and Tolich, M. (2003) *Social science research in New Zealand: Many paths to understanding* (2nd edn), Auckland, New Zealand: Pearson Education.

Davidson, C. and Voss, P. (2002) *Knowledge management: An introduction to creating competitive advantage from intellectual capital*, Auckland, New Zealand: Tandem Press.

Davies, H., Nutley, S. and Smith, P. (2000) *What works? Evidence-based policy and practices in public services*, Bristol: Policy Press.

Davies, P., Hamilton, M. and James, K. (eds) (2007) *Maximising the impact of practitioner research: A handbook of practical advice*, London: National Research and Development Centre for Adult Literacy and Numeracy (NRDC), accessed at www.nrdc.org.uk.

Davies, R. and Dart, J. (2004) *The Most Significant Change (MSC) technique: A guide to its use*, accessed at www.clearhorizon.com.au/wp-content/uploads/2008/12/dd-2005-msc_user_guide.pdf.

Davys, A. and Beddoe, L. (2010) *Best practice in professional supervision: A guide for the helping professions*, London: Jessica Kingsley Publishers.

D'Cruz, H. and Jones, M. (2004) *Social work research: Ethical and political contexts,* London: Sage.

De Vos, A.S., Delport, C.S.L., Fouché, C.B. and Strydom, H. (2011) *Research at grass roots: For the social sciences and human service professions*, Pretoria: JL van Schaik Publishers.

Denscombe, M. (2009) 'Item non-response rates: a comparison of online and paper questionnaires', *International Journal of Social Research Methodology*, vol 12, no 4, pp 281–91.

Dodd, S.J. and Epstein, I. (2012) *Practice-based research in social work: A guide for reluctant researchers*, New York: Routledge.

Drew, S.E., Duncan, R.E. and Sawyer, S.M. (2010) 'Visual storytelling: a beneficial but challenging method for health research with young people', *Qualitative Health Research*, vol 20, no 12, pp 1677–88.

Dudley, J.R. (2010) *Research methods for social work: Being producers and consumers of research*, Boston: Allyn & Bacon.

Duignan, P. (2002) 'Building social policy evaluation capacity', *Social Policy Journal of New Zealand,* vol 19, pp 179–94.

Elgesem, D. (2002) 'What is special about the ethical issues in online research?' *Ethics and Information Technology*, vol 4, no 3, pp 195–203.

Engel, R.J. and Schutt, R.K. (2013) *The practice of research in social work* (3rd edn), London: Sage.

Epstein, I. (2001) 'Using available clinical information in practice-based research: mining for silver while dreaming of gold', *Social Work in Health Care*, vol 33, nos 3–4, pp 15–32.

Epstein, I. (2009) 'Promoting harmony where there is commonly conflict: evidence-informed practice as an integrative strategy', *Social Work in Health Care*, vol 48, no 3, pp 216—31.

Epstein, I. (2010) *Clinical data-mining: Integrating practice and research*, New York: Oxford University Press.

Epstein, I., Stevens, B., McKeever, P. and Baruchel, S. (2006) 'Photo elicitation interview (PEI): using photos to elicit children's perspectives', *International Journal of Qualitative Methods*, vol 5, no 3, pp 1–11.

Fargion, S. (2007) 'Theory and practice: a matter of words. Language, knowledge and professional community in social work', *Social Work and Society: International Online Journal*, vol 5, no 1, accessed at www.socwork. net/sws/article/view/121/537.

Fischer, J. (1973) 'Is casework effective? A review', *Social Work*, vol 18, pp 5–20.

Fleming, M., Burnham, E.L. and Huskins, W. (2012) 'Mentoring translational science investigators', *Journal of the American Medical Association*, vol 308, no 19, pp 1981–2.

Fletcher, S. (2012) 'Research mentoring teachers in intercultural education contexts; self-study', *International Journal of Mentoring and Coaching in Education*, vol 1, no 1, pp 66–79.

Fleury, J., Keller, C. and Perez, A. (2009) 'Exploring resources for physical activity in Hispanic women, using photo elicitation', *Qualitative Health Research*, vol 19, no 5, pp 677–86.

Fook, J. (ed) (1996) *The reflective researcher*, New South Wales, Australia: Allyn & Unwin.

Fook, J. (2002) *Social work, critical theory and practice*, London: Sage.

Fook, J. (2011) 'Developing critical reflection as a research method', in J. Higgs, A. Titchen, D. Horsfall and D. Bridges (eds), *Creative spaces for qualitative researching*, Rotterdam: Sense Publishers, pp 55–64.

Foster, V. (2007) 'Ways of knowing and showing: imagination and representation in feminist participatory social research', *Journal of Social Work Practice*, vol 21, no 3, pp 361–76.

Fouché, C. and Light, G. (2011) 'An invitation to dialogue: the world café in social work research', *Qualitative Social Work*, vol 10, no 1, pp 28–48.

Fouché, C. and Lunt, N. (2009) 'Using groups to advance practice-based research', *Journal of Social Work with Groups*, vol 32, no 1, pp 47–63.

Fouché, C. and Lunt, N. (2010) 'Nested mentoring relationships: reflections on a practice project for mentoring research capacity amongst social work practitioners', *Journal of Social Work*, vol 10, no 4, pp 391–407.

Fouché, C. and Lunt, N. (2011) 'A framework of opportunity for practitioner research', in I.M. Saleh and M.S. Khine (eds), *Practitioner research in teacher education: Theory and best practices*, Germany: Peter Lang, pp 199–217.

Fouché, C., Beddoe, L., Bartley, A. and Brenton, N. (2013) 'Strengths and struggles: overseas qualified social workers' experiences in Aotearoa New Zealand', *Australian Social Work,* doi: 10.1080/0312407x.2013.783604.

Fox, J. (2011) 'The view from inside: understanding service user involvement in health and social care education', *Disability & Society*, vol 26, no 2, pp 169–77.

Fox, M., Martin, P. and Green, G. (2007) *Doing practitioner research*, London: Sage.

Frank, F. and Smith, A. (2006) *Community development and partnerships: A handbook for building community capacity*, Bentley, WA: Curtin University of Technology.

Fraser, M.W., Richman, J.M., Galinsky, M.J. and Day, S.H. (2009) *Intervention research: Developing social programs*, New York: Oxford University Press.

Galinsky, M.J., Turnbull, J.E., Meglin, D.E. and Wilner, M.E. (1993) 'Confronting the reality of collaborative practice research: issues of practice, design, measurement, and team development', *Social Work*, vol 38, no 4, pp 440–9.

Gambrill, E.D. (2003) 'Evidence-based practice: sea change or the emperor's new clothes', *Journal of Social Work Education*, vol 39, no 1, pp 3–23.

Gauntlett, D. (2007) *Creative explorations: New approaches to identities and audiences*, New York: Routledge.

Gibbs, A. (2001) 'The changing nature and context of social work research', *British Journal of Social Work*, vol 31, no 5, pp 687–504.

Gilgun, J.E. (2005) 'The four cornerstones of evidence-based practice in social work', *Research on Social Work Practice*, vol 15, no 1, pp 52–61.

Giuliano, K. (2003) 'Expanding the use of empiricism in nursing: can we bridge the gap between knowledge and clinical practice?' *Nursing Philosophy*, vol 4, pp 44–50.

Glaser, B.G. and Strauss, A.L. (1967) *The discovery of grounded theory: Strategies for qualitative research*, New Brunswick, USA: Aldine Transaction.

Glendinning, C. (2002) 'Partnerships between health and social services: developing a framework for evaluation', *Policy and Politics*, vol 30, pp 115–27.

Grasso, A.J. and Epstein, I. (1992) *Research utilization in the social services: Innovations for practice and administration*, New York: Haworth Press.

Gray, D.E. (2004) *Doing research in the real world*, London: Sage.

Gray, M., Plath, D. and Webb, S.A. (2009) *Evidence-based social work: A critical stance*, New York: Routledge.

Gray, M. and Schubert, L. (2012) 'Sustainable social work: modelling knowledge production, transfer, and evidence-based practice', *International Journal of Social Welfare*, vol 21, no 2, pp 203–14.

Greene, C. and Ruane, E. (2011) 'Collaboration in the cloud', *College & Research Libraries News*, vol 72, no 8, pp 454–60.

Greenaway, A. and Witten, K. (2006) 'Meta-analysing community action projects in Aotearoa New Zealand', *Community Development Journal,* vol 41, no 2, pp 143–59.

Grimes, M. (2010) 'Strategic sensemaking within funding relationships: the effects of performance measurement on organisational identity in the social sector', *Entrepreneurship Theory and Practice*, vol 34, pp 763–83.

Grinnell, R.M. and Unrau, Y.A. (2005) *Social work research and evaluation: Quantitative and qualitative approaches* (7th edn), New York: Oxford University Press.

Groundwater-Smith, S., Mitchell, J., Mockler, N., Ponte, P. and Ronnerman, K. (2013) *Facilitating practitioner research: Developing transformational partnerships*, London: Routledge.

Groves, R.M., Fowler, F.J., Couper, M.P., Lepkowski, J.M., Singer, E. and Tourangeau, R. (2009) *Survey methodology* (2nd edn), Hoboken, NJ: John Wiley & Sons.

Guillemin, M. and Gillam, L. (2004) 'Ethics, reflexivity and ethically important moments', *Research in Qualitative Inquiry*, vol 10, no 2, pp 261–80.

Gulbrandsen, M. and Smeby, J. (2005) 'Industry funding and university professors' research performance', *Research Policy*, vol 34, no 6, pp 932–50.

Hall, R. (2008) *Applied social research: Planning, designing and conducting real-world research*, Sydney: Palgrave Macmillan.

Hamilton, M. and James, K. (eds) (2007) *Practitioner-led research initiative impact report*, London: National Research and Development Centre for Adult Literacy and Numeracy (NRDC), accessed at www.nrdc.org.uk.

Hamilton, M. and Wilson, A. (eds) (2006) *New ways of engaging new learners: Lessons from round one of the practitioner-led research initiative*, London: National Research and Development Centre for Adult Literacy and Numeracy (NRDC), accessed at www.nrdc.org.uk.

Hamilton, M., Davies, P. and James, K. (eds) (2007) *Practitioners leading research*, London: National Research and Development Centre for Adult Literacy and Numeracy (NRDC), accessed at www.nrdc.org.uk.

Hammersley, M. (2005) 'Is the evidence-based practice movement doing more harm than good? Iain Chalmers' case for research-based policy-making and practice', *Evidence and Policy*, vol 1, no 1, pp 85–100.

Hansford, B., Tennent, L. and Ehrich, L.C. (2003) 'Educational mentoring: is it worth the effort?' *Education Research and Perspectives*, vol 30, no 1, pp 42–75.

Harper, D. (2002) 'Talking about pictures: a case for photo elicitation', *Visual Studies*, vol 17, no 1, pp 13–26.

Health Research Council of New Zealand (2005) *Guidelines on Pacific health research*, accessed at www.hrc.govt.nz/sites/default/files/Overview%20 of%20the%20Pacific%20Health%20Research%20Guidelines.pdf.

Healy, K. (2001) 'Participatory action research and social work', *International Social Work*, vol 44, no 1, pp 93–105.

Heisenberg, W. (1958) *Physics and philosophy: The revolution in modern science*, London: Allen & Unwin.

Hickson, H. (2012) 'Reflective practice online – exploring the ways social workers used an online blog for reflection', *Journal of Technology in Human Services*, vol 30, no 1, pp 32–48.

Himmelman, A.T. (2001) 'On coalitions and the transformation of power relations: collaborative betterment and collaborative empowerment', *American Journal of Community Psychology*, vol 29, pp 277–84.

Hocoy, D. (2002) 'Cross-cultural issues in art therapy', *Art Therapy*, vol 19, no 4, pp 141–5.

Hookway, N. (2008) 'Entering the blogosphere: some strategies for using blogs in social research', *Qualitative Research*, vol 8, no 1, pp 91–113.

Huss, E. (2007) 'Shifting spaces and lack of spaces: impoverished Bedouin women's experience of cultural transition through arts-based research', *Visual Anthropology*, vol 21, no 1, pp 58–71.

Huss, E. (2012) 'What we see and what we say: combining visual and verbal information within social work research', *British Journal of Social Work*, vol 42, no 8, pp 1440–59.

Huss, E. and Cwikel, J. (2005) 'Researching creations: applying arts-based research to Bedouin women's drawings', *International Journal of Qualitative Methods*, vol 4, no 4, pp 44–62.

Huxham, C. and Vangen, S. (2013) *Managing to collaborate: The theory and practice of collaborative advantage*. New York: Routledge.

International Association of Schools of Social Work (IASSW) (2005) *Global standards for social work education*, joint statement by IASSW and IFSW, accessed at www.ifsw.org/cm_data/GlobalSocialWorkStandards2005.pdf.

Jipson, J. and Paley, N. (2000) 'Because no-one gets there alone: collaboration as co-mentoring', *Theory into Practice*, vol 39, no 1, pp 36–42.

Katz, E. and Coleman, M. (2001) 'Induction and mentoring of beginning researchers at academic colleges of education in Israel', *Mentoring and Tutoring: Partnership in Learning*, vol 9, no 3, pp 223–39.

Kirk, S.A. and Reid, W.J. (2002) *Science and social work – a critical appraisal*, New York: Columbia University Press.

Klasen, N. and Clutterbuck, D. (2002) *Implementing mentoring schemes: A practical guide to successful programmes*, Oxford: Butterworth Heinemann.

Knights, D. and Scarbrough, H. (2010) 'In search of relevance: perspectives on the contribution of academic–practitioner networks', *Organization Studies*, vol 31, nos 9–10, pp 1287–309.

Kochan, F.K. and Pascarelli, J.T. (eds) (2003) *Global perspectives on mentoring: Transforming contexts, communities and cultures*, Connecticut: Information Age Publishing Inc.

Kochan, F.K. and Trimble, S.B. (2000) 'From mentoring to co-mentoring: establishing collaborative relationships', *Theory into Practice*, vol 39, no 1, pp 20–8.

Kreuger, L.W. and Neuman, W.L. (2006) *Social work research methods: Qualitative and quantitative applications*, Boston: Pearson & Allyn Bacon.

LaMendola, W., Ballantyne, N. and Daly, E. (2009) 'Practitioner networks: professional learning in the twenty-first century', *British Journal of Social Work*, vol 39, no 4, pp 710–24.

Lave, J. and Wenger, E. (1991) *Situated learning: Legitimate peripheral participation*, Cambridge: Cambridge University Press.

Leedy, P.D. and Ormrod, J.E. (2005) *Practical research: Planning and design*, New York: Pearson Merrill Prentice Hall.

Lunt, N., Davidson, C. and McKegg, K. (eds) (2003) *Evaluating social policy and practice: A New Zealand reader*, Auckland: Pearson Education.

Lunt, N. and Fouché, C. (2009) 'Action research for developing social workers' research capacity', *Educational Action Research*, vol 17, no 2, pp 225–37.

Lunt, N. and Fouché, C. (2010) 'Practitioner research, ethics and research governance', *Ethics and Social Welfare*, vol 4, no 3, pp 219–35.

Lunt, N., Fouché, C. and Yates, D. (2008) *Growing research in practice: An innovative partnership model*, Wellington, New Zealand: New Zealand Families Commission, accessed at www.familiescommission.org.nz/sites/default/files/downloads/IP-GRIP.pdf.

Lunt, N., Shaw, I.F. and Mitchell, F. (2009) *Practitioner research in CHILDREN 1st: Cohorts, networks and systems*, report prepared for the Institute for Research and Innovation in the Social Services, accessed at www.iriss. org.uk/news/practitioner-research.

Lunt, N., Ramian, K., Shaw, I., Fouché, C. and Mitchell, F. (2012) 'Networking practitioner research: synthesizing the state of the art', *European Journal of Social Work*, vol 15, no 2, pp 185–203.

Lykes, M.B. and Mallona, A. (2008) 'Towards transformational liberation: participatory and action research and praxis', in P. Reason and H. Bradbury (eds) *The SAGE handbook of action research: Participative inquiry and practice* (2nd edn), London: Sage, Chapter 7, pp 106–20.

Lyons, K. (2000) 'The place of research in social work education', *British Journal of Social Work*, vol 30, no 4, pp 433–47.

Mansell, J. (2011) *Structured observational research in services for people with learning disabilities*, London: School for Social Care Research, accessed at www.lse.ac.uk/LSEHealthAndSocialCare/pdf/SSCR_Methods_ review_10_web.pdf.

Marilyn, C.S. (1999) 'The teacher research movement: a decade later', *Educational Researcher*, vol 28, pp 15–25.

Masson, H., Balfe, M., Hackett, S. and Phillips, J. (2013) 'Lost without a trace? Social networking and social research with a hard-to-reach population', *British Journal of Social Work*, vol 43, no 1, pp 24–40.

McCafferty, P. (2004) 'Group supervision for social work students on placement: an international comparison', *Journal of Practice Teaching in Health and Social Work*, vol 5, no 3, pp 55–72.

McCleary, R. (2007) 'Ethical issues in online social work research', *Journal of Social Work Values and Ethics*, vol 4, no 1, accessed at www.jswvearchives. com/content/view/46/50/.

McDermott, E., Roen, K. and Piela, A. (2013) 'Hard-to-reach youth online: methodological advances in self-harm research', *Sexuality Research and Social Policy*, vol 10, no 2, pp 125–34.

McLaughlin, H. (2007) *Understanding social work research*, London: Sage.

McLaughlin, H. (2012) *Understanding social work research* (2nd edn), London: Sage.

McRoy, R.G., Flanzer, J.P. and Zlotnik, J.L. (2012) *Building culture and infrastructure*, New York: Oxford University Press.

Miller, C. and Ahmad, Y. (2000) 'Collaboration and partnerships: an effective response to complexity and fragmentation or solution built on sand?' *International Journal of Sociology and Social Policy*, vol 20, pp 1–38.

Mills, D., Jepson, A., Coxon, T., Easterby-Smith, M., Hawkins, P. and Spencer, J. (2006) *Demographic review of the UK social sciences*, Swindon: Economic and Social Research Council.

Mitchell, F., Lunt, N. and Shaw, I. (2009) *Practitioner research in social services: A literature review (summary)*, Scotland: Institute for Research and Innovation in Social Services, accessed at www.iriss.org.uk/sites/default/files/iriss-practitioner-research-literature-review-summary-2009–01.pdf.

Monette, D.R., Sullivan, T.J. and DeJong, C.R. (2008) *Applied social research: A tool for the human services* (7th edn), Belmont, CA: Thomson Brooks/Cole.

Moriaty, J. (2011) *Qualitative methods overview*, London: School for Social Care Research, accessed at www.sscr.nihr.ac.uk/methodsreviews.php.

Moya, E.M. (2010) *Tuberculosis and stigma: Impacts on health-seeking behaviors and access in Ciudad Juarez, Mexico and El Paso, Texas*, accessed at http://digitalcommons.utep.edu/dissertations/AAI3409176/.

Mullen, E., Schlonsky, A., Bledsoe, S.E. and Bellamy, J.L. (2005) 'From concept to implementation: challenges facing evidence-based social work', *Evidence & Policy*, vol 1, no 1, pp 61–84.

Muller-Prothmann, T. (2006) 'Knowledge communities, communities of practice and knowledge networks', in E. Coakes and S. Clarke (eds) *Encyclopedia of communities of practice in information and knowledge management*, Hershey, PA: IGI Global, pp 264–71.

Munford, R., and Sanders, J. (2003) *Making a difference in families: Research that creates change*, Sydney: Allen & Unwin.

NASW (National Association of Social Workers) (1964) *Building social work knowledge: Report of a conference*, New York: NASW.

National Co-ordinating Centre for Public Engagement (2012) *Community-based participatory research: A guide to ethical principles and practice*, accessed at www.publicengagement.ac.uk/how-we-help/our-publications/community-based-participatory-research-guide-to-ethical-principle.

National Health and Medical Research Council of Australia (2003) *Guidelines for ethical conduct in Aboriginal and Torres Strait Islander health research*, accessed at www.nhmrc.gov.au/guidelines/publications/e52.

National Institute for Mental Health in England (2004) *Celebrating our cultures: Guidelines for mental health promotion with black and minority ethnic communities*, accessed at www.nmhdu.org.uk/silo/files/cultures-black-minority.pdf.

Neiman, S. (2008) *Moral clarity: A guide for grown-up idealists*, Orlando, FL: Harcourt.

Netten, A. (2011) *Overview of outcome measurement for adults using social care services and support (Methods review 6)*, London: School for Social Care Research.

Northen, H. and Kurland, R. (2001) *Social work with groups* (3rd edn), New York: Columbia University Press.

Nosek, B.A., Banaji, M.R. and Greenwald, A.G. (2002) 'E-research: ethics, security, design, and control in psychological research on the internet', *Journal of Social Issues*, vol 58, no 1, pp 161–76.

O'Leary, Z. (2010) *Researching real-world problems: A guide to methods of inquiry*, London: Sage.

Onwuegbuzie, A.J. and Leech, N.L. (2005) 'On becoming a pragmatic researcher: the importance of combining quantitative and qualitative research methodologies', *International Journal of Social Research Methodology: Theory & Practice*, vol 8, no 5, pp 375–87.

Orme, J. and Powell, J. (2008) 'Building research capacity in social work: process and issues', *British Journal of Social Work*, vol 38, no 5, pp 988–1008.

Orme, J. and Shemmings, D. (2010) *Developing research based social work practice*, London: Palgrave Macmillan.

Orme, J., Ruckdeschel, R. and Briar-Lawson, K. (2010) 'Challenges and directions in social work research and social work practice', in I. Shaw, K. Briar-Lawson, J. Orme and R. Ruckdeschel (eds) *The SAGE handbook of social work research*, London: Sage, pp 463–76.

Osmond, J. (2005) 'The knowledge spectrum: a framework for teaching knowledge and its use in social work practice', *British Journal of Social Work*, vol 35, pp 881–900.

Patton, M.Q. (2002) *Qualitative research and evaluation methods* (3rd edn), Thousand Oaks, CA: Sage Publications.

Payne, M. (2005) *Modern social work theory* (3rd edn), Illinois: Lyceum Books.

Pololi, L.H., Knight, S.M., Dennis, K. and Frankel, R.M. (2002) 'Helping medical school faculty realise their dreams: an innovative, collaborative mentoring programme', *Academic Medicine*, vol 77, no 5, pp 377–84.

Pope, C. (2003) 'Resisting evidence: the study of evidence-based medicine as a contemporary social movement', *Health*, vol 7, no 3, pp 267–82.

Posavac, E.J. (2011) *Program evaluation: Methods and case studies*, Boston, MA: Pearson Education.

Powell, J. (2007) 'Promoting older people's voices – the contribution of social work to interdisciplinary research', *Social Work in Health Care*, vol 44, nos 1–2, pp 111–26.

Powell, J. and Ramos, B. (2010) 'The practice of social work research', in I. Shaw, K. Briar-Lawson, J. Orme and R. Ruckdeschel (eds) *The SAGE handbook of social work research*, London: Sage, Chapter 14, pp 231–45.

Proctor, B. (2000) *Group supervision: A guide to creative practice*, London: Sage.

Radermacher, H., Karunarathna, Y., Grace, N. and Feldman, S. (2011) 'Partner or perish? Exploring inter-organisational partnerships in the multicultural community aged care sector', *Health & Social Care in the Community*, vol 19, no 5, pp 550–60.

Reason, P. and Bradbury, H. (eds) (2008) *The Sage handbook of action research: Participative inquiry and practice* (2nd edn), London: Sage.

Rehr, H. and Berkman, B. (1978) 'Social work undertakes its own audit', *Social Work in Health Care*, vol 3 (March), pp 273–86.

Rehr, H. and Caroff, P. (eds) (1986) *A new model in academic–practice partnership: Multi-instructor and institutional collaboration in social work*, Lexington, MA: Gunn Press.

Reid, W.J. and Hanrahan, P. (1982) 'Recent evaluations of social work: grounds for optimism', *Social Work*, vol 27, no 4, pp 328–40.

Ripley, J.S. and Yarhouse, M.A. (2012) 'Mentoring Psy.D. students in meaningful research', *Journal of Psychology and Christianity*, vol 31, no 4, pp 308–13.

Rosen, A. and Proctor, E.K. (eds) (2003) *Developing practice guidelines for social work intervention: Issues, methods, and research agenda*, New York: Columbia University Press.

Rosen, A., Proctor, E. and Staudt, M. (1999) 'Social work research and the quest for effective practice', *Social Work Research*, vol 23, pp 4–14.

Rothman, J. and Thomas, E.J. (1994) *Intervention research*, New York: Haworth Press.

Roy, A. (2012) 'Avoiding the involvement overdose: drugs, race, ethnicity and participatory research practice', *Critical Social Policy*, vol 32, no 4, pp 636–54.

Royse, D., Staton-Tindall, M., Badger, K. and Webster, L.M. (2009) *Needs assessment*, New York: Oxford University Press.

Ruckdeschel, R. and Chambon, A. (2010) 'The uses of social work research', in I. Shaw, K. Briar-Lawson, J. Orme and R. Ruckdeschel (eds) *The SAGE handbook of social work research*, London: Sage, Chapter 12, pp 195–209.

Rymer, J. (2002) '"Only connect": transforming ourselves and our discipline through co-mentoring', *The Journal of Business Communication*, vol 39, no 3, pp 342–63.

Rynes, S.L., Bartunek, J.M. and Daft, R.L. (2001) 'Across the great divide: knowledge creation and transfer between practitioners and academics', *Academy of Management Journal*, vol 44, no 2, pp 340–55.

Sabah, Y. and Cook-Craig, P. (2010) 'Learning teams and virtual communities of practice: managing evidence and expertise beyond the stable state', *Research on Social Work Practice*, vol 20, no 4, pp 435–46.

Sarantakos, S. (2005) *Social research* (3rd edn), New York: Palgrave Macmillan.

Schön, D.A. (1983) *The reflective practitioner: How professionals think in action*, New York: Basic Books.

Scriven, M. (1999) *Evaluation thesaurus*, London: Sage.

Scullion, P.A. (2002) 'Effective dissemination strategies', *Nurse Researcher*, vol 10, no 1, pp 65–78.

Shamoo, A.E. and Resnik, D.B. (2003) *Responsible conduct of research*, New York: Oxford University Press.

Shaw, I.F. (2003) 'Cutting edge issues in social work research', *British Journal of Social Work*, vol 33, no 1, pp 107–20.

Shaw, I. (2005) 'Practitioner research: evidence or critique?' *British Journal of Social Work*, vol 35, no 8, pp 1231–48.

Shaw, I. and Faulkner, A. (2006) 'Practitioner evaluation at work', *American Journal of Evaluation*, vol 27, no 1, pp 44–63.

Shaw, I. and Holland, S. (2014) *Doing qualitative research in social work*, London, Sage.

Shaw, I. and Norton, M. (2008) 'Kinds and quality of social work research', *British Journal of Social Work*, vol 38, no 5, pp 953–70.

Shaw, I., Briar-Lawson, K., Orme, J. and Ruckdeschel, R. (2010) *The SAGE handbook of social work research*, London: Sage.

Sheldon, B. and Chilvers, R. (2000) *Evidence-based social care: A study of prospects and problems*, Lyme Regis, UK: Russell House.

Sheppard, M. (1995) 'Social work, social science and practice wisdom, *British Journal of Social Work*, vol 3, pp 265–93.

Sheppard, M. (1998) 'Practice validity, reflexivity and knowledge for social work', *British Journal of Social Work*, vol 5, pp 763–81.

Sheppard, M. (2004) *Appraising and using social research in the human services: An introduction for social work and health professionals*, London: Jessica Kingsley Publishers.

Sheppard, M. and Ryan, K. (2003) 'Practitioners as rule using analysts: a further development of process knowledge in social work', *British Journal of Social Work*, vol 33, pp 157–76.

Sitter, K.C. (2012) 'Participatory video: toward a method, advocacy and voice (MAV) framework', *Intercultural Education*, vol 23, no 6, pp 541–54.

Sixsmith, J. and Murray, C.D. (2001) 'Ethical issues in the documentary data analysis of internet posts and archives', *Qualitative Health Research*, vol 11, no 3, pp 423–32.

Smith, L.T. (2012) *Decolonising methodologies: Research and indigenous peoples*, London: Zed Books.

Smith, R. (2009) *Doing social work research*, Maidenhead: Open University Press.

Somekh, B. (2006) *Action research: A methodology for change and development*, Maidenhead: Open University Press.

Steinberg, D.M. (2004) *The mutual-aid approach to working with groups: Helping people help one another* (2nd edn), New York: Haworth Press.

Stern, S.R. (2003) 'Encountering distressing information in online research: a consideration of legal and ethical responsibilities', *New Media & Society*, vol 5, no 2, pp 249–66.

Steyaert, J., Spierings, F. and Autant Dorier, C. (2011) 'Promoting a practice-minded culture in research organizations', *European Journal of Social Work*, vol 14, no 1, pp 123–39.

Straus, S.E., Johnson, M.O., Marquez, C. and Feldman, M.D. (2014) 'Characteristics of successful and failed mentoring relationships: a qualitative study across two academic health centers', *Academic Medicine*, vol 88, no 1, pp 82–9.

Streng, J.M., Rhodes, S., Ayala, G., Eng, E., Arceo, R. and Phipps, S. (2004) 'Realidad Latina: Latino adolescents, their school, and a university use photovoice to examine and address the influence of immigration', *Journal of Interprofessional Care*, vol 18, no 4, pp 403–15.

Stringer, E.T. (2007) *Action research* (3rd edn), London: Sage.

Suchman, E.A. (1967) *Evaluation research: Principles and practice in public service and social action programmes*, New York: Russell Sage Foundation.

Thomas, D.R. (2006) 'A general inductive approach for analyzing qualitative evaluation data', *American Journal of Evaluation*, vol 27, no 2, pp 237–46.

Thompson, N. and Pascal, J. (2012) 'Developing critically reflective practice', *Reflective Practice*, vol 13, no 2, pp 311–25.

Thyer, B.A. (2004) 'What is evidence-based practice?' *Brief Treatment and Crisis Intervention*, vol 4, no 2, pp 167–76.

Trevithick, P. (2000) *Social work skills: A practice handbook*, Buckingham: Open University Press.

Trevithick, P. (2008) 'Revisiting the knowledge base of social work: a framework for practice', *British Journal of Social Work*, vol 38, no 6, pp 1212–37.

Uggerhoj, L. (2011) 'What is practice research in social work – definitions, barriers and possibilities', *Social Work & Society*, vol 9, no 1, pp 45–59.

Van Maanen, J. (2011) *Tales of the field: On writing ethnography*, Chicago: University of Chicago Press.

Wadsworth, Y. (2011) *Do it yourself social research: The bestselling practical guide to doing social research projects* (3rd edn), Sydney: Allen & Unwin.

Walter, I., Nutley, S., Percy-Smith, J., McNeish, D. and Frost, S. (2004) *Improving the use of research in social care practice (Knowledge Review 7)*, London: Social Care Institute for Excellence (SCIE).

Wang, C.C. (1999) 'Photovoice: a participatory action research strategy applied to women's health', *Journal of Women's Health*, vol 8, no 2, pp 185–92.

Wang, C.C., Cash, J.L. and Powers, L.S. (2000) 'Who knows the streets as well as the homeless? Promoting personal and community action through photovoice', *Health Promotion Practice*, vol 1, no 1, pp 81–9.

Wang, C.C., Yi, W.K., Tao, Z.W. and Carovano, K. (1998) 'Photovoice as a participatory health promotion strategy', *Health Promotion International*, vol 13, no 1, pp 75–86.

Warren, J. (2007) *Service user and carer participation in social work*, Exeter: Learning Matters.

Webb, S.A. (2001) 'Some considerations on the validity of evidence-based practice in social work', *British Journal of Social Work*, vol 31, no 1, 57–79.

Weeden, M.R. (2012) 'Ethics and on-line research methodology', *Journal of Social Work Values and Ethics*, vol 9, no 1, pp 40–51.

Weinbach, R.W. (2005) *Evaluating social work services and programs*, Boston, MA: Pearson Education.

Wenger, E. (1998) *Communities of practice: Learning, meaning, and identity*, Cambridge: Cambridge University Press.

Wenger, E.C. and Snyder, W.M. (2000) 'Communities of practice: The organizational frontier, *Harvard Business Review*, vol 78, no 1, pp 139–45.

Wenger, E., McDermott, R. and Snyder, W.M. (2002) *Cultivating communities of practice*, Boston, MA: Harvard Business Press.

White, S.A. (ed) (2003) *Participatory video: Images that transform and empower*, New Delhi: Sage.

Whittaker, A. (2012) *Research skills for social work* (2nd edn), London: Sage.

Wicks, P.G., Reason, P. and Bradbury, H. (2008) 'Living inquiry: personal, political and philosophical groundings for action research practice', in P. Reason and H. Bradbury (eds) *The SAGE Handbook of action research: Participative inquiry and practice* (2nd edn), London: Sage, Chapter 1, pp 15–30.

Williamson, T.K. (2007) 'The individual in research', in T. Long and M. Johnson (eds) *Research ethics in the real world: Issues and solutions for health and social care*, Edinburgh: Churchill Livingstone, pp 9–28.

Wilson, G. (2014) 'Building partnerships in social work education: towards achieving collaborative advantage for employers and universities', *Journal of Social Work*, vol 14, no 1, pp 3–22.

Wood, K.M. (1978) 'Casework effectiveness: a new look at the research evidence', *Social Work*, vol 23, pp 437–58.

Woolf, S.H. (2008) 'The meaning of translational research and why it matters', *Journal of the American Medical Association*, vol 299, no 2, pp 211–13.

Wysocki, D.K. (2008) *Readings in social research methods*, Belmont, CA: Thomson Wadsworth.

Yawn, B.P., Pace, W., Dietrich, A., Bertram, S., Kurland, M., Graham, D., Huff, J., Rocca, L. and Wollan, P. (2010) 'Practice benefit from participating in a practice-based research network study of postpartum depression: a National Research Network (NRN) report', *The Journal of the American Board of Family Medicine*, vol 23, no 4, pp 455–64.

Yegidis, B.L. and Weinbach, R.W. (2009) *Research methods for social workers* (6th edn), Boston, MA: Pearson Education.

Yin, R.K. (2014) *Case study research: Design and methods* (5th edn), London: Sage.

Zerwekh, J. and Claborn, J.C. (2006) *Nursing today: Transition and trends* (5th edn), Philadelphia: Saunders Elsevier.

Index

Note: page numbers in italic type refer to Figures; those in bold type refer to Tables.